"Write What You See…"

"Write What You See..."
THE REVELATION OF JESUS CHRIST

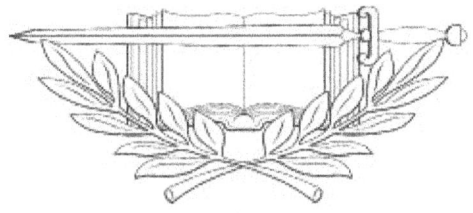

NANCY J. KITCHEN

"Write What You See...": The Revelation of Jesus Christ
   Nancy J. Kitchen
 Copyright © 2016, 2018

All Scripture quotations, unless otherwise indicated are taken from the *New American Standard Bible*.
Copyright 1975 by The Lockman Foundation.

All rights reserved. No part of this publication may be reproduced or transmitted by any means without prior permission of the author.

Cover Art by Pat Marvenko Smith / www.revelationillustrated.com
Cover Design by Karin Buchak

Published in the United States of America
ISBN 10: 0692572651-10: 0692572651
ISBN 13: 978-0692572658
ISBN-13: 9780692572658
Library of Congress Control Number: 2015918470
Get It Write, Rockwall, TX.

---

01 02 03 04 05 06 07 08 09 10

Table of Contents

Dedication · xi
Preface · xiii

PART I: Prologue

Chapter 1	Prologue ·	3
	The Bible ·	5
	Introduction ·	6
	God's Promise ·	7
	Prophecy ·	8
	A Time of Tribulation ·	9
	Definition of Terms ·	10
	The "Last Days" or "End times" ·	11
	Jesus Christ, The Revelation ·	13
	Schools of Interpretation ·	16

PART II: INTRODUCTION and the CHURCHES

Chapter 2	"The things which thou hast seen" ·	23
	Introduction (Rev. 1:1-19) ·	23
	Who, Where, When, and Why ·	23
	The Patmos Vision (Rev. 1:4-10) ·	27
	The Symbols (Rev. 1:12-20) ·	30
Chapter 3	"The things which are" ·	35
	The Churches (Rev. 2 & 3) ·	35
	Background ·	36
	Message to the Church of Ephesus (Rev. 2:1-7) · · · · · · · · · · · · · · · ·	39
	Message to the Church of Smyrna (Rev. 2:8-11) · · · · · · · · · · · · · · ·	42

  Message to the Church of Pergamum (Rev. 2:12-17) · · · · · · · · · · · · · · · 47
  Message to the Church of Thyatira (Rev. 2:18-29) · · · · · · · · · · · · · · · 50
  Message to the Church of Sardis (Rev. 3:1-6) · 52
  Message to the Church of Philadelphia (Rev. 3:7-13) · · · · · · · · · · · · 55
  Message to the Church of Laodicea (Rev. 3:14-22) · · · · · · · · · · · · · · 58
  End of the Church Age · 61

PART III: The Tribulation as Seen from Heaven

Chapter 4 "The things which shall be hereafter" · 65
  "After these things..." (Rev. 4:1-11) · 65
  The Prophetic Events · 66
  John's Vision of Heaven (Rev. 4:1) · 67
  The Throne Room (Rev. 4:2-11) · 69
  The Sealed Book/Scroll (Rev. 5:1-14) · 74
  The Lamb - The Redeemer (Rev. 5:6-14) · 76
  Heaven Rejoices (Rev. 5:9-14) · 78

Chapter 5 Breaking the Seals · 81

  The Seals (Rev. 6:1-17) · 81
  Four Horsemen of the Apocalypse (Rev. 6:1-17) · · · · · · · · · · · · · · · · 82
  Breaking of the First Seal (Rev. 6:1-2) · 83
  Breaking of the Second Seal (Rev. 6:3-4) · 85
  Breaking of the Third Seal (Rev. 6:5-6) · 86
  Breaking of the Fourth Seal (Rev. 6:7-8) · 87
  Breaking of the Fifth Seal (Rev. 6:9-11) · 88
  Breaking of the Sixth Seal (Rev. 6:12-17) · 89

Chapter 6 A Moment of Praise · 93
  An Interlude (Rev. 7:1-3) · 93
  The 144,000 (Rev. 7:4-8) · 95
  The Scene in Heaven (Rev. 7:9-17) · 97

Chapter 7 Sounding of the Trumpets · 99
  Breaking of the Seventh Seal (Rev. 8:1) · 99
  Preparation for the Trumpets (Rev. 8:2-5) · 100
  Sounding of the Trumpets (Rev. 8:6 - 9:21) · 102
  A Heavenly Proclamation (Rev. 8:13) · 104
  The Trumpets and the Spirit World (Rev. 9:1-12, 13-21, 11:15-19) · · · · · · 105

	The Impact on Satan's Realm	108
	The Sixth Trumpet (Rev. 9:13-21)	109
	The Little Book/Scroll (Rev. 10:1-11)	111
	No More Delay (Rev. 10:5-11)	113
Chapter 8	Dealing with the Nation of Israel	117
	General Comments	117
	Israel's History Prophesied	118
	Restoration of the Temple (Rev. 11:1-2)	121
Chapter 9	The Two Witnesses	123
	The Two Witnesses (Rev. 11:3-14)	123
	Conditions of the Times	127
Chapter 10	The Seventh Trumpet	131
	The Sounding of the Seventh Trumpet (Rev. 11:15-19)	131

PART IV: The Tribulation as Seen from Earth

Chapter 11	The Tribulation as Seen from Earth	137
	Interpretations of the Participants (Rev. 12:1-17)	139
	The Woman (Rev. 12:1-2)	141
	The Child (Rev. 12:4-5)	143
	The Great Red Dragon (Rev. 12:3-4)	145
	The War in Heaven (Rev. 12:7-12)	147
	Those Left Behind (Rev. 12:13-17)	150
Chapter 12	Daniel's Prophetic Dreams	153
	Similarities in End-Time Prophecies	153
	Daniel's First Vision (Dan. 2:1-45)	154
	The Second Vision (Dan. 7:1-27)	157
	The Third Vision (Dan. 8:1-27)	157
	Consistency of the Scriptures	158
Chapter 13	Rise of the Antichrist	159
	Signs of the Time (Matt. 24:3-44)	159
	The Build-Up to a World Crisis	161
	Time of Great Deception (2 Thess. 2:1-4, 9-10)	164
	Three Great Crises for the Jews and Israel	165
Chapter 14	The Rapture	169
	Rapture (1 Cor. 15:52; 1 Thess. 4:16-18; Rev. 12:2-5)	169
	The First Prong of the First Resurrection (1 Thess. 4:16-18)	170

	The Days of Noah (Matt. 24:37-44)	172
	Summary to Date	174
Chapter 15	The Participants	175
	The Beast from the Sea (Rev. 13:1-8)	176
	The Antichrist Resurrected (Rev. 13:3; 17:8, 11)	178
	The False Prophet (Rev. 13:11-18)	180
	The Lamb and the 144,000 (Rev. 7:4-8; 14:1-5)	182
Chapter 16	The Harvest and God's Mercy	187
	The Horsemen and Angels (Rev. 6:1-8; 14:6-20)	188
	The Harvest (Rev. 14:14-20)	191
Chapter 17	A Time of Praise	195
	Revelation 15:1-4	195
Chapter 18	God's Timeline	199
	Sequence of Events *	199
Chapter 19	God's Wrath	203
	The Seven Bowls of God's Wrath (Rev. 15:5 - 16:21)	203
	Introduction to the Plagues (Rev. 8:2, 6; 15:5-8)	203
	God's Wrath Poured Out (Rev. 16:2-17)	204
	The Prophesied Nations (Ezek. 38:1-16)	208
	The Fulfillment of Prophecy	212

PART V: The Tribulation as Seen from Satan's Realm

Chapter 20	Babylon	215
	Babylon, the System (Rev. 17:3-7)	215
	The Woman (Rev. 17:1-18)	220
	The Beast (Rev. 17:3, 8-18)	222
Chapter 21	Babylon, the City	225
	The City of Babylon (Rev. 18: 1-24)	225
	The Fall of Babylon (Rev. 18:2-24)	226
	After Babylon	227
	A Time of Praise (Rev. 19:1-6)	228
Chapter 22	The Marriage	231
	The Marriage (Rev. 19:7-9)	231
	The Bridegroom and Bride (Rev. 7:7-9)	231
	The Wedding and the Feast (Rev. 19:9)	233
	Fellow Messenger (Rev. 19:1-10)	234

	Rider on a White Horse (Rev. 19:11-16)	235
Chapter 23	The Battle of Armageddon	239
	The Final Conflict (Rev. 19: 17-21)	239
	The Feast of the Birds (Rev. 19:17-18)	239
	Christ Returns (Rev. 19:11-16)	240
	Satan Bound (Rev. 20:1-3)	241

PART VI: The Final Events

Chapter 24	The Millennium	247
	The Period of Restoration (Rev. 20:1-15)	247
	Views of the Millennium	248
	The Thousand Years (Rev. 20:1-15)	250
	Thrones of Judgment (Rev. 20:4)	252
Chapter 25	The Judgments	255
	Judgment of the Saints (Rev. 12:10)	255
	Judgment of the Nations (Matt. 25:31-33)	256
Chapter 26	After the Thousand Years	259
	Satan's Doom (Rev. 20: 1-3, 7-10)	259
	The Great White Throne (Rev. 20: 11-15)	261
	Punishment or Rewards	263
Chapter 27	All Things Made New	265
	The New Heavens and New Earth (Rev. 21: 1-27)	265
	The New Jerusalem (Rev. 21:2-27)	269
	The City of God (Rev. 21:9-27)	272
	The River of Life (Rev. 22:1) (Ezek. 47:1-6)	274
	The Tree of Life (Rev. 22:2) (Ezek. 47:7-12)	275
	The Thrones (Rev. 22:3)	276
	Further Description	277
Chapter 28	The Epilogue	281
	The Final Scene (Rev. 22: 7-21)	281
	The Conclusion (Rev. 22:16-21)	284
	BIBLIOGRAPHY	287
	Indexes	289

Dedication

This book is dedicated to a few of the people who contributed to making it a reality.

- Cynthia Sowa, who first lit the spark in me to know more and more about the unfathomable message of the end times:
- The strong Christian women of our prayer group, who reinforced my belief that all things are possible,
- Camay Jennings for being my spiritual and physical right hand for so many years,
- Rick Rofman, who brought both a Jewish and Christian perspective to the editing of this manuscript,
- Pat Marvenko Smith and Karin Buchak, who captured my vision of the Shekinah Glory of God for the cover,
- And above all, Jesus Christ for never ceasing to reveal Himself and guide me every step of the way.

Preface

In the late-1990s, I was blessed to be a part of a very special group of seven women, who became fast friends, prayer partners, confidants, and a soft place to fall. We shared one another's lives, our love of God, our personal pain and struggles, our victories and failures, our hopes, and our fears. We laughed together; we cried together; we encouraged and supported one another; but most importantly, we prayed through the situations that arose in each of our lives, as well as the lives of others—praising God and interceding as we went. This was a group of women whom I am convinced God set apart for a particular purpose. We were all convinced of that and treasured His gift.

One of the things that originally brought us together was a Bible study on the teachings and interpretation of the Book of Revelation, which one of the women in our group taught in her home and later in her church. During ten months of weekly classes, the seven of us forged a personal bond that lasted some years and few women have an opportunity to experience. In addition to the personal connections we shared for over five years, I received a double blessing. Not only did I find extraordinary Christian friends, but I also acquired an unexpected passion to understand more deeply God's ultimate plan for this world and His people.

Because of this mounting interest, I went through the class twice, taking copious notes, as is my nature. This unanticipated zeal for increased knowledge of the topic, plus forty-five years as a librarian and bibliophile, seemed to drive me to dig deeper and deeper into other interpretations of what seemed to be a much-misunderstood book. It was as if I were being pressed to capture a unique perspective on John's visions of the last days, so as not to allow it to slip into oblivion, which I am convinced is Satan's intent.

After about five years, for reasons unrelated to this writing, our little band of prayer warriors began to dissipate—several moved away, circumstances changed, and the season that had meant so much to each of us gently slipped away. As great a loss as it was, God evidently had accomplished His purpose for that time.

For me, however, this was not an end of the experience. This burning desire for greater understanding of The Revelation of Jesus Christ could not seem to be quenched. I began to collect, read, and study everything I could find on the subject, and continued to expand the notes that I had thus far accumulated. I don't consider myself a writer, however; I am an editor and researcher. For that reason, the material that follows is not a typical presentation of the topic, but rather an outlined guide to Christ's revelation of *"what is soon to take place."*

Because God has been very explicit throughout the Bible concerning His plans and purposes for mankind, my eagerness to understand His revelations, relative to end-time events, only intensified. Repeatedly, God has revealed, through the words of the prophets, His intentions and will for all creation. For whatever reason, however, we have not seemed to grasp the significance of this information. Therefore, either due to our own failure to understand or accept His Word, or because of an unwillingness to recognize Satan's efforts to blind us to the truth, we are destined to miss Jesus' Second Coming, unless we open our minds. Sadly, there will be no more chances after the last days.

The notes I originally accumulated during the Bible studies continued to increase and expand in depth until about the year 2000. Unclear about what I was to do with them, it seemed that it was evidently not in God's timing for me to share them at that point. My friend was not interested in having them; a class I proposed to teach did not take place as planned, and thus, for over thirteen years, this project, begun some fifteen years ago, was set aside for another time or purpose.

During a period of prayer in the fall of 2013, to my utter amazement, God seemed to urge me to take out my notes and reread them with a new eye. For some time, I had been hearing an increasing number of questions concerning the last days and what the signs and symbols meant. The responses I heard were either inaccurate or confusing at best. It was obvious that interest was increasing, but clear understanding was not. As a result, as much as I tried to ignore this unexplained pressure to resume this project, it was as if God were telling me, "Now is the time to take <u>My</u> teaching off the shelf." So, the pages that follow are humbly offered at what I believe is God's bidding. How He intends to use them, I still do not know; it is totally up to Him. When He told me to "wait," I waited. However, because He has given me no peace about what I believe is His "now," I feel obliged to open the book again, expand parts of it, and share His revelations. This commentary is not a proposal of how to interpret <u>current events,</u> in light of John's visions in the Book of Revelation. It is purely a God-driven interpretation of the end-time events as revealed in the scriptures.

We are closer to the end times than ever in history, and there is little left to be accomplished before Christ's return. He does not wish us to be confused or fearful of what He revealed to John some 2000 years ago. That is Satan's desire. Unlike Daniel, John was told to *"write those things which he saw,"* so that we could *"...be blessed by the reading and hearing of what is to come."* There is hope in understanding, and I believe it is God's desire that this time we be prepared for His coming. The time is near, so, *"look up, for our redemption draws nigh..."*

PART I
Prologue

CHAPTER 1
Prologue

IF YOU WERE TO RESEARCH existing prophetic literature relative to end-time events, it would quickly become evident that mankind, male and female, has always had a burning desire to know the unknown. Almost every culture and religion—Greek, Hindu, Mayan, Native American, to name just a few—have produced stories and legends about how the world began and will end. It seems to be human nature to want to know what the future holds—to know what lies ahead, to be able to distinguish between what is good and true from that which is false or evil, to understand one's options in order to make wise choices, and to feel prepared for what is to come. Because life is comprised of an ongoing series of choices, and because the future is a mystery, uncertainty seems to lead to a fear of being unable to survive the great cataclysms that have been foretold.

In an attempt to soothe that anxiety, men and women have always been seeking answers to how the future might unfold—will it be better than the present, will decisions made today lead to positive or negative outcomes, is there any hope of a victorious ending? Throughout the ages, people have searched the stars, interpreted dreams, consulted soothsayers, fortunetellers, and prophets, in an attempt to gain some grasp of what is looming just around the next corner. There would appear to be an illusion that knowledge will bring some level of comfort and a sense of being in control of one's own destiny.

Mankind has been plagued with this curious spirit to know the unknown since the beginning of time. In fact, it was this overpowering desire to know all things that resulted in man's original fall from grace and state of perfection. God knew from the beginning that nothing and no one would ever remain perfect. Nevertheless, He created all things according to His perfect plan. This plan included human beings with whom He could be in relationship, and a perfect world over which man could have dominion. Because of His infinite wisdom, however, He also prepared a contingency plan to address man's weaknesses and human nature.

The Creator of all things is a God of love and mercy, and it was never His desire, or intent, to create spiritual robots over which He could exercise dominant control. He has a deep desire to love and be loved in return—by choice rather than by manipulation. It was for this reason that God planted the Tree of Knowledge of Good and Evil in the Garden of Eden. It was a test to reveal whether Adam and Eve would be obedient to His command or rebelliously follow their own desires and will. Because He is God, He knew in advance what choices each of His children would make, but unlike what some believe, choices are not predestined. There are those who will accept the will of God and those who will not. He and He alone knows the choice each will make. This means, therefore, that man's future ultimately lies in his own hands. God provides guidance and sets boundaries, but He never overrides man's free will in order to assure His own.

God created all beings, angelic and human, to have free will—a gift that was first given to the angels, before the creation of the universe. Unfortunately, that gift was abused and sin came into being. Because of a prideful nature, the Archangel Lucifer, desiring to possess the knowledge and a position equal to that of God and Jesus Christ, rebelled against God's will. This presumptuous act was rightfully punished, and he, plus a third of the angels who chose to follow him, was cast out of heaven. This was the beginning of the battle between light and darkness, good and evil—between God and Lucifer, who came to be known as Satan or the Devil.

This war of opposing forces is both spiritual and physical in nature. The participants are also physical (human) and spiritual (demons or supernatural spirits), and mankind is the battlefield upon which the struggle takes place. Free will is, therefore, imperative to the triumphant conclusion of this conflict. Life is a journey through the minefields of this battle, and, to navigate it successfully, the participants must fully understand the opposing forces, the environment in which it takes place, the motivating influences, tools of combat, and the ultimate cost. Only with such essential information is one able to make the best choice, fight from a place of wisdom and power, and predict the experiences he or she may encounter. God allows evil to come into this world and our lives, in order to test us and make us stronger for the battle. In His wisdom and almighty judgment, God provides the opportunity to choose right or wrong, good or evil—Satan merely provides the incentive to make bad choices. Because of His endless love, it is God's plan that all who so choose be victorious and once again made perfect.

"Write What You See..." is a chronicle of this conflict, particularly in its last days. Throughout history, accounts of these final events, and interpretations of what they mean, appear in every culture and religion around the world. For that reason, no matter what one's perspective might be, most people have some knowledge and interest in what the end of time will look like.

One of the most detailed and well known explanations is the last book of the Bible—The Revelation of Jesus Christ. *"Write What You See..."* is a line-by-line, deconstructed analysis of this often misunderstood record of what the last days on this earth, as we know it, will be like. It is intended to provide an in-depth study of God's plan for the redemption of mankind and this world. It is presented as a compass and guidebook to understanding what the future may hold and how we can influence our own destiny through the choices we make. How this book is received and followed, or not, is up to the reader. It is merely presented as one more choice in this experience called life.

THE BIBLE

Millions of books and manuscripts have been written throughout history—books filled with thoughts, beliefs, hopes, fears, and opinions—books meant to inspire, encourage, entertain, as well as create dissension, doubt, and conflict. Some books have been widely read and long remembered; others progressed no farther than the pages upon which they were written.

Of all the books written, however, one, and one alone, stands head and shoulders above all others, as the most well known, most widely distributed, possessed by the greatest number of people, and treasured for its message. At the same time, it is one of the most controversial, debated, little understood, and, in some cases, feared books ever compiled. It is loved; it is hated. It has been guarded and protected, as well as sought out and destroyed. Some believe it is the absolute truth; others consider it a fairy tale, a fable, an allegory written merely to convey universal ideas.

What book is this that possesses the distinction of being one of the oldest, best preserved, most widely owned but little-read books in history—the Bible. It is a book that took 1,500 years to write and records the history of mankind from his creation until the much-prophesied end of days yet to come. It is a mystery book, an adventure story, a romance novel, and a biography. Though thought by some to be a book of fiction, it is considered by others to be the consummate, non-fiction book of truth.

The *Guinness World Book of Records* reports that more than five billion copies have been printed since 1815. Prior to that time, countless numbers were copied by hand. It has been translated in full into approximately 350 languages, with parts translated into some 2,100 languages.

The Bible is a collection of books penned by many writers, but with only one author—God. It is, therefore, His Word that the reader either accepts or rejects as truth. Once again, this is one of those freedoms of choice.

"Write What You See..." is an in-depth study of The Revelation of Jesus Christ—the last book or chapter of this masterwork that has outlasted the test of time. Focused on the events prophesied to occur during the last days, *"Write What You See..."* attempts to bring some degree of clarity to what the scriptures actually say—those words that have caused

so much debate and confusion over time. Again, acceptance or rejection becomes the responsibility of the reader.

INTRODUCTION

1. The Bible is a library of 66 divinely inspired books housed between two covers.
    a. These books were originally written over a period of approximately 1,500 years in one of three languages—Hebrew, Aramaic, or Greek.
    b. They were also most likely penned on possibly three different continents—Asia, Africa, and Europe.
2. This collection of works have at least 44 writers, but only one Author.
    a. They are the *logos,* the Word of God, and He is the author.
    b. Through His Word, He communicates His plan and program for mankind and the earth.
3. As a whole, the Bible, is written with the future in mind, rather than the past.
    a. It is as if one were standing at the beginning of time and looking toward the end.
    b. This is God's perspective as He reveals and inspires His book.
4. Genesis, written some 1,400 years before the birth of Christ, tells of the beginnings—the creation of the universe, the fall of man, the judgment of God, and the promise of His redemption.
    a. Man was created in righteousness and holiness and was given dominion over all else that was created.
    b. By his own choice, however, he gave it all away to Satan.
    c. Thus began the <u>degeneration</u> of God's creation.
5. The Book of Revelation, written approximately 1,500 years later, records the <u>regeneration</u> process.
    a. God's plan is to restore mankind, and all creation, to its original state of perfection.
    b. What God does not regenerate, He judges.
    c. He leaves nothing unfinished.
6. Satan understands this; he knows that all things lead to his destruction.
    a. His greatest efforts, therefore, are directed toward convincing people that they can ignore the contents of these books.
    b. He even uses some leaders in the church to further this point of view by causing confusion.

c. Christ foretold this in Luke 21:8.
   d. As a result, the world rejects *Genesis* and ignores *Revelation*.
7. It has now been over 1,900 yrs. since the last word of the Bible was written, but the story is not yet finished.

God's Promise

God does not want His children to go through life uninformed and fearful of what is to come. *"He did not give us a spirit of fear..."* (2 Tim. 1:7). He wants His people to be well armed and prepared for the battles they will face in life—the greatest battle, between good and evil, to be fought in the last days. Man is an active participant in the progression of God's plan toward restoration. Throughout the scriptures, He communicates His Word through His chosen few. He reveals prophecies and signs to prepare His people for what is to come. They must pay attention, be alert, or they will again miss an opportunity to recognize Jesus, when He returns to establish His kingdom on earth.

1. God tells us that not a thing will happen that He does not first reveal through His prophets (Amos 3:7).
   a. Throughout the Bible, He is faithful to this promise.
   b. It is not His fault if we misinterpret what He says, or refuse to accept what we are told.
2. The first coming of Christ is a good example of a promise unheeded.
   a. The details of His birth and death were foretold in the Old Testament (Is. 7:14; 9:6-7; 53:3-9) (Mic. 5:2).
   b. There was no reason to fail to recognize Him.
3. God tells us to ask when we do not understand His Word, or its meaning (James 1:5).
   a. He will answer and reveal mighty things.
   b. We are to search His Word and seek His answers.
   c. As a result, He will give us understanding and wisdom (Eph. 1:17).
   d. In the Book of Revelation, He tells us seven times to *"...listen...,"* for it is His desire that we should be prepared for what is to come (Rev. 2:7, 11, 17, 29; 3:6, 13, 22).
4. God will honor those who seek Him.
   a. He will give crowns to those who long for His coming (2 Tim. 4:7-8).
   b. Understanding strengthens that longing.
5. We have been given a second chance to recognize Christ's coming.
   a. The Book of Revelation tells of that event (Rev. 1:7).

(1) There are seven references to this return in Revelation alone (Rev. 1:7; 2:25; 3:3; 11; 22:7, 12, 20).
(2) It shall take place in public and is not to be confused with the Rapture of the church, which will be in secret.
  b. If we delve into His Word, He will show us how to recognize that the time is at hand (Matt. 24:4-14).
  c. We are given another opportunity to be ready for Christ's return, if we so choose.

Prophecy

Throughout the ages, God has repeatedly spoken through certain carefully chosen men and women—prophets—in order to reveal Himself, His will, His plans and purposes, and what is to come, so that His people should not be caught off guard. He does not wish that His children be at a loss about how to respond to experiences in which they find themselves.

He knows the future and what man will be asked to endure should he choose to follow Jesus Christ. Because of His mercy and undying love, God reveals bits and pieces of that prophetic knowledge in order to strengthen, encourage, and comfort the Church (1 Cor.14:3). He knows how important this will be during, and in anticipation of, the hard-times that are inevitable. For the duration of this life, God's people may only understand in part, but when Christ returns, all that has been foretold will be made clear.

1. In The Revelation of Jesus Christ, prophecy is a message given to John, of the unfolding of God's program of redemption and the restoration of all things defiled by sin.
2. It is a catalyst—a mechanism—which speeds up the process of the spreading of God's Word.
   a. It opens the door to understanding, so one can be prepared for what is to come.
   b. While nothing is changed by prophecy, it facilitates a process that is already in motion.
3. Prophecy is history from God's point of view.
4. There are three main categories, or combinations of prophecy in the Bible.
   a. Prophecy concerning what will happen to The Nations (Dan. 7:13-14).
      (1) The goal is the end of Satan's reign and the beginning of Christ's.
   b. Prophecy dealing with Israel and the Jews (Ezek. 36:25-28).
      (1) The goal is a righteous nation and the Kingdom of David.

         c. Prophecy with respect to the Church (& the kingdom)—Revelation.
            (1) This goal is a new heaven and a new earth.
    5. Satan crosses between, and affects, all of these prophetic lines.
    6. Types of Old Testament prophetic books:
         a. The following books deal with, and describe, both events of their own times and future events.
            (1) If referring to their own time, a date and place is given.
                    Isaiah   Jeremiah   Ezekiel
                    Daniel   Hosea   Amos
                    Micah   Zephaniah   Haggai   Zechariah
            (2) If referring to the future, no date or place is given. It is assumed the reference is to the future.
                    Joel   Obediah   Naham
                    Habukkuk   Malachi

A Time of Tribulation

So..., when do the last days begin? We are told repeatedly throughout the Bible, in both the Old and New Testaments, just how to recognize when the end times are upon us:

- The Antichrist will be revealed,
- The temple rebuilt,
- There will be a falling away of Christians from the faith.
- A one-world government formed.
- A great display of heavenly events—stars fall from the sky, the sky darkens, the moon turns blood red, and
- The Antichrist desecrates the temple.

Leading up to these events, however, the whole world will watch and experience an increase in trials and tribulations. Just since the beginning of the current millennium in 2000, we have observed an unbelievable increase in terrorist activity. Wars and rumors of wars are far beyond Afghanistan, Iraq, Iran, and Palestine, etc. There have been earthquakes, hurricanes, floods, fires, tornadoes, and drought, as seldom, if ever, seen before, resulting in increased famine and scarcity. Diseases and pestilence, such as pandemic, avian and swine flues, Ebola, ongoing HIV, and a resurgence of TB, are out of control. Even the weather has become extreme. Violence has moved from the streets into the classrooms. The financial crash of the economy has devastated lives of both rich and poor. Leadership becomes increasingly corrupt and inept. Morals continue to be compromised, and no one—Christian or non-Christian—will escape the consequences of living in this world in which evil and wickedness have become a way of life. Even today, there is a total disregard for, and perversion of, moral standards—good has become evil and evil good. Anything and everything goes. These are only the birth pangs of the last days, but such will be the times as the end of days approach.

Even so, there is much debate about whether we are currently in a time of tribulation and when the end times begin? If we consider the fact that Jesus came to save mankind from sin and evil, which is Satan's prevailing approach to destroying God's children, then we can say that the Devil's demise begins with the First Coming of Jesus Christ. It concludes with His Second Coming, when Satan is cast into the great abyss. We must remember that God does not measure time as man does—a thousand years is as a day, and a day is as a thousand years. The last days are, therefore, a slow but progressive process.

Jesus told us in John 16:33, that we would have trials and tribulation in life, because we live in a sinful and wicked world. His life was no exception. He demonstrated this fact to the extreme. No one ever suffered or was persecuted more, and yet Jesus taught us how to overcome and be victorious. He stepped down from the Throne of God to live on this earth and grow into a man of sorrow. He suffered all of the betrayal, persecution, and torment unto death that this world could mete out, in order to provide hope to a fallen humanity.

What does this all mean? Obviously, we have been in a time of tribulation for almost 2000 years. How long it will last only the Father knows. We are just not yet in the Period of Tribulation of the last days. Nevertheless, if we know and watch the signs of the times, we <u>can</u> be prepared for the *"Day of the Lord."*

DEFINITION OF TERMS

There are certain terms, phrases, and symbols that appear throughout the Old and New Testaments. These have specific meanings attached to them that enable the reader to understand better what is being described or explained about a specific topic. This is particularly true in the Book of Revelation. The following are a few that are repeatedly used in reference to end times:

1. *"The Day of the Lord"* - the day, or days and events, leading up to His return.
2. *"In that day"* - the Day of the Lord, or the end times.
3. *"After these things…"* - what is to come in the last days.
4. "Pre-tribulation" - the Rapture before the tribulation period begins.

5. "Mid-tribulation" - the Rapture midway through the seven-year period
6. "Post-tribulation" - the Rapture at the end of the seven-year period just before the return of Christ.
7. The Bride - the tried and tested saints who overcome—the Church.
8. Overcomers - saints (people) who persevere and overcome the evil of the world and hold fast to their faith in Jesus Christ.
9. Tribulation Saints - those who accepted Jesus as Lord and Savior following the Rapture.
10. God's program - His purpose and plan in creation and redemption.
11. Significance of certain numbers:
    4 = the Earth - N,S,E,W; elements - air, water, fire, earth (dirt)
    6 = Satan's number = incompleteness 666 = unholy trinity
    7 = completeness (7 days = a week, 7 churches = the completed church)
    7 = 4 (the earth) + 3 (heavens)
    10 = indefinite number
12. "dead in Christ" - those who have already died believing in Christ. When we die as believers, our spirit immediately goes to be with the Lord; the body remains in the grave, or wherever, until "that day" (the Rapture), when the two are reunited in glorified bodies.
13. Mankind - male and/or female alike

The "Last Days" or "End times"

Just as it is important to have a shared understanding of certain terms associated with complex subject matter, it is imperative to have similar views on concepts related to those topics. Without a clarity of meaning, individuals often reach differing, or conflicting, conclusions. It is not that there is only one interpretation, but for the purpose of discussion, like must be compared with like.

This is particularly critical in a study of the Book of Revelation. Because of the symbolic nature of its content, there have been many opposing interpretations of what is presented—some misleading and others merely a source of confusion. This is not in accord with God's will and the reason why parameters should be spelled out from the onset.

Because of the abstract nature of John's visions, the most important issue that needs to be clear is the difference between what is meant by the phrases "the last days" and "the end times." Do they refer to the same time period? Are they synonymous with the last days of the existence of this earth, as we know it? How can we know they have been rightly interpreted, and does it even matter? Based upon <u>this</u> study, it most assuredly matters, and without clear insight, the entire book is often misunderstood. As scripture is the only real source of explanation, it is necessary to examine it carefully, in order to gain proper insight. It is vital to speaking the same language.

First of all, the "last days" and "end times" are not synonymous. They are differing time periods relative to differing groups of people. The Old Testament tells of God's creation of mankind and the universe, as well as the history of the Jewish people and their relationship with Him. The New Testament deals with the life of Christ and the development of the Church. Revelation is the culmination of all that has gone before and is yet to come. With this framework, we are told by the prophets that the "last days" refer to the current Church Age, ending with the Rapture of all true believers. The "end times" are reflected in the Tribulation Period leading up to the return of Christ, the Messiah, as He comes to set up His kingdom on earth.

With this in mind, the question of whether we are living in the last days, or not, takes on new meaning. Yes, we are in the last days of the Church Age, which will end when Christ *"comes in a twinkling of an eye,"* to take the true believers—the visible church—to be with their Father in heaven. Their trials and tribulations will be over, and there will be no more pain or suffering for them. God Himself will wipe away every tear, and they will know joy. This is not the end of time, however. There is still more to come.

When this has been accomplished, the seven-year Period of Tribulation will begin. Often called "the latter days" in the Old Testament, it is that time, when God turns His attention to the redemption of His chosen people and the nation of Israel. This will mark the true "end times"—the end of days as they currently exist.

Thusly, as the Church, we are in our last days, and the signs clearly show that our redemption draws nigh. However, according to Old Testament prophecy, the end times are still to come. Only then will we see a New Heaven and New Earth.

1. One of the most often asked questions of our day is, "Are we currently living in the last days, or are they the end times, as described in the Book of Revelation?"
   a. These terms or concepts must first be defined in order to answer that question rightly; even then, they are used interchangeably at times.
   b. The answer, however, is dependent upon clarifying "the last days or end times of what."
2. In the context of <u>this</u> study, these terms refer to differing time periods and involve differing groups of people.
3. Upon examination of the scriptures, we are told that God spoke through the prophets and His Son about the last days, end times, and how to identify them.
   a. Sometimes He was speaking to Jews and sometimes to the Gentiles (Heb. 1:1-2).

b. Only by considering to whom and about what He spoke can we reach defensible conclusions.
4. The interpretation of <u>this</u> study is that the "last days" refer to the Church Age, which began with Pentecost and will end with the Rapture of the true church, or believers in Christ as Lord and Savior.
   a. This is supported by both Old and New Testament prophets, as well as Christ Himself, as they describe what to look for as this period approaches its end.
   b. If we examine scripture, and accept it as truth, along with the conditions of our time, we are living in the "last days."
   c. These are not the last days of time, but the last days of the Church Age—the Age of the Gentiles.
5. Old Testament prophecy often calls the "end times," "latter days," or a time of *stress* (Deut. 4:30).
   a. *Stress* in Hebrew means tribulation.
   b. Both Daniel and Jeremiah describe the conditions of the latter days as indicative of the Tribulation Period—that time when God will pour out His anger upon His people until they repent and His purpose of love is accomplished (Jer. 30:24; 48:47) (Dan.: 10:14).
   c. He clearly states that this time is in the future, and He will bring peace and rest to those who return to His will for them.
6. Thusly, it is possible to say that we are living in the "last days," which have not yet come to an end.
   a. These will end when the Rapture and the gathering of the Tribulation Saints occurs.
   b. However, only God knows the day or time.
7. The "end times" will then follow, during which God will deal with the nation of Israel and the wicked of the world.
   a. This period will encompass the seven-year Period of Tribulation, indicated by the opening of the seventh seal.
   b. During that time, God will pour out His wrath upon the wicked world.
8. When all that is foretold is finished, Christ the Messiah will return to destroy sin, restore the earth and mankind, and set up a new kingdom.

Jesus Christ, The Revelation

In His infinite wisdom, God knows that what man does not fully understand, he tends to ignore, or forget—even if he has been told or shown the facts. Throughout the Bible, God has repeatedly revealed Himself, His love, His will, and the laws He has given man to guide him through the challenges of life. The Word says that there will be trials and tribulations, but God has made a way for man to endure and overcome. All that is required is an understanding of the way and a willingness to obey.

Throughout the ages, God spoke through the prophets. He sent miracles, signs and wonders, and finally His own son, Jesus Christ, to reveal the way and all truths—to know the Son is to know the Father (John 14:7). By leaving the Godhead and coming to earth as a man, Jesus brought the Word personally and provided an example of how man should live, in order to have eternal life. He then paid the ultimate price by dying on the cross, as a sacrificial offering for man's sins—*"the wages of sin is death"* (Rom. 6:23). In this way, He provided a means for man to be saved.

Even in the Old Testament, God foretold this coming of Jesus, as well as how to recognize Him. Either man did not listen and believe, or he simply did not understand. In either case, the first coming of Jesus Christ was missed, and man did not recognize his Savior. Jesus then foretold that He would come again and take all who believed in His message of love and truth with Him to the Father. This time, Satan, sin, and death would be defeated and destroyed forever. When that is accomplished, all things will be made new and God's perfect creation restored.

The Revelation of Jesus Christ, the last book of the Bible, is God's final attempt to inform and prepare mankind for the last days and this Second Coming. It is His desire that all should be saved, but He knows that not all will. We have been given the freedom to choose who and what to follow—Jesus and an eternity with Him and the Father, or an eternity with Satan and the consequences of our own choices. Under both the direction of our Creator, as well as the influence of the Evil One, we have the opportunity to choose which option to elect.

The Book of Revelation describes in very graphic terms how to identify that the end times have come, what to expect, and the choices with which one will be faced. This time, the vision is given to another of God's chosen prophets, and it provides a supernatural revelation of the return of Jesus Christ—this time as Judge and King. During His First Coming, He rode on a donkey in peace. At His Second Coming, He will appear on a mighty steed to do battle. The prophetic vision discloses in detail a great battle, which will be waged against Satan and his powers of darkness. In typical apocalyptic form, it provides a last-chance effort to show mankind that there is hope for a victorious future, but severe consequences for poor choices.

1. The New Testament book of The Revelation of Jesus Christ is an "apocalypse"— a vision—and means the supernatural unveiling, or revelation, of divine truths unknown to man and incapable of being otherwise discovered (Rom. 16:25).

a. It is a part of God's promise to reveal His secrets and impart knowledge of His plans.
   b. In this case, it deals with the belief that the power of evil (Satan), who is in control of human behavior, is to be overcome by the direct intervention of God, who is the power of good.
      (1) As a result, an entirely new, perfect, and eternal age will be created for the righteous.
      (2) True apocalyptic writings are concerned with the events of the "last days," the end of the present age, and life in the age to come.
      (3) This sets Revelation apart from the works of prophecy in the Old Testament, which deal with life in that time period, rather than the next.
   c. Revelation reveals two opposing, supernatural powers that are both personal and universal in character.
      (1) Both of these powers have human and supernatural followers.
      (2) Those followers are in conflict throughout history.
2. The Book of Revelation is both the revealing of Jesus Christ as the object and the subject of the writings, and His revelation to mankind of the plan for "*what must soon take place*" (Rev. 1:1; 22:6-7).
   a. One point of view is that, like the belief of the early church that the events being described in Revelation were about to take place, they describe the persecution that the church would suffer under Roman domination.
   b. Since Christ Himself said "*...this generation will not pass away before all these things take place...,*" this interpretation has flaws (Mark 3:30).
   c. The generation of Christ's time has passed away, and "the last days" are still to come.
   d. This is God's revelation, however, and time is measured in His terms, not necessarily ours.
      (1) To God, "*A day is as a thousand years, and a thousand years as a day*" (2 Pet.3:8).
      (2) "Soon" not only means in the near future, but can also mean suddenly, or swiftly.
      (3) When the events of the last days begin, they will take less than one generation to be accomplished (Mark 3:30).
3. The Gospels tell of Jesus as Man, while Revelation reveals Jesus as God.
   a. The Gospels are the apostles' first-person accounts of Jesus as a man.
   b. Revelation is John's first-person account, through his visions, of Jesus as God.
4. The book tells of the redemption and restoration of all that was lost by sin (our bodies, our souls, and the planet itself).

a. God will regenerate, or restore, all to its original, perfectly created condition.
   b. He will give us glorified (not regenerated) bodies.
   c. Christ will reclaim that which He created and make it perfect, as it once was.
   d. That which cannot be redeemed shall be destroyed by God's Wrath.
5. Christ's coming for His Bride (the Church), the judgment of the wicked, and the set-up of His eternal kingdom are all revealed in great detail.
6. The account of John's vision is God's revelation <u>to</u> the churches and <u>about</u> the Church.
7. Paul's words in Acts 28:27-31 are indicative of the fact that it was God's intent that all should know of His Word.
   a. It was Paul's mission to take that Word to the Gentiles.
   b. God's revelation of Jesus to the Church was the last until the Book of Revelation.

SCHOOLS OF INTERPRETATION

Because this revelation was written in a different time and to a different culture, much of the symbolism is foreign and unfamiliar to our age. Consequently, people of today either totally discount the prophecy as a piece of fantasy, or have interpreted the descriptions from their own perspectives—to support their particular agendas. As a result, there are numerous interpretations of what the images used throughout the book mean. Unfortunately, their differences have led to much confusion and controversy, even within the Church. Disagreement has actually fostered a separation in beliefs. This is to the delight of Satan, who is the Father of Deception. Nothing makes him more pleased than to watch discord among the brethren.

The fact is, modes of interpretation are not salvation issues. However, acceptance of the ultimate truth that Jesus will return for His own, conquer sin and death for the last time, and bring judgment upon Satan and his followers is vital. Unless people study the scriptures carefully and understand their implications, they will be unprepared to rightly interpret the Word and make wise choices. The Bible states very emphatically that we are to neither add to, nor remove from, the Word of God, or there will be dire consequences (Deut. 4:2; Prov. 30:5; Rev. 22:18). For that reason, it is imperative that God's people be enlightened and able to choose wisely between what is honest and true and that which is in error or deceptive.

"Write What You See..." is a comprehensive examination of the Revelation of Jesus Christ from a pre-tribulation, dispensational, pre-millennial perspective, providing detailed evidence to support that point of view. It does not attempt to apply meaning to modern-day events in order to fit them into scriptural context, however. As mentioned previously, this

is a verse-by-verse commentary on what the Word actually says. Interpretation is then up to the reader.

1. John says that "*the time is at hand*," and through the ages, many who have read this have looked at the events of their day and attempted to associate world conditions with Christ's warnings of what shall take place just before His return.
   a. It is true that everything that has thus far occurred is leading up to the "last days."
   b. It is necessary to read carefully the Word, however, in order to rightly interpret "*what must take place*."
2. Unfortunately, there is little unanimity with respect to the interpretation of the events, signs, and symbols described in the Book of Revelation.
   a. In the context of this study, a symbol is considered to be something that often represents or suggests something else, because of its relationship with, or resemblance to, another person, object, or event—a visible sign of something invisible, intended to clarify or give greater meaning to what is being described. It may have multiple meanings or interpretations.
   b. A sign either stands for something other than itself, or is a message that points toward something that will occur. Normally, it has only one meaning.
   c. The visions, which John sees, are generally not common to man's typical experience—especially in today's culture.
      (1) He didn't know what the future would look like, so he described what he saw in relation to what he did know, or was understandable in the first century—much of which was viewed in mythical terms.
      (2) A great deal of his symbolism is, therefore, difficult for us to interpret in modern-day terminology.
      (3) Many of the images seem both impossible and/or highly improbable to our times.
      (4) Because time references are also often unclear, much confusion has occurred in that regard.
   d. As a result, people have applied many different interpretations and meanings to this book throughout the ages.
   e. Many of these interpretations are in direct conflict with one another; others lend themselves to various explanations.
   f. Only through the leading of the Holy Spirit, as well as careful study of the entire Word and how it builds upon itself, can one reach a decision of how to interpret the events of John's vision.

  g. The following are various interpretive approaches to explaining the Book of Revelation.
3. Symbolic/Idealist View
  a. This is an allegorical view, which bears <u>no</u> relationship to historical events.
  b. The interpretation of the symbols used is based on the assumption that what is revealed are simply universal truths of good and evil in conflict.
  c. Nothing that either has happened, or is yet to take place, is seen as real or actual.
  d. Revelation is merely a story written by a man to make certain points about what the prophecies of the Old and New Testaments might have meant.
4. Preterist (Past) View
  a. This view describes conditions existing during the first century or shortly thereafter.
  b. All prophesized events were considered to be fulfilled by 70 A.D.
  c. Events illustrate the persecution of the Christians under the domination of the Roman Empire.
  d. The "last days" in this interpretation mean the last days before the destruction of the temple.
  e. 70 A.D. is seen as the end of the age—the age of the old covenant and redemptive plan through animal sacrifice.
  f. Most end events are believed to have already occurred.
  g. Christ's return was expected to be imminent.
  h. The problem with this interpretation is that it is meaningless to subsequent generations, except as a history of the early church.
  i. Most modern scholars do incorporate a part of this view into their interpretation.
5. Historical View
  a. From the historical perspective, events are seen as a chronological preview of the whole Christian era.
  b. The seals, trumpets, and bowls of judgment are viewed as different periods history.
  c. They are symbolic of western church history through the ages.
  d. This outlook, however, keeps changing its interpretation of events based upon the times.
  e. Its approach holds the Bible in one hand and a newspaper, or history book, in the other, and tries to make them agree.

6. Futurist View
    a. Futurists interpret the events of Revelation as referring literally to those of the end times yet to come—immediately before the Second Coming of Jesus Christ.
    b. They relate John's visions to ones of a great tribulation before the establishment of God's kingdom described in the Old Testament and in Matthew.
    c. Any relationships to historical events are viewed as merely "similar to" or "rehearsals of" those things that will take place in the last days of time, as we now know it.
    d. This provides a perspective that has relevance and meaning for succeeding generations of Christians.
7. Amillennialist View
    a. Though this is a widely accepted view, it is not consistent with what scripture says, if one believes that the Word is *"honest and true."*
    b. It contends that there is no literal 1,000 year reign of Christ on earth.
    c. This period is simply symbolic of the present or Church Age.
    d. It is spiritual in nature.
8. Dispensational Pre-millennialist View
    a. Related to the Futurist View, this perspective holds that the Second Coming of Christ, and the subsequent millennial kingdom, are preceded by a seven-year period known as the "Tribulation."
    b. It also considers the millennium to be a literal 1,000 years.
    c. During this time, the nation of Israel will be saved and restored to a position of preeminence during the millennium.
    d. This is the point of view of <u>this</u> study.
9. The interpretation given to the symbolism and meaning of Revelation often depends upon the reader's approach to interpreting the Bible as a whole.
10. The only agreement between these views is that this is a powerful affirmation of God's triumph over evil.

PART II
INTRODUCTION and the CHURCHES

CHAPTER 2
"The things which thou hast seen"

INTRODUCTION (REV. 1:1-19)

AS RECORDED SO GRAPHICALLY IN the Book of Revelation, this prophetic vision is a foretelling of the events of the end times and all that one might expect to see and experience during those days. Who had it, and when and where did it occur? How and why was it written in such detail and yet made to be so mysterious and symbolic? What was its purpose, and how can one believe whether it is honest or true? These are all questions that are systematically addressed in the book that has survived the test of time.

Following the life, death, and resurrection of Jesus Christ, His disciples took seriously His command to *"go into all the world and spread the gospel..."*—a gospel of God's love and saving grace (Mark 16:15). As they carried out their commission to make Jesus and God's plan known to mankind, the numbers of believers multiplied exponentially, and they established churches everywhere they went. At the same time, however, this small band of advocates for Jesus was actually feared and distrusted, hated and severely persecuted by the Roman government and non-believers alike. As the years passed, most of the entire original group was ultimately put to death in some horrific manner—all because of their unwavering commitment to spreading the gospel of truth and love.

WHO, WHERE, WHEN, AND WHY

Only the Apostle John, the youngest of the twelve disciples, who was often referred to as *"the disciple whom Jesus loved,"* lived to die a natural death in his late 90s. However, throughout his ministry, he too was persecuted and tortured to the point of death for preaching the Word of God. Very late in his life, about 96 A.D., he was imprisoned on the Isle of Patmos, by the Emperor Domitian, for teaching the Way, as it was first called. It was in that desolate place that God gave him a vision of *"what must soon take place."* This was a vision intended to prepare mankind to make life-changing choices that would seal their destiny and determine their eternal life. It would provide notice of what is to come in the last days and how to survive.

Over a thousand years earlier, God gave Daniel and Ezekiel, two Old Testament prophets, very similar visions. He very specifically told them, however, not to share their visions, as it was not the time. John, on the other hand, was firmly instructed to *"write what you see..."* and share it with the seven churches of Asia Minor (Rev. 1:11)—churches he had helped establish and knew well. His written account was then to be read and heard by all believers of all times. This was not simply a prophecy for that period in history. It was intended to be a foretelling of the pain and judgment one could expect throughout life and during the last days in particular. At the same time, it was also to be a guide aimed at leading Christians toward a life of hope and eternal life with God and Jesus Christ. All that is asked of mankind is a willingness to be open to the teachings of the scriptures and a decision as to whom to follow—the Lord, God Almighty, or Satan, the *"deceiver of the brethren."*

1. Some disagreement still exists about who the John of Revelation is.
    a. Because of the difference in writing style between The Gospel of John, 1 John, 2 John, 3 John, and Revelation, some believe the author might not be one and the same.
    b. The gospels of John were <u>inspired</u> by God, but Revelation was <u>revealed</u> to him by God in a vision.
        (1) It was God's message, not John's.
        (2) It uses much of the format and style standards found in prophetic writings throughout the Bible, thus explaining a difference in writing style.
        (3) An example is the telling and retelling of a story from different perspectives in order to cover all of its aspects.
        (4) This same approach is used in the description of Daniel and Ezekiel's visions.
        (5) The difference in John's writing styles is also evidence that, what he has written in Revelation is not merely his own writing or thoughts.
    c. Some believe the gospel of John could have been dictated to a secretary—most likely Polycarp, his disciple.
        (1) This was often the custom in those days.
        (2) Polycarp's Greek style of writing might have been more formal than John's education could have allowed.
    d. Because of his advanced age and failing eyesight, he might also have had someone else copy the account of his vision, as he had written it—explaining some differences in style.
    e. The consensus, however, is that the author of this book was the Apostle John.
        (1) Such early writers as Justin Martyr, Irenaeus, Tertullian, and others confirm this identity.

(2) It was not until the third century that Dionysius raised arguments that produced other conclusions.
2. There is also some disagreement concerning <u>when</u> Revelation was written.
   a. One belief is that it was written during the reign of Nero, after the 64 A.D. burning of Rome.
      (1) Hostility against Christians was increasing to the point of persecution.
      (2) Because the Hebrew letters for Nero add up to 666, he was believed to be the Antichrist.
      (3) It was also foretold that Nero would reappear in the East after his death.
      (4) This interpretation fits the historical belief that Revelation foretells the tribulation leading to the destruction of Jerusalem and the temple in 70 A.D., which marks the end of the Judaic Age.
   b. There is stronger evidence, however, that John wrote the book around 96 A.D., near the end of the reign of Domitian.
      (1) Early writers such as Irenaeus, a disciple of Polycarp, supported this view.
      (2) As John probably did not leave Jerusalem to preach to the Gentiles until shortly before its destruction in 70 A.D. there would not have been sufficient time to have established a ministry and reputation such as he developed with the churches of Asia Minor.
      (3) Those churches had existed long enough, by the time John wrote his letters, for them to have lost some of their original fervor.
      (4) Also, Domitian was the first emperor to demand worship of himself while he was still alive, thus explaining a heightening of persecution of those who refused.
3. In his 90s, John was exiled to the Isle of Patmos, most likely by Domitian, for his Christian beliefs and for preaching the Word of God (Rev. 1:9).
   a. Despite the oppressive, barren, hostility of this place, however, it was in this environment that John had the miraculous visions about which he wrote in the Book of Revelation.
   b. The place that was intended to be a place of torment in fact became a place of indescribable wonder.
   c. John was the last living Apostle, well known and highly revered by the churches of that day.
   d. Despite his position, however, he was a humble man, as evidenced in his reference to himself as *"a brother and companion in suffering..."* of those to whom he wrote (Rev. 1:9).

e. He was the only apostle to die a natural death, which he did at a very old age in Ephesus, following his release from Patmos.
4. While on the Isle of Patmos, John was given a vision of Jesus Christ and those things *"which would shortly take place"* (Rev. 1:1).
   a. What he recounts is not just what he was told, but what he actually experienced in the vision of days that are yet to come.
   b. This revelation, of what would occur just prior to Christ's return, was actually given by God to Jesus, who then imparted it to John.
   c. Prior to this time, even Jesus did not know the day or time of His return (Matt. 24:36).
      (1) It was not being kept a secret so that man would be taken by surprise.
      (2) It was being hidden from Satan, whose greatest desire is to prevent that event from occurring.
   d. John's visions were God's way of communicating this information to His people.
5. The Book of Revelation is not simply <u>about</u> Jesus, though that is evident, but <u>Jesus'</u> revelation, or unveiling, of what is to take place in the future, during the end times.
   a. Through an "angel," God gives John a vision of *"what must soon take place"* (Rev. 1:1).
   b. Based upon the description of the "angel," it was most likely Jesus Himself.
   c. He is often described as an "angel" in various other instances throughout the Bible and called 'Angel of the Lord' (Rev. 8:3-5; 10:1-3).
6. John is instructed to bear witness to *"what he sees,"* and write of it to those in the seven churches of Asia Minor, who have embraced Christ, as the Son of God (Rev. 1:2).
   a. While each church is an actual church, with which John was intimately familiar, they are also representative of the types of churches, with their strengths and weaknesses, to be seen throughout the Church Age.
      (1) The seven original churches were in Turkey (Asia Minor) within 80 miles of one another.
      (2) Though they were close in proximity, they were very different from one another and exemplary of the complete Church.
      (3) They serve as a model of how a church should function, and what they need to do to correct their weaknesses.
   b. Any church throughout history that does not fit within one of these formats is not a part of the completed Church.
   c. This is important to understand as one considers the validity of such modern-day movements as Mormons, Jehovah's Witnesses, Scientologists, etc.

7. Throughout the Book of Revelation, seven blessings or beatitudes are given to the faithful.
   a. The first is *"Blessed is the one who reads the words of this prophecy..., and who hears it and takes it to heart..."* (Rev. 1:3; 22:7).
      (1) This is the only book in the Bible that promises a blessing to those who read it.
      (2) Christ did say, however, in Luke 11:28 that *"...those who hear the Word and observe it are blessed."*
      (3) God obviously wants the prophesies of this book known, and it would seem to indicate that they were intended to be read in public.
      (4) In this way, He could bless those who would follow and heed His Word.
      (5) As a part of the scriptures, it was to be read aloud, so that it could be heard.
      (6) There is power in hearing the Word.
   b. The later blessings are:
      (1) *"Blessed are the dead who die in the Lord..."* (Rev. 14:13).
      (2) *"Blessed is he who stays awake..."* (Rev. 16:15).
      (3) *"Blessed are those who are invited to the wedding supper of the Lamb"* (Rev. 19:9).
      (4) *"Blessed and holy are those who have part in the first resurrection"* Rev. 20:6).
      (5) Again, *"Blessed is he who keeps the words of the prophecy in this book"* (Rev. 22:7).
      (6) *"Blessed are those who wash their robes, that they may have the right to the tree of life..."* (Rev. 22:14).
   c. By ignoring this book, the Church is not following God's command.
   d. Scripture is a guide to conduct, as well as a source of doctrine, and is not to be ignored.

THE PATMOS VISION (REV. 1:4-10)

John begins his description of what he sees by identifying himself and the One through whom the revelation comes. He describes the state he was in at the time, what he hears, who and what he sees, and why he is being given a vision of the Second Coming of Jesus Christ. This revelation results in a step-by-step record of John's experience throughout the vision. The analysis of this teaching, *"Write What You See...,"* is an interpretation of John's scriptural account.

1. John begins by greeting the seven churches and by identifying from whom this revelation comes (Rev. 1:1, 4, 9; 22:8).

a. The message is "...*from Him who is, and who was, and who is to come, the Almighty*" (*Rev.* 1:4) (Heb. 13:8).
   (1) This is the eternal God the Father.
   (2) He is the source of all things and encompasses all things.
   (3) The fact that He is "almighty" speaks to His omnipotence.
b. It is also "...*from the seven spirits before His throne*" (the Holy Spirit). The seven spirits include: (Rev. 1:4 & 5) (Is. 11:2-3)
   (1) The Spirit of the Lord, which encompasses everything the others do not.
   (2) The Spirit of Knowledge,
   (3) The Spirit of Wisdom,
   (4) The Spirit of Counsel,
   (5) The Spirit of Understanding,
   (6) The Spirit of Strength, and
   (7) The Spirit of Fear of the Lord.
c. The seven spirits represent the sevenfold ministry of the Holy Spirit, as described in Isaiah 11:2.
   (1) They are the various aspects or the totality of the Holy Spirit, which is a part of the trinity.
   (2) They represent the distinct roles the Holy Spirit plays to accomplish God's will.
   (3) They are given authority over the Churches among which Jesus walks.
   (4) Because they are before the throne, we can surmise that they will be sent out onto the earth to accomplish differing events about to befall mankind in the last days.
d. And "*from Jesus Christ.*"
   (1) He is the faithful witness. (Ps. 89:37)
      (a) He communicates to John the revelation given to Him by God.
      (b) And because of what He suffered in life and death, He can act as a model to those who are about to be persecuted.
      (c) He bears witness to the fact that He has prepared a way of salvation.
   (2) He is the firstborn of the dead (2 Cor. 15:20) (Col. 1:18).
   (3) The one who loves us and died for our sins.
e. Though He has physically left this realm, His work is not yet finished.
f. He still must be a warrior and judge.
g. Even in this prophetic account of the last days, the message begins with the gospel of salvation (Rev. 1:5).

(1) We have been saved from our sins for a purpose—to rule and reign with Jesus in eternity.
(2) *"He has made us to be a kingdom, priests..."* (Rev. 1:6) (Ex. 19:6) (Is. 61:6).
(3) For Christ's sacrifice, we are to give Him *"...glory and honor forever and ever. Amen"* (Rev. 1:6).
(4) The Holy Spirit reveals all things to us, if we will but listen and heed Him.

2. The Second Coming of Jesus Christ is described to remind us that He is coming again (Rev.1:7).
   a. He did not return to heaven to stay there; He went to prepare a place for us (John 14:2-3).
   b. He would then one day return for those who would rule and reign with Him for eternity.
   c. As He ascended, He would come back with the clouds to reclaim His own (Matt. 24:30) (Mark 14:62) (Acts 1:11).
   d. The saints or elect, who are gathered from the heavens, are often referred to as clouds (Jude 14).
   e. All shall see Him, *"...even those who pierced Him."* (Jews)
   f. The unsaved will wail and mourn, for they do not want to see Him return (Matt. 24:30).
      (1) The only ones left on the earth, upon His return, will be the unsaved and the Jews.
      (2) Because the unsaved know they will be punished even more severely than they already have, they "wail" at His coming.

3. With that, it is stated, *"So be it. Amen"* (Rev.1:7).
   a. As it begins, so does the book end: *"So be it. Amen"* (Rev. 22:20-21).
   b. The first and the last—one in the same.

4. Jesus then states, as He does on numerous occasions, that He is the *"Alpha and Omega,"* the *"first and the last"* (Rev. 1:8; 2:8; 21:6 & 22:13) (Is. 41:4).
   a. He is the Lord God Almighty, *"who is, who was, and who is to come."*
   b. Jesus and God—separate and yet one.

5. John tells us that he was *"in the spirit,"* in prayer on the Lord's Day.
   a. This is the first and only reference in the scriptures to *"the Lord's Day."*
   b. All do not agree on an interpretation.
   c. Based upon similar references to the last days, however, most Jews of that time would interpret it to refer to events of the end times.
   d. It is possible, however, to believe it is a reference to that day on which Christ was resurrected into heaven.

  e. This is the day the Church reserved as a day of prayer and worship.

  f. Being "*in the spirit*" could mean that he was in deep prayer and meditation, and in the process had an amazing mystical experience.

6. On this day, as he was in the spirit, John hears a voice, crystal clear like a trumpet, telling him to write all that he would see, and send it as a message, to the churches of Asia Minor (Rev.1:10-11).

  a. The voice John hears is that of Jesus/the Lord/God.

   (1) Though somewhat different, he knows that voice.

   (2) He had spent three years listening to it.

  b. Often throughout the scriptures, this voice is likened to a trumpet.

THE SYMBOLS (REV. 1:12-20)

Because the things which John sees are so bizarre and improbable, especially to our day and times, he uses a great deal of symbolism to explain his meanings. Additionally, prophetic language tends to be poetic and symbolic in form. Therefore, it is important to understand that, as mentioned earlier, a symbol is generally used to represent something other than itself—a visual sign of something often invisible or difficult to explain. It is an image <u>like</u> something more common to one's understanding. In John's account of what he sees and hears, he often likens something to an image or sound that is more familiar or imaginable to the reader. Throughout the Book of Revelation, it is important to remember that a sign or symbol is intended to clarify meaning.

1. As John turns to see who speaks, he sees seven lampstands, which represent the seven churches.

  a. Lampstands are not candles, and do not give off light (symbolic of truth and knowledge) themselves.

   (1) They hold the candles, which give forth the light.

   (2) Jesus is the light, and the Church holds that light up for the entire world to see.

  b. Jesus is then observed walking among the lampstands—ever in their presence.

   (1) He is, and shall be, always in the midst of His people (Matt. 28:20) (John 14:18).

   (2) He never takes His eyes from them.

   (3) He knows them intimately.

  c. In the midst of the lampstands is the *"son of man."*

(1) This was Jesus' favorite name for Himself, which He used more often than any other to identify Himself (Dan. 7:13).
(2) He saw Himself as a servant and took on the likeness of man (Phil.2:6-11)
(3) In His humility, He actually experienced all that would be required to save mankind from sin.
(4) His love for us is so great He gave up His character of God to take on the nature of man.
(5) God had to watch this happen in order for His plan to be accomplished.
(6) As a result, God exalted Jesus above all and gave Him a name above all names (Phil. 2:8-9).

d. Jesus reveals Himself to John, at this point, in His glorified body and as God (Rev. 1:13-20) (Dan. 7:9; 10:5-6) (Is. 53:2).
 (1) He has a robe reaching to His feet = Priestly attire.
 (2) A golden girdle across His breast = Kingly attire.
 (3) His hair is white like wool and snow = Incarnate purity and wisdom (Dan. 7:9).
 (4) His eyes are like a blazing fire = Perfect knowledge and understanding of all things.
 (5) His feet are as burnished bronze = Feet denote dominion over, and bronze signifies judgment; i.e. His feet are coming in judgment (Ezek. 1:7) (Ps. 110:1).
 (6) His voice is like rushing water = Power and majesty (Ezek. 43:2) (Ps. 29:3).
 (7) He holds seven stars in His right hand = Angels (or ministers) of the seven churches.
 (8) He walks among the churches holding their angels (ministers) in His right hand, signifying authority over the church.
  (a) The Churches are the lampstands.
  (b) The ministers are the stars.
  (c) And Christ is the sun or light.
 (9) He has a tongue like a two-edged sword = The Word of God—Judgment and the Good News (Is. 55:11) (Heb. 4:12) (Eph. 6:17).
 (10) And His face is like the sun—bright and strong.

e. John knows this is Jesus, but unlike how he had known Him before, this is a bigger-than-life, regal Jesus.

f. The power of seeing the "Shekinah Glory" of God is so great that John falls into a faint.

- (1) This was a common reaction to experiencing the divine glory of God (Ezek. 1:28) (Dan. 8:17).
- (2) As only the pure in heart can see God and live, this was a protection in the presence of such power.
- g. Jesus touches John, however, and tells him to *'fear not'*, reminding him of who He is: (Dan.10:10-12)
  - (1) The "*first and the last*" (Rev. 1:17) (Is. 41:40, 48:12).
  - (2) The Living One.
  - (3) He who was dead and now lives forevermore.
  - (4) He who holds the keys and has authority over death.
  - (5) Because of who He is, John need not fear.
  - (6) This is the message of the entire Bible.
2. John is then told again to write what he sees (the vision of Jesus/God), what is (the churches as he shall describe them), and what shall take place in the future "*after these things*" (Rev.1:19).
   a. "*After these things...*" is what is yet to come following the Church Age.
      - (1) The Church Age is that period between the beginning of the Church, on the Day of Pentecost, and the return of Jesus Christ for His Church—the Rapture.
      - (2) If "*these things*" are to occur after the Churches, it must mean the Church is removed or Raptured before they take place.
   b. "*After these things...*" is the consummation of God's redemptive plan and the coming of His kingdom.
   c. It is at this point that prophecy begins, and all that is described in the first three chapters <u>must take place and end</u>, before the events of Chapter Four can commence.
   d. Despite all that lies ahead, Christ's word to John is to "*Fear not*" (Rev. 1:17).
3. There are those (Post Tribulationists) who believe that nearly everything up to the 18th chapter of Revelation has already occurred, and the prophesies have been fulfilled.
   a. Considering that history repeats itself until it is completed, often prophetic events do also.
   b. There have been a number of examples and rehearsals of events of the last days, but they obviously were not the end of time, as we currently know it.
   c. They have been like dress rehearsals.

d. There are things that yet need to occur before the <u>final</u> events can begin to take place.
4. We are told never to add or take away anything from what is written (Rev. 22:18-19).
   a. If anything is added, God will add plagues.
   b. If anything is taken away, He will remove one's place in the *Book of Life*.
   c. These are serious consequences and should warn men not to interpret the Word according to their own wishes or beliefs.

CHAPTER 3
"The things which are"

THE CHURCHES (REV. 2 & 3)

FROM THE VERY BEGINNING OF his vision, John is specifically told to write *"the things which thou hast seen," "the things which are,"* and *"the things which shall be"* (Rev. 1:19). What does that mean, and does it really matter if one understands or not? It absolutely does! Unless one has a defensible understanding of the differences between these three situations, as well as the importance and significance it has to the whole of God's revelation, it is not possible to interpret rightly the message it imparts. Prophecy follows a chronology and, if the events are not delivered in a chronological order, recognition of the truth may be unidentifiable.

When it comes to an analysis of John's vision and the meaning of what he conveys, it is imperative to grasp that these three perspectives are based on differing conditions. If it were not so, no distinction would be necessary. To this point, John has seen and heard Jesus in all His glory and majesty. He describes His appearance and the many attributes of His nature. John also identifies the seven spirits, or aspects of the Holy Spirit, through whom the revelation is also imparted. He then explains the symbolism of what he has seen. All of this encompasses *"the things which thou hast seen."*

Because of the instruction to write about the details of his vision, John records what he is told and sends it in the form of letters to the seven churches of Asia Minor. *"The things which are"* are the seven churches. These are actual churches that exist at that moment in time. They are churches that John is intimately and personally familiar with, because he had a hand in starting and growing them from their inception. Following a description of the letters, which he writes to each church, they—the Church—are not mentioned again, until the end of the book. Because only Tribulation Saints are discussed from that point on, it would seem to be a solid indication that they do not make up the Church that is taken up when the Rapture first occurs. These Saints, therefore, are those who come to a realization, during the Tribulation, of the truth of what the Church had been trying to communicate all along—salvation through the acceptance of Jesus Christ as Lord and

Savior. Therefore, since the preponderance of the Book of Revelation is John's vision of what is yet to come—an interpretation of the events leading up to the Second Coming of Jesus Christ, as well as the final battle between good and evil—it is a legitimate conclusion that this is what represents *"the things which shall be."*

BACKGROUND

As stated previously, the seven churches, to which John directs the letters dictated by Jesus Christ, are literal churches located in western Asia Minor. They are each in cities of significant renown and cultural influence. However, in the Book of Revelation, they are also intended to be representative of all churches throughout the Church Age—some fundamental and ritualistic, others radical, liberal, secular, and/or materialistic in nature. These churches exist simultaneously, and yet are also reflective of differing time periods in history. The message conferred in the letters, therefore, is as relevant for today as in the day they were penned.

When John wrote these letters, the Church was, and would be for generations to come, being severely persecuted by the Roman government and non-Christian world. It was a hopelessly evil period, and the Church—made up of the believers in Jesus Christ, with Him as its head—was in jeopardy of total annihilation. It was, and would continue to be, hard to be a Christian, and they needed hope and encouragement. Though originally comprised primarily of Jews—the leaders of which had had Jesus put to death—the Church began to grow among the Gentiles, or non-Jewish community. If His own people would not accept Him, He must be taken to any who would. The disciples took seriously their commission to *"go into all the world and preach the gospel"* (Mark 16:15). The result was that the Church primarily became a body of non-Jewish followers of Jesus Christ.

Each letter follows a distinct structure:

- A characterization of Jesus based on the description of Him in Rev. 1:13-20, but adapted to fit the situation of each church,
- Words of praise or commendation,
- Words of criticism of any faults of each individual church or type, and
- Promises or directions on how to become Overcomers.

Because of His love, Jesus' primary mission was not to judge, but to bring mankind to a state of repentance. The Tribulation Period is intended to be one more opportunity to elect to follow either Jesus Christ or Satan—good or evil. For that reason, the discipline is harsh. Repeatedly throughout the scriptures, God says, *"Those whom He loves He disciplines or chastens"* (Job 5:17; Prov. 3:12; Acts 17:11; Heb. 12:6). This is why the letters are even here. Before He judges the world, He begins with the Church. God wants man to accept His Son as Lord and Savior—their salvation purchased with the sacrifice of His blood. Only in this way is it possible to overcome the trials and tribulations of this life and the last days. Jesus ends His message to the churches with an invitation to fellowship with Him and *"sit with Him on the throne with the Father"* (Rev. 3:21).

1. The emergence of Christianity came at the height of Roman domination and rule.
    a. To strengthen the hold on people, there had been a combining of religious and political control.
    b. Anyone under Roman authority was expected to declare loyalty to the state by worshipping the emperors as gods.
    c. Because of their unbending refusal to acknowledge any but the One True God, Jews had been exempted.
        (1) Theirs had been accepted as an ancient, ethnic religion.
        (2) Fighting this had become useless and too costly.
    d. With the spread of Christianity, this exemption carried over for a time, as most of the early believers were Jews.
    e. As time passed, however, more and more Christians were Gentiles, or non-Jews, and Christianity became a separate religion.
        (1) These Christians, therefore, were expected to declare their allegiance to the state and the deified emperors.
        (2) Their refusal to do so, as well as their profession of love for God and His son, are what prompted the intense persecution that Christians experienced.
        (3) That same condition is increasing in intensity even today.
        (4) Christians are the target of abuse and are actually dying for their faith.
2. Chapters 2 and 3 of the Book of Revelation are a history and prophetic word about, and to, the seven churches of Asia Minor.
3. The seven churches described are literal, historical churches existing at the time that John wrote about his vision.
    a. At the same time, they are representative of all churches throughout the Church Age, with certain ones predominant during certain periods of time.
        (1) Ephesus represents the first century,
        (2) Smyrna the period of greatest persecution,
        (3) Pergamum the age of Constantine,
        (4) Thyatira the Middle Ages,
        (5) Sardis the Reformation era,

The Seven Churches

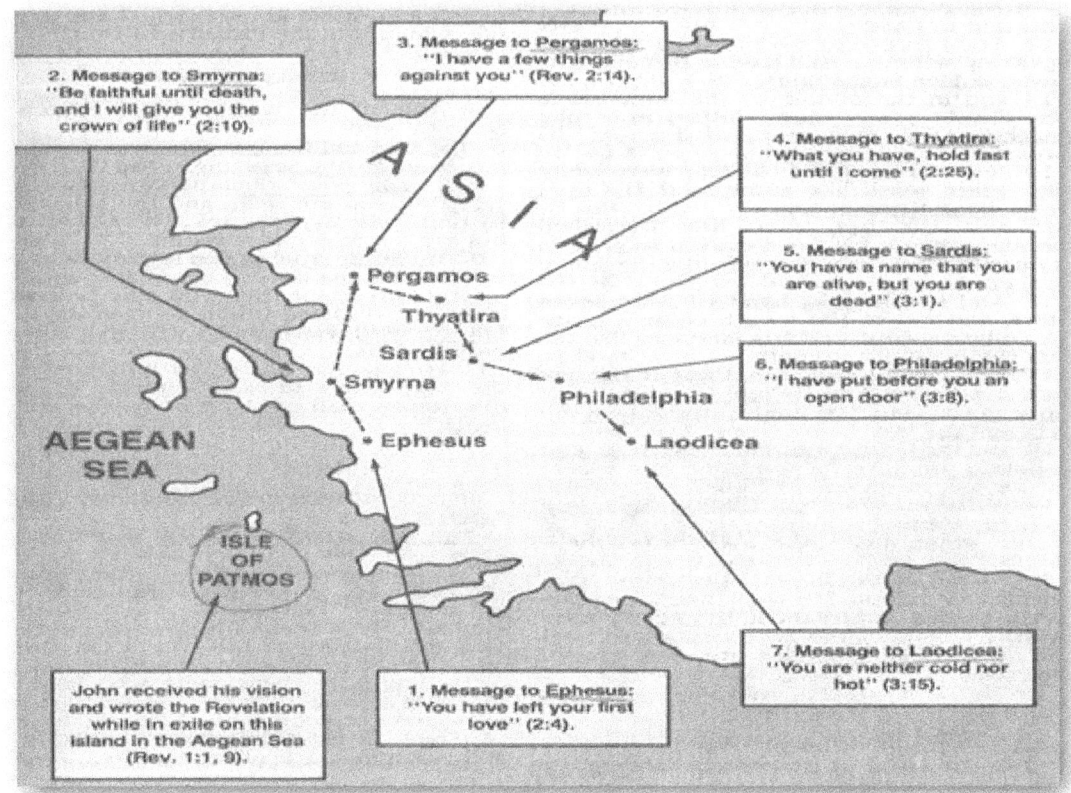

       (6) Philadelphia the modern missionary period, and
       (7) Laodicea the apostate church of the last days.
  b. These churches also exist simultaneously throughout history.
  c. Any of the seven churches can be found some place in the world throughout the Church Age.
  d. The Church is both the people and an organizational entity.
       (1) There will be a period in the last days, however, when the Church, as an organization, will cease to exist.
       (2) There will, however, always be believers.
       (3) The Tribulation Saints are an example of believers who come to Jesus after the Rapture of the Church, thus they are not a part of an organized church.
  e. Seven is indicative of the completed Church.
4. What we find in Revelation are messages aimed at the churches to encourage them to remain loyal to their religion and faithful unto death.

a. The word that is given to these churches is intended for the Christians of all churches, of all nations, throughout history.
   b. The judgments, warnings, and promises are <u>for all time</u>.
   c. The promises are <u>to all Overcomers</u> (the invisible church) in each congregation.
5. Satan will stop at nothing to destroy the Church.
   a. However, God will <u>never</u> let the true Church disappear completely, no matter what Satan does.
   b. He, Satan, <u>shall not</u> prevail (Matt. 16:18).
6. Jesus identifies Himself differently to each church according to their particular need.
   a. The characteristics He uses to identify Himself are taken from Rev. 1:13-16.
   b. He appears in some aspect of His divine nature and person.
7. To each church He says, *"He who has an ear, let him hear what the Spirit says to the churches..."* (Rev. 2:7, 11, 17, 29; 3:6, 13, 22).
   a. He does not say *"...to the <u>church</u>...,"* but *"...to the <u>churches</u>..."*
   b. It is His intent that <u>all</u> should know what is to come.
   c. It is the purpose of this book that none should be left uninformed.
   d. As the Word is written to all mankind, so is Christ's revelation of what is to come.
8. The letters are written to the leaders/ministers of each church.
   a. To them Jesus addresses His words of praise, His criticism of their faults, and a word of promise to those who overcome.
   b. There is one, Laodicea, for which He finds nothing to praise.
   c. Two (Smyrna and Philadelphia) are found faultless.
9. The following messages are sent to all Christians regardless of time or place.
   a. Unfortunately, the Church has chosen not to study these epistles in depth.
   b. They convict and rebuke, and it is not comfortable to realize that judgment begins in the House of the Lord.
   c. Jesus says, *"I love you, but you need to reform."*
   d. The Church has always been resistant to reform. It doesn't like to hear about its short-comings.

MESSAGE TO THE CHURCH OF EPHESUS (REV. 2:1-7)

The Church of Ephesus represents the apostolic church—the church of the First Century. It was established around 50A.D. by the Apostle Paul and was blessed with a number of strong, dynamic pastors. Building on a sound foundation created by Paul, Timothy continued to guide the young church toward becoming an exemplary model of a Godly congregation.

Because Ephesus was also John's home, and where he took Mary, the Mother of Jesus, following the crucifixion, he too was one of the church's pastors for a time. This church was highly blessed, therefore, with first-hand accounts of Jesus' life and teachings. As a result, their faith was well established upon sound doctrine.

This church functioned, however, in the midst of a pagan society, and they were faced with ongoing pressure to relax their beliefs. The word "Ephesus" actually means to relax or let go—to backslide. This became their primary challenge.

1. Background
    a. Ephesus was an important and magnificent city—the center of government, art, learning, and religion.
        (1) The Temple of Diana, one of the Wonders of the World, was located there and provided a center for pagan worship.
        (2) A reverence for gods and goddesses was commonplace in the everyday life of many.
    b. Paul lived in Ephesus, started its church, and the spiritual condition of the city guided much of his teaching.
        (1) Some of his greatest ministry took place in this city.
        (2) He healed and cast out demons; he confronted the exorcists and magicians prevalent in that day, and taught the great doctrines of Jesus.
    c. Ephesus was John's home also—where he died after being released from Patmos.
    d. It was the place to which Mary, Mother of Jesus, went following His death.
    e. Today, the city is a ruin.
    f. The Church of Ephesus came into existence at the end of the Apostolic Age.
        (1) Because the period of this Church was during and just following the time of the apostles, it began by being filled with love and commitment to Christ.
        (2) He was truly their first love.
        (3) Everything they did was out of love and a desire to honor Him.
    g. It is to this church that Jesus identifies Himself, as the one *"who holds the seven stars and walks among the lampstands or churches"* (Rev. 2:1).
        (1) He is in the midst of every church, but is only evidenced in some.
        (2) <u>He</u> should be the reason for a church's existence.
2. Commendations
    a. This is a Godly church that joyously does many good works.
    b. It is zealous and generally sound in its doctrine.

      c. When persecuted in Jesus' name, the people suffer cheerfully for they know in whom they believe.
      d. This church also has a hatred for what God hates—referring to the deeds of the Nicolaitans. (Nico = conquerors Laitan = layity (lay people)
         (1) This is a heretical sect within the church that has as its agenda the creation of confusion and unrest among the people.
         (2) These are leaders who come to lead the people astray from their first love.
         (3) They attempt to put layers between God and man by creating a hierarchy or priesthood. They are increasingly bureaucratic in their structure.
         (4) They also advocate a compromise with pagan ideas.
      e. This church, however, puts these deceivers to the test and finds them false.
      f. During his ministry, Paul warned the church leaders that they must keep the flock safe from such deception (Acts 20:28-32).
      g. Because the majority heeded this warning, the church as a whole persevered and resisted accepting the doctrines of the Nicolaitans.
  3. Faults
      a. This church looks good to the world—only Jesus sees their faults.
      b. As time passes, it begins to lose its first love—Jesus Christ (Matt. 24:12)
      c. The <u>doing</u> of good deeds becomes all-important, i.e. ministries, outreaches, missionary programs.
         (1) They begin doing them for the wrong reasons.
            (a) When going into battle with evil, it is imperative that it is God's battle and not just our own agenda.
            (b) Jesus must guide the way, and all that is done be done in righteousness.
         (2) Many in this church become prideful of their good works.
         (3) The caring for others becomes almost institutionalized.
            (a) Good deeds becomes their purpose.
            (b) They have committees for everything.
            (c) Church work is all-important.
      d. Focus turns to works rather than to Jesus and love.
      e. Though this church looks good to the world, Jesus sees into the hearts of these people and knows their weaknesses.
  4. Directives and promises.
      a. This church is told to *"repent and return to earlier ways"* (Rev. 2:5).
      b. Failure to do so can result in their removal as a part of The Church.
      c. Overcomers will be granted the right to eat of the Tree of Life and live forever.
         (1) This right was lost in the Garden of Eden, when Adam and Eve sinned.

(2) Their sin unleashed suffering and disease, not only on themselves but upon the whole world and generations to come.
(3) God was merciful, however, and allowed death as an escape from this consequence of sin.
(4) Access to the Tree of Life was the first blessing lost and the first to be restored to the Overcomers.
(5) God will restore eternal life to all who are faithful.
(6) Once sin was dealt with by Jesus on the cross, death could be lifted.

MESSAGE TO THE CHURCH OF SMYRNA (REV. 2:8-11)

The Church of Smyrna came to be known as the suffering church. The word Smyrna actually means "myrrh," which is a bitter herb, but when crushed releases a sweet fragrance or perfume. This is how God experiences this church. Though small in number and poor in material wealth, they suffer some of the most horrendous persecution of all the churches, and for the longest period of time. Because of their faithfulness and resolve to stay committed to Jesus Christ no matter what, they are tortured and tormented not only by the Roman government and the ungodly of the world, but by Jews who consider themselves children of God, but are only Jews by race, not by religion. These professed "Jews" are actually a part of Satan's army intended to participate in the eradication of the Church from the face of the earth.

This body of believers from the Church of Smyrna is hated to the point of death for their steadfastness of spirit and unrelenting devotion to the Savior, who was willing to die for them. Jesus finds no fault with this church. In His eyes, they are rich in spirit, and He tells them not to fear, for though they may die a martyr's death, they will be saved from the judgment, which is the "second death."

1. Background
   a. Smyrna is mentioned nowhere else in the scriptures but in Revelation.
   b. The message to it is the shortest of the letters to the churches.
   c. Jesus knows this church is walking into 200 years of hell and Imperial persecution.
      (1) It will be persecuted by Rome, as well as by false Jews, who claim they are Godly but are not (Rev. 2:9) (Rom. 2:29).
      (2) He finds nothing wrong with this church, but holds out no hope of its survival.

d. Despite the beauty and opulence of the city, Smyrna was a poor church with regard to worldly goods, but they were faithful to the teachings of Christ unto death.
   (1) It corrects what was wrong with the Church of Ephesus.
   (2) Their total focus has to be upon Jesus in order to bear their torment in His name.
e. These Christians are persecuted, by the following for their faithfulness, more severely than any other church:
   (1) Domitian - 81-96 A.D.
      (a) It was under him that John was sent to the Isle of Patmos.
      (b) Christians were a nuisance and threat.
   (2) Nerva - 96-98 A.D.
      Unknown
   (3) Trajan - 98-117 A.D.
      (a) He did not seek out Christians to persecute them, but when they were brought to him, or to his attention, he was ruthless.
      (b) It was common practice for them to be thrown to the beasts in the amphitheater.
   (4) Hadrian - 117-138 A.D.
      (a) He also persecuted in moderation.
      (b) Things were getting worse, but it was still far from as bad as it would get.
   (5) Antoninus Pius - 138-161 A.D.
      (a) He rather favored Christians and admired their perseverance, but...
      (b) He was a "law and order" man, and it was against the law to be a Christian, so it was his responsibility to enforce the law.
      (c) He persecuted the Christians, but his motivation was to uphold the law.
      (d) Polycarp, the Bishop of Smyrna, was a much-revered student of John's and was put to death by Antonius Pius, though with reluctance.
      (e) He would have liked to have let this wonderful little man go, but Polycarp gave him little choice, because he refused to deny his Lord or the fact that he was a Christian.
      (f) He was burned alive, but willingly died for his Savior.
   (6) Marcus Aurelius - 161-180 A.D.
      (a) This was a barbarous man and unbelievably cruel toward the Christians.

- (b) He used horrible methods to persecute them.
- (c) He beheaded them, threw them to the beasts, and used hot griddles and racks to torture them.
- (d) To get them to deny Christ, he would even slowly drown children in front of their parents, but they remained faithful.

(7) Commodus - 180-192 A.D.
   Unknown

(8) Septimius Severus - 193-211 A.D.
- (a) He set out to find Christians in order to kill them.
- (b) He had them crucified, beheaded, boiled in oil—anything to break the spirit of these faithful people, who would not deny their Lord.

(9) At this point, several emperors tolerated the Christians and gave them a bit of a break. - 193-234 A.D.
- (a) The persecution let up to some degree and there was a breathing spell.
- (b) However, it was just the lull before the storm.

(10) Maximinus - 235 - 248 A.D.
- (a) He decided they had been going about this in the wrong way.
- (b) He believed the way to be rid of the Christians was to do away with their leaders.
- (c) As he had the leaders killed off, however, more kept springing up.

(11) Decius - 249-251 A.D.
- (a) It was his intent during his rule to remove Christianity from the face of the earth.
- (b) His plan was to wipe out every Christian.
- (c) This was empire-wide.
- (d) A method he used to identify the Christians was to require everyone to have a certificate of faithfulness to the gods in order to buy and sell.(forerunner of the sign of the Beast).
- (e) Since Christians did not have this, they stood out and were killed.

(12) Valerian - 253-260 A.D.
- (a) He was even more horrible than Decius.

(13) Gallienus - 260-268 A.D.
- (a) He again favored the Christians, but it was very short-lived.

(14) Aurelian - 270-175 A.D.
- (a) He began the horrendous persecution all over again.

(15) Diocletian - 284-305 A.D.

INTRODUCTION and the CHURCHES 45

                (a) He was the last of the imperial persecutors.
                (b) He also said he would wipe the name of Christianity off the face of the earth.
                (c) It was his intent that no one would ever remember a man named Jesus or this sect called Christians.
                (d) He used <u>every</u> form of torture and method to kill these people.
                (e) He obviously did not succeed.
            (16) Constantine - 306-335 A.D.
                (a) Constantine marked the end of this horrendous period of persecution.
                (b) Though he never became a Christian, his mother Helena did, and he honored her by acknowledging her beliefs and religion.
    f. The persecution, which the Church of Smyrna experiences, is beyond our comprehension, and yet they never wavered.
    g. Jesus does not tell this church He is returning, because He knows they will be martyred and die.
        (1) Their possessions, their children, their very lives will be taken because of their faithfulness.
            (a) They have to claim Jesus repeatedly, as they are even forced to watch their own children dropped repeatedly into water to be drowned, if they do not deny Christ.
            (b) Most of this church holds fast to its faith in a merciful Savior.
        (2) Two to seven million Christians are killed before the times change.
            (a) During this period, Christians live in catacombs under the city.
            (b) The names of martyrs are written on the walls.
    h. To this church Jesus identifies Himself as *"the first and the last"* (Alpha and Omega) (God), *"He who was dead and is now alive"* (Rev. 2:8).
        (1) He knows their suffering, because He suffered all that the world of sin could do to Him.
            (a) He Himself was martyred and served as the supreme example.
            (b) He wants them to know that He understands and is with them; they will never be alone.
            (c) We go through nothing He does not already know about.
        (2) Just as He died and now lives, so will this Church—for their faithfulness.
        (3) He provides a way.
        (4) Nothing Satan sends against these people can destroy their love of Christ.
        (5) Scripture says that the gates of Hell shall not prevail against them (Matt. 16:18).
        (6) Although Satan will not prevail, he keeps trying.

2. Commendations
    a. While this church is poor in things, they are rich in their faith.
    b. They are given what is important to God, not what is important to the world.
        (1) Regardless of their circumstances, they have Jesus and are rich.
        (2) The riches of the world do not save us for eternity—Jesus does.
        (3) Crowns will be received for loving Him.
        (4) These people have that love and are rich in God's eyes.
    c. God's grace enables them to be martyred for their beliefs.
        (1) That same grace will see us through anything Satan puts in our way.
        (2) As sin increases, "*grace doth more abound*" (Rom. 5:20).
        (3) Jesus is our intercessor and we can overcome.
        (4) The Bible does not teach that we will not suffer *(2 Cor. 6:4-10)*.
        (5) Any teaching that claims such a fantasy is not scriptural.
        (6) Life is an endurance contest, and God blesses us with the opportunity to endure through His strength and grace (James 1:12)
            (a) How much more He is honored, when we overcome our trials, than when we are delivered from them.
            (b) To honor Him is our purpose for being, and we should rejoice that He finds us worthy (James 1:2).
    d. This church sets an amazing example of perseverance and faithfulness in the face of indescribable persecution, and the church grows in spite of all that is heaped upon them. People see something in these followers that they admire and want.
    e. Christianity could not be wiped out.
    f. The Word tells us that, if we obey His commands, have faith, and love Him, we can overcome the world (1 John. 5:3-4).
3. Directives and promises.
    a. Jesus tells this church not to fear.
        (1) God did not give us "*a spirit of fear, but of love and power and a strong mind*" (2 Tim. 1:7).
        (2) Fear is a spirit, and it is sent by Satan to destroy us.
        (3) When we resist that spirit, we are victorious.
    b. Jesus understands what this church must go through, because He first experienced all that they will have to endure.
        (1) Because He overcame death and Satan, they can also.
        (2) He will give them the grace and strength to persevere.

    c. For their faithfulness, they will have the crown of life and be saved from judgment, or the second death.
        (1) This second death was the second thing lost in the Garden of Eden and the second thing imposed upon man.
        (2) What greater evidence of God's faithfulness than to restore to original perfection that which was lost in sin.

MESSAGE TO THE CHURCH OF PERGAMUM (REV. 2:12-17)

The city of Pergamum was not a place conducive to peaceful worship of Jesus Christ. It was the center of paganism and imperial idol worship, as well as a time of internal problems. Even within the church, certain groups—the Nicolaitans who purported to be Christians—were living a lifestyle of the world. To rationalize this, they worked very hard to excuse behaviors that were strictly prohibited by Christian doctrine. It was no wonder that this city was often referred to as *"the place where Satan has his throne."*

Because Pergamum was an environment of major deception and compromise, it was also considered to be a city of concessions—a mixed marriage between idolatry and Christianity. The people are encouraged, both by the local community and from within their own ranks, to indulge in immoral practices so as not to be conspicuous for their beliefs. They are told that, since they do not actually believe in the pagan gods, or are only making a show of loyalty to the emperor, there is nothing wrong with participating in non-Christian activities. This mindset, however, went a long way toward eroding the church's commitment to the One True God and Jesus Christ. This is where the Sword of the Word battles against the deceit of Satan. As a two-edged instrument of combat, on one hand the Sword warns the unbeliever of condemnation, while simultaneously promising salvation and grace to those who trust in the Lord.

The Overcomer in this setting is promised the "hidden manna," or tools of salvation. They are guaranteed a white stone, which protects the believer from judgment, and a new name, which often occurred when one was given a new life. This is consistent with God's promise to *"make all things new"* (Rev. 21:5).

  1. Background
    a. This city too was sumptuous and the home of many rich chiefs and royal figures.
    b. It was a center of learning, with a 200,000 vol. library, as well as the heart of "modern," medical practice in its early development.
    c. Pergamum was also a city of idolatrous and occultic, mystery religions.

(1) It took the place of ancient Babylon and became a focal point of satanic worship.
    (a) Satan has a religion and his intent is to be worshipped.
    (b) The focus of this worship is to acknowledge him as God.
    (c) In the last days, this will become a <u>world</u> religion—in the person of the Antichrist.
    (d) He has a plan—an organization and hierarchy.
    (e) His throne, at this time, is not in Hell; it is in Pergamum.
    (f) Satan rules the earth and his throne is in this place.
(2) Hell was created by God to hold Satan and the wicked, but only after the second coming of Christ.

d. There are those in the Church of Pergamum who follow the teachings of Balaam (Rev. 2:14).
    (1) They lead the people to believe that they can mix with heathens and not be judged (Num. 22-25).
    (2) This is a belief that the church can be wedded to the world and still serve God.
    (3) This cannot be so.
    (4) One cannot serve two gods (Matt. 6:24).
e. Jesus knows this is the environment in which the Christians of Pergamum live.
f. It is Satan's desire that the Church should be obliterated, and when he cannot make that happen in one way, he changes his strategy.
    (1) He then moves to pervert it.
    (2) He introduces an attitude of compromise and tolerance for the ungodly.
g. The persecution of the Christians lessened for this church, because Constantine ended the period of severest oppression and torture.
h. The Christian church, therefore, becomes alive and active, but it does not strongly resist what is happening around it.
i. For safety sake, this becomes a time of compromise and the melding of religions.
j. The clergy, therefore, began to develop a system of organization and perverted doctrine.
    (1) The <u>beliefs</u> of the Nicolaitans become formalized into <u>doctrines</u> within this church.
    (2) Only the <u>true</u> church still hate them.
k. This church unites with the world.
l. To it, Jesus identifies Himself as the one with the two-edged sword, to divide the good from evil.

(1) As mentioned before, the sword is the Word.
(2) It provides the direction for our lives.
(3) This church begins to leave the Word for the ways of the world.
2. Commendations
   a. The true believers of the Church of Pergamum are faithful and courageous in their own practices, despite the fact that they live in a Satanic environment.
   b. They are Overcomers in a perverse society.
3. Faults
   a. This church, however, overlooks the teachings of some in their midst who are enticing the flock to turn to the idolatrous and immoral ways of Balaam and Balak—destroyers of the people.
   b. By being connected to the world, they can have worldly advantages.
   c. Because many of their forefathers died being persecuted for their faith, this church instituted the use of statues to honor their martyred ancestors and venerated them in an heretical way.
      (1) Pergamum is where idolatry enters the Church, and the people begin to worship saints.
      (2) They are instructed to pray to the Virgin Mary and confess their sins to priests.
      (3) Layers (priests, bishops, archbishops, a Pope) are slowly placed between God and man, separating him from direct access to God.
   d. The church lets too much of the world into its worship.
      (1) It mixes with other cultures, governments, and religious practices, in the name of tolerance.
      (2) This is the beginning of a melding of church and state.
   e. They are willing to compromise with other religions and tolerate many ungodly practices
      (1) When we compromise our beliefs, however, God takes away His blessings.
      (2) He is a jealous God and desires our complete faithfulness (Ex. 20:5; 30:14).
   f. This church also tends toward false pride and a lofty spirit.
4. Directives and promises
   a. Christ's directive to the Church of Pergamum is to *"Repent of your weaknesses and overcome the temptations of the world, or I will make war with you with my word"* (Rev. 2:16).
   b. In response to repentance, God will provide, protect, and restore His relationship with them.
      (1) To the Overcomers, He will give of the hidden manna.

(2) This gift to the Hebrews was hidden in the Ark of the Covenant, along with the Ten Commandment tablets, Aaron's rod, and some of the manna God gave the Israelites as they wandered through the wilderness.
(3) That manna, meant to sustain them, was the "hidden manna."
(4) In giving His people this gift, He would restore life, remove judgment, and re-establish an intimate, personal relationship with them.
  c. He will also give them a new name, written on a white stone—a ticket for admittance into heaven— that only they and God will know.

MESSAGE TO THE CHURCH OF THYATIRA (REV. 2:18-29)

The believers of the Church of Thyatira are faced with a great dilemma. Do they hold fast to their Christian doctrine and beliefs, or do they elect to do what is most expedient to maintain a position of acceptance within the community. Thyatira was an active military center and guild society. For that reason, everyday life was controlled by ungodly practices, rules, and regulations. If one wanted to have and/or keep a job, however, it was necessary to belong to one of the guilds—most of which incorporated pagan rituals and immoral perversions into their organizational activities. In hard times, when individuals are already being persecuted for their beliefs, it is very difficult to decide to forego the ability to provide for one's family and be safe.

From both within and without the church, the Christians are encouraged to compromise their convictions and principles, in order to survive. To turn one's back on them is an act of apostasy, making it a false church. This becomes the greatest fault of this body of believers. Many have listened to the exhortations of a Jezebel woman and elected to at least tolerate her teachings. She was severely punished for her life, and any who follow her teachings can expect similar consequences. This church is directed to repent and return to their faith in order that they be allowed to share in the millennial reign with Christ. Their destiny depends upon their choice.

1. Background
    a. Thyatira was a significant town in which many craftsmen lived, and they formed guilds that exercised a great deal of influence over people's lives.
        (1) These guilds set the tone of society, and that tone tended toward perversity.
        (2) Much pressure was placed upon people to be tolerant of all types of behavior.
    b. The Church of Thyatira, which becomes the church of the Dark Ages, was predominant during a period of aberrant and depressing life styles.
        (1) Truth ceases to have value.

(2) Little in life is clear and positive in nature.
(3) There is little spiritual guidance from the priesthood, as they become increasingly corrupt themselves.
(4) "Compromise" becomes a driving force, and slowly the church comes to tolerate false beliefs and religions, because it is "politically correct."

c. Jesus identifies Himself to this church as "the Son of God with eyes like fire and feet of bronze" (The metal of judgment.) (Rev. 2:18).
(1) Jesus generally referred to Himself as *"the Son of Man."*
(2) Because this church is now worshipping mortals, He wants to impress upon them in this case that He is God.
(3) He comes with perfect knowledge and judgment.
(4) The eyes signify His perfect knowledge, and He knows their works.
(5) He sees with clarity the evil ways the people are accepting, and He is aware that they are being deceived.
(6) The bronze feet refer to the fact that He is coming in judgment of their deeds.
(7) We saw this previously, when He first revealed Himself in Rev. 1:13-20.

2. Commendations
 a. There are people of faith during this time, who do many good works and are zealous about their beliefs.
 b. Great numbers of them are brought before the Inquisition for this very reason.
 c. Despite the times and current practices, many believers begin to repent and return to their earlier enthusiasm for Christ.
 d. Though many people are good, the structure of the church becomes increasingly perverted.
 e. This is the beginning of reformation in this church.
   (1) During this period, John Huss, a simple priest, was an example of those who spoke out against the perversion within the church, and consequently, he was burned at the stake.
   (2) Huss meant "goose," and at his death he proclaimed, "You may cook this goose, but a swan is coming you can neither cook nor boil."
   (3) The swan, being his sign, was prophetic of Martin Luther.

3. Faults
 a. The Church of Thyatira tolerates the ways of Jezebel—wife of King Ahab and a corrupting prophetess of the Old Testament (1 Kin. 16 - 2 Kin. 1:10).
   (1) The Jews understand this reference, because they understand the Old Testament.

(2) Jezebel claimed to speak for God, but gave corrupt messages of adultery and idolatry.
　(a) Her name means "pure and chaste," but she was the very opposite.
　(b) What she proclaimed was supposed to be true, but was not.
　(c) She taught a false doctrine—a Nicolaitan doctrine.
(3) Just like Jezebel, this church also professes one thing and acts in another.
(4) Although she was given a chance to repent, she did not and was condemned to a life of suffering and the loss of her children.
(5) Any who follow her can expect to receive the same reward.
　b. This church actually incorporates these false teachings into their religion, where Pergamum only tolerated them.
4. Directives and promises
　a. Christ directs this church to repent, but, like Jezebel, many do not.
　　(1) They, therefore, will be repaid according to their deeds.
　　(2) Despite their professions, as the ungodly are judged, so will they be judged.
　b. Those that will follow the righteous way are told to ignore the wicked, because they will be unable to save them.
　c. True believers must hold fast to their faith, and in the end, they will be given authority over the nations.
　　(1) Earth ultimately belongs to the Overcomers (1 Cor. 6:2) (Ps. 115:16).
　　(2) The "squatter" (Satan) <u>will</u> be removed.
　　(3) God will take away authority from the false believers and give it to those who overcome.
　d. They will also be given the "*morning star*"—Jesus, who will rise up in their hearts (2 Pet. 1:19).

MESSAGE TO THE CHURCH OF SARDIS (REV. 3:1-6)

Like most cities of this time, Sardis was also predominantly pagan and a society of many mystery cults. Obviously, Christians can be neither welcome nor comfortable in such an environment. Their doctrines and beliefs are viewed as much too restrictive and judgmental of pagan practices. Because they are in the minority, the Church of Sardis is greatly persecuted in an attempt to eliminate them from the community. They pose both a threat to accepted, immoral behaviors and traditions, as well as an irritant to a free life-style.

This church appears to be spiritually alive, but in fact, they are like dead bones—dried up and lifeless. Although they are not persecuted to the level of many other churches, in order to survive and have jobs, it was necessary to be acceptable as members of the guilds, or other entities that controlled the workplaces. Christians are considered a "peculiar people" to be avoided at all costs, so many in the Church of Sardis are not strong enough in their faith to resist turning their backs on the teachings of Jesus Christ. There is no power in their faith, and in so doing, their bad choices soil their garments with the filth of ungodly practices. Such choices render them spiritually dead and in jeopardy of having their names removed from the *Lamb's Book of Life.*

The message to this church is almost entirely one of condemnation. The word 'Sardis' actually means 'remnant' or 'escaped few.' Those who do heed the warning, however, are all that is left of what the church once had been. They, and they alone, will be safe from the judgment that can come unexpectedly like a thief in the night. This is true even in this present day—our choices determine our eternal destiny.

1. Background
   a. The Church of Sardis was predominant at the end of the Dark Ages and into the time of the Reformation.
      (1) It is a time of separation from ways that are more perverse and a return to the rule of Christ.
      (2) Fortunately, the Reformation comes from <u>within</u> the Catholic Church, because of its excesses and perversion of doctrine.
   b. Many good things are restored at this time, but this church is not given over to the Holy Spirit.
   c. They think they are alive, yet they are dead in Spirit.
   d. They are not dependent upon the Holy Spirit to empower them, and they need it.
   e. This church is very orthodox and has doctrine and structure, but is not given over to the Holy Spirit.
      (1) Anything that replaces the Holy Spirit is either dead or dying.
      (2) There is no greater force within us, if we are living for God.
      (3) God is spirit, and we must worship Him in spirit (John 4:24).
   f. Jesus identifies Himself to this church as *"He who has the seven spirits of God,"* because He knows it is the complete spirit of God that is most needed in their lives.
   g. We are probably in this church today, and have been since the 1500s.
   h. It will also exist at the same time as the church of the Leodiceans.
   i. The Sardis church does not know prophecy and does not wish to.
      (1) This means that Jesus can come at any time, and again they will miss Him—just as they did at His first coming.

(2) God does not want this to happen again, and is why each of these epistles ends with "*He who has an ear, let him hear what the Spirit says to the churches.*"
(3) Seven times this is said, because He wants us to know what lies ahead and how to be prepared to overcome (Rev. 2:7, 11, 17, 29; 3:6, 13, 22).

2. Commendations
   a. Some in this church remain faithful, in spite of the corruption.
   b. They never deny Jesus' name.
3. Faults
   a. Many others, however, are weak and do not hold fast to the Word.
   b. They are easily deceived by false doctrine.
   c. They are self-righteous and smug for all their orthodoxy.
   d. All need the Holy Spirit and to allow it to guide and direct them.
   e. Many of these people are powerless and not even aware of it.
   f. They have the Church, but not God.
   g. Their reputation is good in the world, but they look dead to Christ.
   h. Emphasis is on <u>right belief</u> rather than a <u>right relationship</u> with God.
4. Directives and promises
   a. The Church of Sardis needs to wake up and repent, for they have not held fast to, or obeyed, what they have been taught.
      (1) Unless they do so, Christ will come like a thief in the night, and they will not be prepared (Rev. 3:3).
      (2) If they do not acknowledge Him before men, He will not acknowledge them before the Father (Luke 12:8).
         (a) What we do with Christ determines what He does with us.
         (b) Our fate is a result of our own choices.
   b. The faithful will be clothed in white garments of purity and worthiness (Rev. 3:4).
      (1) This is the first reference to a description of the redeemed.
      (2) It also appears in latter parts of the book (Rev. 6:11; 7:9, 13; 19:14).
      (3) Regardless of what we think of ourselves, our own righteousness is as filthy rags, and only Christ can purify us and make us white as snow.
         (a) Throughout the Bible, garments signify one's righteousness.
         (b) We either have *our* righteousness or God's (Phil. 3:9).
         (c) We can either clothe ourselves in "strange garments" or God's (Zeph. 1:8).
         (d) Only Christ can take away our sin and give us new garments. (Zech. 3:3-5)

            (e) Those who insist upon wearing their own will be found unworthy to enter into communion with God—the Father and the Son (Matt. 22:1-14).
        (4) If we do not come to the Father in the righteousness of Jesus, we do not come.
    c. The faithful will <u>not</u> have to fear having their names removed from the *Book of Life* (Rev. 3:5; 13:8; 20:12, 15; 21:27) (Ex. 32:32-33).
        (1) Everyone's name was written in the *Book of Life* before the world began.
            (a) This is why, until the age of accountability, <u>all</u> are safe.
            (b) Any of God's children, who never attain that state, still belong to Him.
        (2) One's decision, to accept Christ as Lord and Savior or not, determines whether his/her name <u>stays</u> in the *Book of Life*, and is then written in the *Lamb's Book of Life*.
        (3) Names can only be removed by one's own actions (Ps. 69:28).

MESSAGE TO THE CHURCH OF PHILADELPHIA (REV. 3:7-13)

Unlike the Church of Sardis, the message to the Church of Philadelphia is primarily one of praise for its patience and faithfulness. Though small in number, the fruit of this church is that of brotherly love and an unwavering commitment to Jesus Christ and His teachings. For that reason, He would use the key of David to open the door to the storehouse of God's blessings for them and allow them access to the Father. He promises that one day their enemies—referring even to unsaved Jews who considered themselves superior to Christian Jews and Gentiles—will bow down at their feet, acknowledging the love of God for this church. They will also be kept 'from' the Great Tribulation—*"the hour of trial that is going to come upon the whole world to test those who live on the earth"* (Rev. 3:10). This is another reference to God's plan to remove all believers before the outpouring of His Wrath upon a defiled and sinful world.

It is a fair assumption that when Jesus says He will keep His people 'from' the Tribulation period, not 'through' it, He is speaking the truth. He is not a man that He should lie, since one of His greatest attributes is that He is honest and true. Alternatively, the 144,000 Jews will go 'through' this time, but have a shield of protection around them.

1. Background
    a. This is a glorious church without spot or wrinkle, but it does not last long.
    b. It is the perfected church for which Jesus will return, and something phenomenal must occur in order to bring it into existence.

      (1) There will be a period of great political, economic, and social turmoil, in which mankind brings himself to the edge of destruction, but a <u>man</u> will come upon the scene who will restore peace and safety, as well as prosperity to the world.
      (2) That man will be the Antichrist.
      (3) He will create an environment that sets in motion the final events of the last days.
      (4) The people of this church are the only ones who will recognize the signs of the time, as the coming of the Lord draws nigh.
  c. With this church, Jesus finds no fault, and He loves them as He loved the Church of Smyrna.
      (1) These people are ready for His return.
      (2) They know from the Word that when He comes, it will be in the twinkling of an eye.
      (3) There will be no time to hesitate or get prepared.
      (4) To wait, until He comes, to make a wholehearted decision to accept Him, is to miss Him.
      (5) Like the Church of Smyrna, this church loves Jesus with their whole beings.
      (6) For them, there is no other God.
  d. This church also displays love for one another as never seen before, and it is by this love that the world shall know them.
  e. They are united in love and doctrine and adhere closely to the written word.
  f. Jesus reveals Himself to this church as *"He, who is holy and true, and holds the keys to the kingdom of David"* (Is. 22:22).
      (1) This key is the power of resurrection and the entrance into the kingdom of God.
      (2) He has the power and authority to open the door for the church and bring them in.
      (3) Only He can open and close that "door" (Matt. 24:32-33; 25:10) (Luke 13:25) (James 5:9) (Rev. 4:1).
      (4) When He comes for His own, the graves will open for those who died believing in their God, along with those living, who know His voice.
      (5) They will be brought into the kingdom of heaven.
      (6) Those who do not acknowledge Him as Lord will find the door closed.
  g. Some believe we are in the Philadelphia Church Age now.
      (1) If you look closely at the church of today, however, there is little evidence of that.

    (2) Catholics war with Protestants, Baptists with Methodists, and Christians with Christians.
    (3) The church has not yet attained a true attitude of peace and harmony.
  2. Commendations
     a. Love and unity is the hallmark of this church.
     b. They keep God's word and do not deny His name.
     c. They know no compromise.
        (1) This is the *invisible church,* which exists within a new world order that accepts everyone and everything in a seeming attitude of "tolerance and love."
        (2) Because the Philadelphia Church will not compromise itself, however, they and their beliefs are the object of ridicule and rejection.
        (3) As in any true church of Jesus Christ, Satan plants tares to discredit true believers (Matt: 13:24-30).
           (a) These people are condemned for being stiff-necked and intolerant for saying that there is no other way to salvation than through Jesus Christ.
           (b) They are ridiculed for being unloving in the belief that not all "spiritual roads" lead to God.
        (4) Nevertheless, those who bring that condemnation will one day be brought to their knees before the faithful ones.
        (5) They will come to know whom Jesus loved.
     d. This church will be small but powerful and will do miraculous things "*in Jesus name*" (John 14:12).
  3. Faults
     a. Jesus finds no fault with this church.
     b. They are without condemnation.
  4. Directives and promises
     a. For their faithfulness, these believers are given 'the open door—eternal life, resurrection.
     b. The world will one day acknowledge them and their truth.
     c. Because they do not waver in the face of condemnation, they will be kept from the trials of "that day" (the Day of the Lord) that *"is going to come upon the whole world to test those who live on the earth"* (Rev. 3:10; 3:5-10) (Matt. 24:4-28).
        (1) The Lord will keep them from that hour—the Wrath of God—that the world is prophesied to suffer.
        (2) This is why we are to pray that we may escape that which is to come upon the world (Luke 21:36).

(3) To believe that we must go through the Wrath, therefore, is to disbelieve God's Word.
(4) We would not be told so, if it were not true.
d. This church will become pillars in the Temple of God.
(1) Jesus and God are that temple.
(2) This church holds up the Temple for all to see.
e. The name of God, Jesus' new name, and the name of the Holy City will be written on their foreheads.
(1) This will be a sign that every Overcomer belongs to God.
(2) They have citizenship in the New Jerusalem.
(3) And Jesus will be present <u>with</u> them in a way He has never been before.

MESSAGE TO THE CHURCH OF LAODICEA (REV. 3:14-22)

Laodicea is a city of great wealth, and the people are proud of their successes in life. They are self-sufficient and believe they have no need of any help. This is even true of the Church of Laodicea. They display all the trappings of a church of God, but they no longer have a heart for the truth of His word. They are rich in material goods but bankrupt in spirit. Their seeming acts of service and compassion are overpowered by their concern for an outward appearance of faith and propriety. This is a church ruled by the people, which is exactly what 'Laodicea' means. The bureaucracy of this church consumes much more of its attention than spreading the gospel or serving God.

Jesus, however, considers this church to be lukewarm—neither hot nor cold. This is disgusting to Him, and He wishes to spit them out of His mouth. They are satisfied, however, that they display a religious adherence to the moral principles of Christ. They practice a belief in Him, but they have no understanding or dependence on a power greater than themselves. In God's eyes, they are poor in spirit, blind to the truth, and naked of garments of righteousness. This is the other church for which Jesus has no commendations.

This will be the predominant church in the last days—willing to be "tolerant" and compromise with the social mores, self-sufficient, and totally oblivious to their need for spiritual understanding. Unfortunately, the majority within this church will miss the Rapture. They will become a large portion of the Tribulation Saints.

1. Background
   a. Laodicea was a wealthy, banking city.
      (1) It was also a medical center and was particularly known for a special ointment used for the treatment of serious eye problems.

INTRODUCTION and the CHURCHES

(2) Because of the riches of this city, the people believe they have need of nothing.
(3) Even the church of this city thrives on the prosperity of the times.

b. This church does not belong to Christ, however, and is not one for which He will return (2 Tim. 3:1-9; 4:9).
  (1) It belongs to, and is ruled by, the people. It is thus called the Church of the Laodiceans—the people.
  (2) It is rich in money and things, but claims no need of Jesus, the Holy Spirit, or the Word.
  (3) Though self-sufficient, their things are worthless in God's sight.
  (4) This church cares for no one but themselves.
  (5) It no longer teaches sound doctrine.
  (6) It teaches what the people want to hear; i.e. self-help, feel-good messages.
  (7) Its purpose is to entertain.

c. To this church, Jesus reveals Himself as *'the Amen'*—so be it.
  (1) He is the true and faithful Witness of God and the Beginning of the Creation of God (Rev. 3:14).
    (a) He knows their hearts and their deeds.
    (b) He knows they are neither hot nor cold.
    (c) They are complacent, indifferent, and lukewarm.
    (d) They are sickening to Him, and He desires to spit them out of His mouth (Rev.3:16).
  (2) His identification, as *"a faithful Witness of God...,"* is in contrast to the unfaithfulness of <u>their</u> witness for God.
    (a) They wear His name—Christian—but they do not profess Him.
    (b) In the eyes of Jesus, this is worse than denying Him.
  (3) This is the church that first truly embraces the theory of evolution, not the creation.
  (4) Satan's influence is evident, because he fights against creation.
  (5) Creating is the one thing he cannot do.

d. Laodicea is also a church to which Jesus says nothing about coming back, because He will not take them upon His return.
  (1) The other church is Smyrna, because their end will be physical death.
  (2) The end for the Church of Laodicea is spiritual death.

f. This will likely be the predominant church of the last days before Christ's return.

2. Commendations
   a. There are a few faithful ones in this church, but they shall eventually leave before the end comes.
   b. True believers are not comfortable in this church.
3. Faults
   a. The Church of Laodicea is self-righteous and totally self-sufficient.
   b. It is boastful and rich, and feels it has need of nothing, yet is poor in Spirit.
      (1) It believes it is wealthy; Jesus sees it as poor (in spirit).
      (2) The city is known for its cloth; Jesus sees the church as naked.
      (3) They make salve to heal eyes; Jesus says these believers are blind.
   c. This church sees itself as perfect, but is completely self-deluded.
   d. It is an apostate church and scoffs at true believers.
   e. Those who are a part of this church worship themselves rather than Jesus.
      (1) They are "little gods."
      (2) They believe they have the power within themselves to order their own lives.
      (3) They do not seek God's will to direct them.
      (4) We are moving increasingly toward this today, but it will become even worse.
   f. There is no humility in this body.
   g. Jesus finds nothing good in them.
   h. The church proclaims a belief in Christ, and yet has none. Jesus said it is better not to profess Him, than to be dishonest (Titus 1:16).
   i. In love, He stands outside this church and knocks (Rev. 3:20).
      (1) But, as a whole, this church does not let Him in.
      (2) There may be some individuals who do, but they are few.
      (3) It is for these that He knocks.
4. Directives and promises
   a. God tells this church to repent, so He can give them <u>His</u> riches.
   b. Jesus finds them to be pitiable, poor, blind, and naked.
      (1) They are poor in spirit, blind to the truth, and totally unclothed in the righteousness of Jesus Christ.
      (2) Their riches are as rags.
   c. He will spit them out and cast them from Him, because their condition is by their own choice.
   d. He will dine with the Overcomers, however, and serve them, because His love is so great (Luke 12:35-40).

e. The true Christian will sit with Him on His throne (Rev. 3:21).
      (1) This is the ultimate gift toward which all believers strive.
      (2) We will sit with Him, as He sits with His Father.
      (3) This is what life in Christ is all about.

END OF THE CHURCH AGE

The Church Age is that historical period between the day of Pentecost—the seventh Sunday after Easter—and the Rapture of the Church in the last days. The Old Testament encompasses the Age of Law as presented to Moses in the Ten Commandments, while the New Testament records the development and growth of the Church, following the baptism in fire, as the Holy Spirit descended upon the disciples in the Upper Room. From that moment forward, the Church became the body of Christ, with the responsibility of spreading the gospel to all mankind.

Because this is a wicked world, the Church is composed of sinners who have been saved through God's grace and mercy. As a part of the Church, it should be our desire to love, serve, honor, and glorify God in obedience to His Word. How well we carry out the commission to *"go into all the world..."* is the basis of the letters to the seven churches. They are intended to be a warning, a comfort, and an encouragement to all people. The end of the world, as we know it, is predicted repeatedly. Based on man's choices, however, there is hope for a glorious new beginning.

1. All of the seven churches exist at any time throughout the Church Age, but Sardis is probably the predominant church of today.
   a. Deceived,
   b. Self-righteous, and
   c. In need of the Holy Spirit and its power.
2. In the last days, the Church of the Laodiceans will be the predominant church.
   a. Rich in wealth, but poor in spirit,
   b. Blind to the truth,
   c. Self-sufficient, and
   d. Unrepentant.
3. Our goal, however, should be to move toward becoming the Church of Philadelphia.
   a. Loving but uncompromising,
   b. Holds fast to the Word and is faithful,
   c. Is the church for which Jesus will return, and
   d. Is not, and never will be, the predominant church.

4. There is a lesson to be learned from each Church that is vital to our salvation and redemption.
    a. From Ephesus - never lose our first love,
    b. From Smyrna - only God can see us through sorrow,
    c. From Pergamum - never dilute what we believe,
    d. From Thyatira - do not compromise our morality and integrity,
    e. From Sardis - avoid becoming complacent,
    f. From Philadelphia - never cease sharing the gospel in love, and
    g. From Laodicea - do not become self-sufficient and self-righteous.
5. Jesus wants all to be Overcomers that we might sit and reign with Him, as He sits with the Father.
    a. He loves us and wishes to give us of His abundance.
    b. His greatest gift is eternal life with Him.
    c. Nothing in this life is too great to overcome, if we look to what waits for us.
6. Thus ends the Church Age, but we are not out of it yet.
7. It merely marks the end of "*these things*."
8. What John now will see will be that which "*...comes <u>after</u> these things*" (Rev. 1:19).

PART III
The Tribulation as Seen from Heaven

CHAPTER 4
"The things which shall be hereafter"

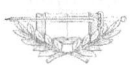

"After these things..." (Rev. 4:1-11)

To this point, John has written about the first two components of what he was instructed to describe— *"The things which he has seen"* and *"the things which are."* The first refers to Jesus Christ, in all His glory and majesty, as He is about to deliver a revelation of what shall occur in the last days. The second is Christ's message to the seven churches of Asia Minor, concerning how to live in a manner that will assure their victorious survival of the trials that lie ahead. His words of encouragement and correction contain both praise and concern for their strengths and weaknesses. The Churches comprise *"the things which are."*

The content of John's testimony thus far is encompassed in the first three chapters of the Book of Revelation. Everything to this point has either been to, or about, the Churches, but from Rev. 4:1 through 19:7, they are not mentioned even once. It would appear that God's concern with the Church, as an institution, has been completed. From a Pre-Tribulationist point of view, this could rightly lead one to conclude that the Church has now been Raptured. It is prophesied that at the sound of a trumpet *"the dead in Christ shall be raised..."*—those who die believing in Christ (1 Cor. 15:52). Then, *"we who are alive and remain shall be caught up... to meet the Lord in the air"* (1 Thess. 4:17). The scriptures do not actually call this the Rapture, but if one methodically searches the Bible concerning the promises made to believers, as well as warnings to those who choose not to accept God's Word, then one can reasonably presume that there is more evidence in support of a Pre-Tribulation Rapture than not.

"Hereafter..."

The subsequent nineteen chapters consume the bulk of the Book of Revelation. What is revealed, following a vision of an "angel" and His message to the Churches, now relates to *"those things which will be hereafter."* This strongly supports a defensible argument that the true Church is not intended to suffer the full wrath of God (I Thess. 5:9). Everything from this point forward concerns what the Tribulation Saints must endure, and if the true Church—the body of Christ—were to be amongst those persecuted by the events of the end times, there would be some indication of this in John's explanation. As this is not the case, what comes *"after these things"* obviously refers to the future and does not include the organized Church, as a suffering part of the outpouring of God's Wrath upon a sinful world.

1. In Rev. 1:19, John is instructed to write about "...*the things which are...*" (The Churches), and "...*the things which shall take place <u>after</u> these things*" (the events of the end times).
    a. Since the Churches continue throughout history until they are removed in the Rapture, the events John is about to see, and is told to describe, would seem to take place <u>after</u> the Rapture, or the removal of the true believers of the Church.
    b. This makes a Post-Tribulationist interpretation of the Rapture somewhat difficult to explain.
    c. Repeatedly, we are told what occurs *"after these things"* (Rev. 4:1; 7:9; 9:12; 15:5; 18:1; 19:1; 20:3).
    d. If the Rapture comes at the end of the Tribulation Period, and Christians are to go through it, why are they not mentioned as suffering the impact of the plagues and cosmic occurances? How does one explain away the fact that the scriptures describe the events of the Tribulation following the removal of the Church?
2. What <u>is</u> described is the terrible conflict between those left behind and the demonic efforts intended to destroy them and their new-found faith.
    a. From an Historical Perspective, this is embodied in Rome of the first century and the Antichrist in the end times.
    b. It is representative of the conflict in the spiritual world between the kingdom of God and the kingdom of Satan.
3. That is not the Pre-Tribulation perspective.

THE PROPHETIC EVENTS

As mentioned earlier, in order to understand a sequence of events, it is necessary that they be presented in a logical chronology. Each fact must build upon the previous one, so as to produce a clear and plausible representation of the theses being considered. To gain a true and complete understanding of the Book of Revelation, it is necessary to look beyond John's visions to the prophesies of Daniel, the prophetic words of Jesus in Matthew, as well as the writings of Paul in Thessalonians. Upon an in-depth study of these prophetic scriptures relevant to the end times, *"Write What You See..."* lays out a depiction of the final events, and an interpretation of their meanings, in relation to modern-day understanding. This provides significant scriptural, supportive evidence for the Pre-Tribulation perspective.

John's vision reflects the last-day occurrences in heaven, on earth relative to those left behind following the Rapture of the organized Church, and from the perspective of the demonic world of evil. It is still God's desire, however, that all who would be saved will make that choice before Jesus' final return.

1. In order to include all of the details of what will occur from the end of the Church Age until the formation of the new Kingdom of God, the events are described three times. Each telling expands upon the previous.
    a. From the vantage point of Heaven (Rev. 4:1-11:19),
    b. From the vantage point of Earth (Rev. 12:1-16:21), and
    c. From the vantage point of Satan's domain (Rev. 17:1-19:21).
2. As all things have their beginnings in heaven, the accounts of what shall soon take place begin from that perspective.
    a. *"After these things"* follow the period of the seven churches (Rev. 1:19; 4:1).
    b. From a Pre-Tribulationist point of view, they also follow the removal of the Church in the Rapture.
        (1) A strong argument for this position is that the word "church" occurs 20 times in the first three chapters of Revelation, but not once after Chapter 4 until Rev. 19:7.
        (2) While the Rapture is not explicitly described, cumulative support for this interpretation is herein presented.

JOHN'S VISION OF HEAVEN (REV. 4:1)

Everyone wonders what heaven will look like, and everyone has an opinion, even if it is that there is no such place—when you are dead, you are dead. However, if an individual has any belief system at all, there is at least some agreement that heaven is the dwelling place of the One True God. It is imagined as beautiful beyond description. The entrance is envisioned as through "Pearly Gates," and someday we will see our saved, loved ones in that wondrous place. Strangely enough, those who have professed to having had a vision of this magnificent place find that there are many similarities in their accounts of what they saw.

The most detailed description of heaven, however, is found in the Book of Revelation—recorded by the Apostle John in the first century. As in the beginning of his vision, John indicates that he slipped into a deep state of meditation in the spirit and saw an open door leading into heaven. A voice like a trumpet, which he heard in Rev. 1:10, calls to him to *"come up"* and enter into the presence of God, the Creator. From this point forward, John relates what he is shown that will soon take place in the last days before the Second Coming of Jesus Christ.

1. John begins his account with *"After this I looked (or saw)..."*
   a. This phrase is used repeatedly to introduce a new vision (Rev. 4:1; 7:1, 9; 15:5; 18:1).
   b. A variation of it is *"After this I heard..."* (Rev. 19:1).
2. The vision John sees is a door leading into heaven.
   a. This way into heaven is open to all who will believe.
   b. A voice like a trumpet, which he had heard in Rev. 1:10, is the glorified Christ telling him to come up and be shown *"what must take place after these things"* (Rev. 4:1)
      (1) The must is important.
      (2) The things that are going to take place are not by chance.
      (3) They are a working out of God's divine plan.
      (4) We are told they must take place *after these things*, or the end of the Church Age.
      (5) Everything from Rev. 4:1 on is prophecy—a foretelling of future events.
   c. At this point, John is supernaturally caught up into Heaven in the Spirit (Rev. 4:1).
      (1) Symbolic of the Rapture, it also is precipitated by the sound of a trumpet (1 Thess. 4:16-18).
      (2) John's translation into the presence of God is an example of the taking up of the "church"— as the Overcomers (dead and alive) shall be caught up *"in a twinkling of an eye"* (1 Cor. 15:52).
      (3) He is able to see, hear, and speak—thus able to write, as commanded, what he observes.
   d. Others have looked into Heaven and seen visions, but were never actually there (Ezek. 1:1) (Dan. 7:2).
3. The visions John sees bear many similarities to the visions seen in Dan. 7:9; 10:2, 12:4.

a. Both prophets identify themselves by name and give the time and place of the experience.
   b. They each see a heavenly Being and then give a very similar description of what they see.
   c. At the end of the portrayal, both men fall to the ground unconscious.
   d. In each case, they are comforted and strengthened by the Being.
4. Following the vision, they are given a long revelation that results in a treatise to the Church.

THE THRONE ROOM (REV. 4:2-11)

Though Jesus said He would go to prepare a place for us, where there would be many mansions or rooms, John's exposure to heaven takes place strictly in the Throne Room, before the very seat of God. As he gazes in awe, he attempts, with the only words he can find, to describe the indescribable. In so doing, he creates a picture of a magnificent God seated on a throne of love, justice, and mercy. Natural and unnatural creatures, Old and New Testament Elders, and a sea of Saints, worshipping and praising the One True God, surround this throne.

Not knowing what the future would be like, John often uses mythological images to describe what he sees. At least it provides some frame of reference in which to suggest a discernible picture. Though it is more difficult for modern-day society to visualize, the poetic nature of the prophecy requires the reader to use a heightened level of imagination and a willingness to accept certain facts by faith.

1. John is taken up, by the power and spirit of God, into the very throne room of heaven. There he sees Him who sits upon the great throne (Ps. 103:19) (Ezek. 1:26, 28) (Is. 6:1).
   a. This is the dwelling place of God.
   b. He is King, and He sits upon a mighty throne in authority, power, and judgment.
   c. He appears as a jasper stone with a sardis stone inside.
      (1) The outward image is of a diamond-like, shimmering white light with flecks of purple—symbolizing purity, holiness, and royalty.
      (2) The inner portion is a red/orange flame exemplifying fiery judgment.
      (3) Here is the Shekinah Glory, which is beyond a human-like description.
   d. What John sees is that, regardless of any evil that takes place, God is still on the throne governing the universe.

2. Encircling the throne is an emerald colored rainbow—a constant reminder of God's covenant and a symbol of His mercy.
    a. Noah saw only an arch in the sky; John sees the complete rainbow.
        (1) What we see today of God's mercy is incomplete.
        (2) When we get to heaven, we will see it in its entirety.
    b. Daniel and Ezekiel also saw this vision of a rainbow (Dan. 7:9-10) (Ezek. 1:26-28; 10:1).
    c. God gave the rainbow—a copy of the one in heaven—to men after the first destruction by flood (water).
    d. He promised He would never destroy the earth <u>by water</u> again (Gen. 9:11).
    e. The next destruction would be <u>by fire</u> (1 Pet. 3:1-18).
        (1) <u>Destroy</u> does not mean annihilate, however, but to dissolve or change into a new form—to pass from one state of existence into another.
            (a) The same word used for "destroy" in 2 Pet. 3:10-11 is used to mean, "loosed" (Matt. 21:2).
            (b) Both cases mean to set free that which has been bound (Rom. 8:21).
            (c) Man and the earth have been bound by sin, and cleansing by fire shall restore them to their original purity.
        (2) Just as the earth was cleansed after the flood, so shall it be restored following the Tribulation.
        (3) This fire will purge everyone and everything of all evil and wickedness.
        (4) Even the heavens will be shaken and restored.
        (5) God shall make <u>all things new</u>, not <u>all new things</u>.
    f. We are told to pray without ceasing that sin might be bound in heaven, so that it might be bound on earth (1 Thess. 5:17; Matt. 16:19).

(1) God gave us power in prayer, if we will but be obedient and use it.
(2) Satan understands that power and will go to great lengths to interfere with its increase.
g. These acts will restore and redeem the earth.
h. Three things purify.
(1) Water - baptism
(2) Fire - last days
(3) The Blood - of Jesus
i. All things must go through, or under, one of these purifications. We can choose to be 'restored by' or 'condemned to' the eternal fire.
j. Whatever comes under God's will, will be redeemed.
(1) Whatever does not, will be destroyed.
(2) God, not man, will carry out the purging of the last days, for not everyone or everything will be touched.
(3) Only God, not man, will know what needs to be cleansed.
3. Around the throne of God, John sees twenty-four more thrones, with twenty-four elders seated upon them (Rev. 4:4).
a. There is not agreement as to who <u>these</u> elders are.
(1) Some believe they are figuratively representative of all of God's people throughout the ages.
(2) That they are the whole people of God from the Old and New Testaments, who will reign with Him; i.e. twelve patriarchs of the Old Testament and twelve apostles of the New Testament.
(3) Another interpretation is that they are angelic beings who act as a part of the heavenly court and help execute the divine rule of the universe.
(a) These would be a host of angels who attend upon the throne.
(b) They are what Paul refers to as thrones, principalities, rulers (Col. 1:16).
(c) They are dressed in white signifying their holiness.
(d) This interpretation is difficult to justify, however, since elders may judge, but angels are never given that authority.
(e) Angels are also never seen seated on thrones or wearing crowns.
(f) They are merely seen standing <u>around</u> the throne and <u>around</u> the elders (Rev. 7:11).
(g) Additionally, throughout Revelation, we are repeatedly told that white garments are reserved only for the saints.

b. The view of <u>this</u> teaching is that these are not angels but human beings—either specific, risen, glorified, Raptured saints, or types of saints gathered from every tribe and tongue on earth.
    (1) They are the Overcomers of old that God promises will rule and reign with Him (Matt. 19:28).
    (2) We are repeatedly told who shall wear white (pure) garments, crowns upon their heads, and sit upon thrones—the Saints.
c. These elders sit in authority and judgment, as did the judges of Israel.
    (1) They are the most senior of those who are gathered to the Lord.
    (2) The later succession of saints are:
        (a) Those who "escape" the tribulation.
        (b) Those that suffer the tribulation and are taken out of it.
        (c) The sealed ones who come later.
        (d) Those "harvested" from the earth, because they refused to worship the Beast and take his sign upon their foreheads or hands.
4. Out of the throne come lightning, voices, and thunder, which denotes that this is a throne of judgment.
    a. God's awesomeness and power are manifested in the lightning and thunder.
    b. Also described in Ps. 18:13; 97:1-4.
5. Before the throne are seven blazing torches representing the seven Spirits of God, or the Holy Spirit.
    a. The Holy Spirit is now seen as cleansing fire—judgment.
    b. This too is power.
    c. The torches are held by seven lampstands seen in Rev. 1:12.
        (1) The seven lampstands represent the seven churches, or church types.
        (2) The Holy Spirit dwells within those of the "true church."
6. Before the throne is a sea of crystal glass.
    a. This vision of the heavenly temple was carried out in the building of the Old Testament temple, with a bronze laver or sea surrounding the Holy of Holies—everything on earth has its beginning in heaven (2 Chron. 4:1-2).
    b. This sea was seen in Ex. 24:10 as sapphire.
    c. The sea, or water, is often used to represent a multitude of people—God's own.
7. Additionally, around the throne John sees four living creatures full of eyes (Rev. 4:6) (Dan.7:4) (Ezek. 1:10; 10:14).
    a. Four is the number of the earth and is a representation of God's covenant with creation.
    b. Gen. 9:8-13 describes the aspects of God's covenant in the living creatures.

(1) One looks like a lion.
(2) The second has the appearance of an ox.
(3) The third has a face of a man.
(4) The fourth is like a flying eagle.

c. There is a rabbinical saying dating back to 300 A.D.:

'The mightiest among the birds is the eagle.
The mightiest among the domestic animals is the bull.
The mightiest among the wild beasts is the lion.
The mightiest among all is man."

(Strack & Billerbeck. *Komentar zum Neuen Testament aus Talmud un Midrasch.* 1922-28)

    (1) This suggests that whatever characteristics in nature, including man, is noblest, strongest, wisest, and swiftest is represented before the throne of God.
    (2) They take part in the fulfillment of the Divine Will and the worship of the Creator.

d. Each of these creatures, or living ones, are seen by John (Rev. 4:6), Ezekiel (Ezek. 1:5-24), and Isaiah (Is. 6:2).

    (1) These three men each saw them from a different perspective, however.
        (a) John and Isaiah saw them with six wings (Rev. 4:8) (Is. 6:2).
        (b) Ezekiel only saw four wings (Ezek. 1:5-10).
        (c) John and Isaiah called them "living ones."
        (d) Isaiah identified them as seraphim (Is. 6:6).
        (e) Ezekiel called them cherubim (Ezek. 1:10-11).
        (f) These are merely different names for the same creatures.
    (2) In either case, they are the greatest of the created creatures.
        (a) Their job is to cover, guard, protect, and keep.
        (b) They have the authority to handle the coals in the golden censures, which are the prayers of the saints.
    (3) These creatures are covered with eyes (Rev. 4:6).
        (a) They see everything that God sees and continually praise Him saying, *"Holy, Holy, Holy..."* (Rev. 4:8; 5:8, 14; 7:11; 19:4).
        (b) He is the Lord God Almighty, and everything He does is holy.
    (4) The creatures lead the elders in adoration of His holiness.
    (5) The elders fall down and worship Him.
        (a) Their glory is His glory.
        (b) They lay down their crowns at His feet and say, *"You are worthy... to receive glory and honor and power, for you created all things..."* (Rev. 4:11).

- (c) Any crowns we are given as rewards for service on earth are intended to be gifts laid at His feet.
- (d) He created us, and all things, for His own purpose and is not about to abandon us, despite how it sometimes feels.
- (e) Evil may be rampant, but it will not be victorious in the end.
- (f) Praise precedes power, for God inhabits our praise.
  - (6) As close as the living ones are to God, so had Lucifer been before he fell from grace.
    - (a) He was the highest and most exalted of the cherubim.
    - (b) He was glorious to behold—the morning star/bearer of light.
    - (c) Unfortunately, he aspired to be <u>above</u> the throne.
8. What John sees in the midst of all this praise and worship is a great release of power.

THE SEALED BOOK/SCROLL (REV. 5:1-14)

And then suddenly, John notices that God is holding a book or scroll in His right hand. It is fastened shut with seven seals. As seen in other cases, there is some debate about the content of this book. Nevertheless, evidence is persuasive that this is the Title Deed to the earth, which has been lost in sin and corruption. Although Jesus paid the price on the cross for its redemption, mankind is still under the influence and power of the Evil One. The actual transfer of possession of the earth, however, is yet to come. This will not happen until all who would be saved are. God alone knows when that has been accomplished. It is only then that Satan and his followers will finally be judged and cast into the pit of fire forever. The breaking of the seven seals will initiate that process.

1. John sees, in the right hand of God, a book, or scroll, written on both sides and fastened with seven seals (Rev. 5:1) (Ezek. 2:9).
   a. It is comforting to see that man's history, and future, rest in God's hands.
   b. While there are various interpretations of exactly what this "book" is, some explanations have little to support their conclusions.
   c. A few of the presumptions are:
      (1) A book of human destiny.
      (2) The Old Testament fulfilled in the New Testament.
      (3) A symbol of the promise of the kingdom of God, which His people are to inherit.
      (4) The *Lamb's Book of Life*.

(5) A book of "*lament and mourning and woe*" similar to the one given to Ezekiel (Ezek. 2:1-10).
d. One interpretation, which supports the belief that the Church goes <u>through</u> the Tribulation, but is sealed from God's "great wrath," views the breaking of the seals as merely a prelude to the actual opening of the book.
  (1) It purports that the breaking of each seal allows a later, specific persecution of those in the Church, by the Antichrist.
  (2) Supposedly, their punishments take place at the same time that God's wrath without mercy is poured out upon the wicked, or unsaved.
  (3) If one carefully analyzes the scriptures, however, this interpretation requires some major stretching to make it justifiable.
e. To consider the scroll to be a prophecy of end-time events—including the salvation of God's people and the judgment of the wicked—is not inaccurate, but it is also not totally complete.
  (1) It asserts that this book with seven seals is God's plan of redemption, the overthrow of evil, and the gathering of the redeemed.
  (2) Such an analysis is more descriptive of the entire Book of Revelation than of the scroll seen in the right hand of God.
f. The interpretation of <u>this</u> teaching is that the scroll is the Title Deed to the Earth.
  (1) It is likened to the Jewish custom for redeeming of lost land (Lev. 25:23-55).
    (a) In the Year of Jubilee, a kinsman could redeem or reclaim any land that had been lost or sold by a rightful owner.
    (b) God gave the earth to Adam and Eve, but through sin they lost everything to Satan, the Deceiver—the earth, their soul, and their bodies to death.
    (c) They gave up their unobstructed communion with God and absolute dominion over the earth and all living things.
    (d) They did not realize the value of what they had, but Satan did, and enticed them to sin, because he wanted control of the earth.
    (e) He hated, and still hates, mankind because the earth was given to him.
    (f) Satan's possession of the earth is only a purchased right, however, and not an inherited one.
    (g) It is, therefore, subject to loss.
    (h) His power over man and the earth lasts only until a kinsman, who is willing and has the resources, pays the price to redeem them.

- (i) Jesus came as that kinsman—the second Adam.
- (j) At one point, as a temptation, Satan offered Jesus the world, because it belonged to him at that time, but Jesus refused.
- (k) It was not the right time.
- (l) It also would not have paid the price that was required for total redemption.
- (m) It was on the cross, as Jesus shed His blood, that the price to reclaim our inheritance had to be paid.
- (n) The only reason that He could even die was because He took on the sins of man. He was sinless, but *"...the wages of sin is death..."* (Rom. 6:23).
- (o) Crucifixion was the price that Jesus willingly paid to restore eternal life, and everything else man had lost.
- (p) With this act, Satan would lose all legal right to the earth, though he still retains power over it until he is defeated in the final battle.
- (q) The time has not yet come for Jesus, the Redeemer, to take possession of the earth and kick Satan out.
2. The breaking of each seal in heaven initiates an action toward the reclaiming of all that is God's and man lost.

THE LAMB - THE REDEEMER (REV. 5:6-14)

Someone must break the seals and open the book. At first, there does not seem to be anyone worthy of this responsibility. However, one of the Elders tells John there is one—*"a Lamb looking as if it had been slain."* Jesus is that Lamb—sacrificed for our salvation. He takes the scroll from the hand of God, and begins the process of reclaiming the earth and all that is within it. This time He will come as Conqueror and Judge, in order to return a purged creation to His Father. Rightly, it will be in a restored condition. All that was evil will have been destroyed and all things made new.

1. At first, it appears there is *"no one in heaven or on earth or under the earth..."* worthy to break the seals of the scroll, and John weeps because of it (Rev. 5:3-4).
   a. He knows what it means if the book is not opened.
   b. All creation cannot be redeemed and will remain in the hands of Satan forever.
2. An elder, however, tells John that there <u>is</u> one who is worthy to open the book and look inside.
   a. *"Blessed are those that mourn, for they shall be comforted"* (Matt. 5:4).

b. The Lion of Judah, the Root of David, has triumphed and is able to open the book (Gen. 49:9-11) (*Is.* 11:1, 10) (Rom. 15:12).
      (1) This is the sum of the Old Testament Messianic hope.
      (2) The Lion is able to conquer, because He first suffered as a Lamb slain.
   c. When John looks for this Lion, he sees instead, standing between the throne and the elders, "*a Lamb looking as if it had been slain*" (Rev. 5:6).
      (1) It has seven horns, referring to complete, aggressive, majestic strength and power, and seven eyes, denoting spiritual power of wisdom and knowledge.
         (a) As seven represents completeness and totality, seven eyes reflects that this is the all-seeing God.
         (b) He sees everyone and everything at all times.
         (c) He is all-knowing and there is no place to hide.
      (2) The seven eyes also represent the seven spirits of God, or the Holy Spirit.
         (a) The Spirit of the Lord, which encompasses everything the others do not.
         (b) The Spirit of Knowledge,
         (c) The Spirit of Wisdom,
         (d) The Spirit of Counsel,
         (e) The Spirit of Understanding,
         (f) The Spirit of Strength, and
         (g) The Spirit of Fear of the Lord.
   d. Jesus is the Lamb who was sacrificed.
      (1) As the Lion, He has the strength and power to administer judgment and reclaim what was lost.
      (2) As the Lamb, He paid the price.
   e. The Bible traces the theme of 'the lamb."
      (1) Isaac asked, "*Where is the lamb?*" (Gen. 22:7).
      (2) John the Baptist answered, "*Behold the Lamb of God*" (John 1:29).
      (3) Now, John says, "*Worthy is the Lamb*" (Rev. 5:12).
3. The Lamb takes the book from the hand of God, in order to go to earth to reclaim it.
   a. What is seen here is a double act of giving and taking.
      (1) It symbolizes a harmony between the will of God and the will of Christ.
      (2) This is evidenced throughout the Book of Revelation.
   b. The assurance is given that this revelation is from God, showing what "*must soon take place*" (Rev. 1:1).
   c. The breaking of each seal is an attack against, and judgment of, an apostate church and a wicked world.

d. The first six seals are a mixture of judgment and mercy. After that, there will be no more mercy.
   e. The world will be subdued, Babylon judged, the Antichrist destroyed, the dragon (Satan) vanquished, death overcome, the curse expunged, the earth made new, and the kingdom established.

HEAVEN REJOICES (REV. 5:9-14)

As Jesus Christ, the Lamb, takes the scroll, all heaven breaks into praise and worship. The prophecies of the past are about to take place, and all that was lost to sin soon made perfect. The prayers of the Saints, over the ages, are about to be realized—*"Thy will be done on earth as it is in heaven."*

A new song is sung in heaven, and only the Saints are able sing it. It was for them that Jesus came to earth so they might be saved from sin and death. Because they are in heaven singing this song, it could be inferred as further evidence of a Pre-Tribulation Rapture. In any case, what John sees is a great outpouring of love and adoration for the Father and the Son. God's children, who were prepared, were spared the pain and torment of the Great Tribulation.

1. The elders and creatures around the throne hold harps and golden bowls of prayers of the ages.
   a. All prayers that *"...Thy kingdom come and Thy will be done on earth as it is in heaven..."* have been kept and saved for this day, and will now be responded to (Matt. 6:9-13).
      (1) It is the power of these prayers that causes Satan to try so hard to keep people from praying.
      (2) He knows that one day these prayers will be answered and his power will be overcome.
2. As the Lamb takes the scroll, a <u>great</u> praise goes up in Heaven (Rev. 4:9).
   a. First, the four living beings and twenty-four elders fall down before the Lamb.
   b. The very fact that He is worshipped, as God is worshipped, confirms His divinity.
   c. He is worthy of the praise, for He has paid the price to redeem all men, regardless of their tribe or nation.
   d. This is acknowledged in a new song (Is. 42:9-10).
      "You are worthy to take the scroll...
      with your blood you purchased men

(from every tribe and nation) for God.
You have made them to be a kingdom of priests...
and they will reign on earth" (Rev. 5:10).

- e. This song of Moses has been sung on earth before, but never in heaven.
  - (1) This explains why it is "new"—new in heaven.
  - (2) Only the Saints can sing this song, for the blood of Jesus purchased only them.
  - (3) This is strong evidence that the Saints are now—before the opening of the seals—in heaven.
  - (4) Then thousands upon thousands and ten thousand times ten thousand angels encircle the throne and add their praises to those of the elders and living creatures (Rev. 5:11).
  - (5) This description is not meant to signify a specific number.
  - (6) It merely indicates that the number is immeasurable.
  - (7) It also notes that the angels do not sing, nor is there any scriptural evidence that they <u>ever</u> do.
  - (8) The Christmas angels praise God by "*saying*" (Luke 2:13-14).
  - (9) Angelic creatures shout.
  - (10) Singing is a privilege reserved for the Saints.
- f. Finally, "*every creature in heaven and on earth and under the earth and upon the sea and all that is in them*" join in the chorus (Rev. 5:13).
  "*To Him who sits on the throne <u>and</u> to the Lamb be praise and honor and glory and power, forever and ever!*"
- g. Anyone who acknowledges the Father, but not the Son, is in conflict with the scriptures and God's intent.
- h. To this, the four living creatures say "*Amen.*"
- i. They began the song, and it is fitting that they should end it.
- j. This is a great praise service.
  - (1) All heaven joins in it and worships the Father and the Lamb.
  - (2) It is a fervent outpouring of love and adoration for who They are.
- k. All nations and tribes are represented in Heaven.

3. While this activity is taking place in heaven, however, it goes unnoticed on earth.

CHAPTER 5
Breaking the Seals

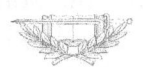

THE SEALS (REV. 6:1-17)

JOHN'S NARRATIVE NOW TAKES A different direction. He has seen and identified Jesus Christ as the messenger of this prophecy concerning the events of the last days. He has received Jesus' message to the seven churches of Asia Minor, which represent church-types throughout history. He has been taken up into heaven and shown the Great I Am, who sits on a mighty Throne. Around the Glory Seat is an assembly of angels and creatures, whose responsibility it is to wait upon the Heavenly Father and His Son.

He has also observed twenty-four elders, who too are seated on thrones before the Supreme Godhead. These elders are the most senior of God's people and represent the 12 tribes of the Old Testament and the 12 disciples of the New Testament. Finally, he is overwhelmed by the sight of myriads of Saints standing and kneeling before the One True God. These are God's children—those who chose to obey His law and accept Jesus Christ as their Lord and Savior.

We are told that the Church Age is ended, as Jesus steps out of heaven for a moment, and *"in a twinkling of an eye,"* catches up the faithful—living and dead—into the presence of their Heavenly Father. From this point forward, God will now deal with the nations—the unprepared, the ungodly, and the demonic forces of Satan. For a short time, those who yet choose to be saved before the final outpouring of God's Wrath will be granted mercy in the midst of judgment. It is God's will that they still have a last opportunity to become a part of the bride of Christ.

At this point, the Lamb—Jesus Christ—has just taken the scroll from the hand of God, and is ready to begin the process of purging and cleansing the earth of its sin and corruption. What John is about to see is another example of the consistency of the scriptures. Scripture interprets scripture. It does not contradict itself (2 Peter 1:20-21). Regardless of time or writer, there are similarities in the content that is surreal. Many individuals go to great lengths to explain it away, but it is hard to deny that there has to be some guiding force behind the likenesses.

As John sees the seals opened, each precipitates an action against the earth and the peoples that dwell upon it. These events directly parallel the sequence of prophesies made by Jesus Himself, to the disciples in the Olivet Discourse of Matthew 24, Mark 13, and Luke 21, with what occurs in Revelation 6 and 8.

> 1st. Seal - Spread of the gospel around the world, but also the revelation of many false christs and false teachers (Matt. 24:5 vs. Rev. 6:2).
> 2nd. Seal - Wars and rumors of wars (Matt. 24:6-7 vs. Rev. 6:3).
> 3rd. Seal - Scarcity and famine (Matt. 24:7 vs. Rev. 6:5-6).
> 4th. Seal - Death to a fourth of the earth (Matt 24:9 vs. Rev. 6:7).
> 5th. Seal - Persecution and tribulation (Matt 24:21-22 vs. Rev. 6:9).
> 6th. Seal - Great cosmic disturbances (Matt. 24:29 vs. Rev. 6:12).
> 7th. Seal - Christ's return with the Saints (Matt. 24:30 vs. Rev. 8:1).

As Jesus breaks the seven seals, cataclysmic phenomenon take place that brings about both punishment and/or restoration to those remaining. Only the One who spoke all things into existence has the power or authority to either destroy, or remold creation into its original, perfect state. This process begins the Day of the Lord.

FOUR HORSEMEN OF THE APOCALYPSE (REV. 6:1-17)

As the Lamb begins to open the seven seals, the judgment of a wicked world is initiated. This will be a period of great tribulation, pain, and suffering, such as never before known. Any misery or adversity that has befallen mankind in the past has only been a dress rehearsal for what lies ahead. In order to be able to survive or overcome this final act, one must be able to identify the times and make wise choices. The consequences are beyond our imagination.

With the breaking of the first four seals, beings on horseback are told by each of the four creatures from around the throne of God to 'come,' or 'go forth.' It is their assignment to carry out a specific action toward the earth and those who remain. There is still time for those who were left behind following the Rapture to repent and accept Jesus as their Lord. The days are numbered, however, and the price will be high.

Nevertheless, the reward will be eternal life in the presence of God, the Father, and God, the Son.

1. Introduction
   a. As the Lamb begins to open the seven seals, the four horsemen who come riding forth have been seen before in other places throughout the Bible (Zech. 1:8; 6:1-8)
   b. They appear as white, red, black, and ashen or pale.
   c. Their job is to patrol the earth.
   d. The riders are not specifically identified, but each has a specific assignment.
2. This sending forth of the horsemen occurs as each of the four living creatures from around the throne sends out a horse.
   a. With a voice like thunder, the first creature like a lion says, *"Come."*
      (1) In Greek, the word means both "come" and "go."
      (2) Because the horsemen are being sent out to do a particular work, the better translation in this case is "go."
      (3) They are being sent to convict the world of its sin and provide a last opportunity for people to come into the Kingdom.
   b. A different horse and rider is sent out as the Lamb breaks the first four seals.
   c. As each seal is broken, something different happens on the earth.
   d. The breaking of these seals, and the actions they precipitate, are in preparation of the Great Tribulation, or Wrath of God.
   e. Their purpose is also to place increasing pressure upon the Antichrist.
   f. This is a period of <u>judgment mixed with mercy</u>.

BREAKING OF THE FIRST SEAL (REV. 6:1-2)

The first horseman, riding on a white horse, is the only one of the four about which there is disagreement over who it is and what his task is. This is another example of where differences in interpretation cause confusion and misunderstanding, even by the most elect. Assuming that what fits one's agenda is true, however, results from failing to examine all of the evidence.

This horse and rider have been seen in scripture before and will appear again just before the Great Battle that will ultimately destroy all evil. We are told from whence the horseman comes, how he will appear, and what his objective will be. With these facts, one can logically reach no other conclusion than that this is Jesus Christ Himself. His first act is to once more try to save all who would be saved from the punishment that is about to befall mankind.

1. A white horse, with rider carrying a bow and wearing a crown, goes forth.
   a. This is the only horseman over which there is any dispute as to his identity.
      (1) One interpretation is that this is the Antichrist.
      (2) It is the beginning of his reign and he appears as an "angel of light."
      (3) He is seen as a savior of the times.
      (4) Such an interpretation is not consistent, however, with what we are told in other places.
   b. Another explanation is that this is the ministry of the church to the world.
      (1) The next three horsemen are viewed as the negative reaction of the world to that ministry.
      (2) This view does not believe the Rapture has yet taken place.
   c. Some interpreters also see this horseman as a conquering warrior going out to wage war against the enemy, causing major destruction and terror.
      (1) In some cases, this is assigned to specific identities in conflict with Rome.
      (2) These are related to first century historical events.
   d. Based upon the description of the first rider, however, and what we have seen previously, it would seem more likely that this is Christ Himself, not the Antichrist, as some believe.
      (1) This rider comes out of heaven—an evil force would not.
      (2) White represents purity and might—not darkness and corruption.
      (3) This is a conqueror, a victor—evil is not.
      (4) The rider wears a crown (stephanos) that is reserved for Jesus and the saints, representing victory over evil.
      (5) Christ knows that Satan and the Antichrist are doomed to fail, and they would never wear such a crown.
      (6) This is righteousness coming out of heaven to direct the work and Word of the gospel.
   e. The bow, which the rider carries, represents the preaching of the Word.
      (1) Because a bow implants the Word of God into the hearts of man, it is a symbol of the power of God.
      (2) There is power in the Word.
      (3) As great tribulation is about to fall upon the world, this is a major part of God's grace.
      (4) We are told that it must be preached in all the world, and <u>then</u> the end will come (Matt. 24:14).
      (5) Currently, a third of the world still has not heard of Jesus.

(6) Before the last day, the entire world will understand who Jesus, the Redeemer, is.
  (a) Those who refuse Him would rather die than change (Rev. 6:15-16).
  (b) By their own choice, they will.
f. The interpretation of this study is based upon the belief that the Rapture has just taken place.
  (1) No saints are left; however, immediately following it, many do come to believe and begin to spread the gospel.
  (2) There are many who profess to be Christians but whose motives are not right with the Lord.
  (3) Only God will know their hearts and decide who is taken up in a cloud.
  (4) Many of the surprised "Christians" left behind will repent and begin to spread the truth.
  (5) The scriptures do not say that all will be saved, or even that everyone would have the gospel, but rather, it would be preached to all nations.
  (6) With today's communication systems, this is not only possible, but probable.
  (7) This horseman initiates the final efforts to spread that Word.
g. This rider will be seen again in Rev.19:13 and is called *"The Word of God."*
h. This assignment continues until the last seal is broken and gives evidence of God's mercy in giving His people a last chance to accept Jesus Christ and His Word.

BREAKING OF THE SECOND SEAL (REV. 6:3-4)

The horseman on a red horse is sent out by the second living creature that looks like an ox. This horseman carries a large sword, and, by removing peace from the world, wars and great bloodshed are an end result. All positive relationships and powers of communication will cease to be, and no one will feel safe.

1. A red horse and rider with a sword goes forth next.
   a. The red indicates the bloodshed and carnage that will result from the opening of this seal.
   b. The sword represents the war and fighting that will be rampant.
   c. This horseman has the power of life and death.
2. His assignment is to remove peace from the world and cause men to war against one another.

    a. Many will even be deceived into believing they will be eternally rewarded for taking the lives of those they consider to be infidels.
    b. There will no longer be any moral compass.
    c. The result is wars between nations, civil strife, confusion, and men murdering one another.
    d. Life no longer has any value.
 3. Prior to this time, we are told there must have been peace.
    a. The Antichrist will create such a period of peace, security, and prosperity, in order for man to be caught off guard.
    b. This rider removes that peace and safety from the world and creates a spirit of terror.

Breaking of the Third Seal (Rev. 6:5-6)

The creature with the face of a man says, "come," and calls forth the third rider on a black horse. He carries a scales in his hand, which measures the world's material resources. Because of the state of the economy, things become increasingly scarce. With all of the unrest and wars being waged worldwide, the production of food and other goods are significantly impacted. Man can no longer provide the mere necessities for his family. Scarcity and starvation become the norm.

 1. A black horse is sent forth with a rider carrying a scales.
    a. Black signifies a mournful time.
    b. The scales suggests that everything is measured and nothing is in balance.
       (1) A measure of wheat is the minimum needed for a person to survive for one day.
       (2) During this time, it will require a day's labor to purchase that measure, and that does not feed one's family, let alone pay the rent, etc.
       (3) Rationing and exorbitantly high prices will become the norm.
       (4) People will die of starvation.
       (5) Such inability to meet typical daily needs leads to lawlessness, violence, and crime.
    c. Their only hope is from those foods such as olives (oil) and grapes (wine), which grow naturally and do not require much tending.
       (1) Man is told not to harm these staple foods (Rev. 6:6).
       (2) They may become all that is available.

(3) This is a rationale for preparing for the times by accumulating the imperishable for such a day.
  d. Money will make little difference—things just are not to be had.
  e. The world mourns its loss.
2. Worldwide famine is the charge of this horseman.
  a. Bounty is taken away from the earth and crops fail.
  b. With widespread war and confusion, transportation comes to a standstill.
  c. Food that does exist cannot be transported and gotten to the people.
  d. There is no point in growing food, if it cannot be gotten to market.
  e. Worldwide scarcity becomes the rule.

Breaking of the Fourth Seal (Rev. 6:7-8)

The fourth of the living creatures, like a flying eagle, calls out the horseman on the pale or ashen horse. This rider is Death, and Hades follows him. They are represented in physical form, as one day they will be thrown physically into the Lake of Fire. It is their assignment to kill one fourth of the wicked on the earth by whatever means—plagues, starvation, warfare, etc.

There will be a period of five months, however, during which people will actually want to die, just to escape the torment they are experiencing. Nevertheless, death will not be possible. It is part of Satan's strategy to torment mankind in this way. He will not even allow death to be an option. When they do die, Hades will store them up until Judgment Day.

1. With the breaking of the fourth seal, an ashen or pale green horse and rider go out.
  a. This is Death followed by Hades.
    (1) They are seen as personas, and will one day be thrown live into the Lake of Fire.
    (2) Death <u>is given</u> the power to take those people who do not belong to God.
    (3) As a part of Satan's torment, Death eludes mankind for five months, because death would be a welcome release from the suffering they will experience (Rev. 9:6).
    (4) God is still supreme and only those things which He allows may take place.
    (5) The Word says, the wicked will "see" Death.
    (6) Men of God will not (John 8:51).
  b. Hades stores those that Death reaps.

2. They kill one fourth of the living creatures of the world—men and beasts.
    a. This is accomplished through wars, civil strife, famine, and pestilence.
    b. Nature is out of balance and everything goes wild.
    c. Man even takes the food of animals, and the beasts become a threat to him (Rev. 6:8).

BREAKING OF THE FIFTH SEAL (REV. 6:9-11)

As mentioned previously, John is observing these events from heaven, so he is not really seeing the consequences of these actions from the perspective of earth. That is yet to happen. With the opening of the fifth seal, John sees an altar in heaven, and under it are all the people who die for their new-found faith, following the Rapture. These are the Tribulation Saints, and they want to know when their death will be avenged. They are told, nevertheless, that they must wait until the last person willing to be saved is saved. In the meantime, they are given the pure, white robes intended for the Saints—the robes they will wear to their marriage to the Bridegroom and upon returning with Him for the Great Battle of Armageddon.

1. At this point, no more horsemen go forth.
2. We have been shown a powerful, worldwide government, eager for conquest, but full of unrest, danger, misery, war, famine, pestilence, and death.
    a. There is no longer a time of peace and safety, as once created by the Antichrist.
    b. It has been removed, and the world becomes a place of anger, death, and fear.
3. With the breaking of the fifth seal, however, John sees an altar in heaven and under it the souls of the saints who have been martyred since the breaking of the first seal.
    a. These are those who turned to Christ after the Rapture, became Christians, and were killed for holding and testifying to the Truth.
    b. Satan's power persecutes them and slays them for spreading the Word.
    c. They die martyr's deaths.
    d. These are the Tribulation Saints.
        (1) There is no difference between them and the Raptured Saints.
        (2) They are all a part of the Bride.
        (3) Because they waited to accept Christ, however, they were required to go through great persecution.
    e. They do not go directly to God upon death, however.

(1) They must wait under the altar until an appointed time, when all who will confess Christ have done so.
(2) They plead for vindication, and ask *"How long?"* before they are avenged (Rev. 6:10).
    (a) They seek retribution and justice for what they have suffered.
    (b) They accept, however, that vengeance belongs to the Lord (Rom. 12:19) (Heb.10:30).
    (c) This is reminiscent of David's cry (Ps. 13:1-6).
(3) These are told they must wait a while longer, until all who shall die for their faithfulness are martyred.
  f. In the meantime, these saints are given their white robes.
    (1) We see them again in Rev. 6:11.
    (2) This is a symbol of their victory over the persecution of the Antichrist.
    (3) It is God's promise to His people that they shall participate in the victory and triumph over the Evil One.
    (4) These are the robes they will wear to the marriage ceremony.

BREAKING OF THE SIXTH SEAL (REV. 6:12-17)

As Jesus breaks the sixth seal, an enormous earthquake, as never seen before, rocks the whole earth, actually shifting it off its axis. As a result, the moon turns blood red, and the sun turns black from the stirring up of the dirt and dust created by the earthquake. At the same time, the heavens also appear to roll back as stars actually fall from the sky. This great cosmic disturbance changes everything in an instant.

Men are terrified by these events, and even seek refuge in mountain caves. It causes them to begin to recognize that this is not by man's hand; it is God's Wrath being poured out on them, and there is no escape or safety. This is a time of dealing primarily with the unsaved Gentiles. Later, emphasis will be placed on restoring God's relationship with the Jews.

1. At the breaking of the sixth seal, great cosmic and terrestrial events occur. It is an omen of the terrible judgment about to be poured out upon the inhabitants of the earth (Is. 13:10) (Luke 21:25-26).
  a. An earthquake, such as never seen before, takes place.
  b. It is the first of three mentioned in the Book of Revelation (Rev. 6:12; 11:13; 16:18-19).

      c. Mountains and islands shake and are moved out of their places.
      d. From the churning up of the dust and soil, the sun becomes black like sackcloth (Is. 50:3).
      e. The moon turns blood red (Joel 2:10, 31) (Is. 13:10) (Acts 2:19-21).
      f. Even the heavens are shaken, and stars fall from the sky (Matt. 24:29) (Mark 13:25).
      g. The sky splits apart, and the starry heavens disappear like a scroll being rolled up (Is. 34:4).
2. The unsaved of the world run in terror, but there is no safe place for them to hide (Is. 2:19).
      a. They even flee to the mountains and caves, asking them to conceal them (Rev. 6:16).
      b. Regardless how great or small, rich or poor, however, there is no escape.
3. All people at this point understand the concept of Jesus, and that the time of God's Wrath is at hand.
      a. They realize that by not turning to God now, they are specifically rejecting Him.
      b. There are no more lukewarm people left on the earth.
      c. Any remaining are there by their own choice, because they reject God and His Word.
4. These events take place so Jesus is recognized as the <u>only</u> hope and salvation.
5. In the three and a half years between the breaking of the first and the sixth seals, God's Wrath is mixed with mercy.
      a. The purpose of this time is to save all remaining souls who choose to be saved.
      b. It also marks the beginning of God's judgment of mankind.
      c. This is the time of the Great Tribulation, but the Great Wrath is yet to come.
6. It is also the period of dealing primarily with the Gentiles.
      a. Because the Jews refused salvation through Jesus Christ, the gospel was taken to the Gentiles.
          (1) They were grafted onto the olive tree and nourished by the original roots (Rom. 11:17-21).
          (2) They share a place with the Jews, who are cut off for a time.
          (3) When Israel decides to believe, they will again be grafted back onto the tree.
          (4) All Israel will be saved, but not necessarily all Jews.
          (5) God alone knows whom to save and whom to condemn.

    b. It is a mystery why the hearts of the Jews are hardened, but such is the case until the full number of Gentiles are saved (Rom. 11:25)
        (1) When that day is accomplished, the saving of all Israel will begin.
        (2) They too will then accept Jesus as their Messiah.
    c. Pentecost began the Day of the Gentiles and ends when the moon turns to blood.
        (1) On that day, the time of grace is over.
        (2) The Day of the Gentiles will be completed.
    d. This will mark the beginning of Jacob's Trouble—Daniel's 70th Week—the seven years of Great Tribulation—the outpouring of God's punishment.

CHAPTER 6

A Moment of Praise

Revelation: 7:1-8

As we have watched the chronology of events to this point, John has systematically been shown a sequence of incidents that are prophesied to take place during a seven-year period of tribulation. He has been abundantly blessed to be chosen as a spectator of this process, as well as its recorder for future generations. The progression of images he sees unveils a revelation of God's plan to wipe out sin and restore His creation to its original condition of perfection. It is the responsibility of Jesus Christ, in the likeness of a Lamb, to carry out this mission on behalf His Father—to reclaim all that has been lost to the rebellious nature of sin.

The consequences of the opening of each seal are not merely random, however. Each event builds on that which precedes it—the final objective being complete restoration. It is God's intent to recreate a perfect world and a perfect relationship with mankind. Nevertheless, He has never chosen to sustain it through domination over one's free will. He wants it to exist because of His love for His children and their choice to love and obey Him as their Heavenly Father.

Although major things have occurred so far, suddenly, following a great earthquake and cosmic disturbance, there is a break between the opening of the sixth and seventh seals. It is as if Jesus said, "Stop!" The torment has been intense thus far, and despite the fact that it has included love and mercy in the midst of punishment, it has been nearly unbearable—in some cases totally. However, there is suddenly a cessation of the torment, and as with any anguish, it is a merciful gift to have it cease, if only for a moment.

An Interlude (Rev. 7:1-3)

Following the roar of the cataclysmic activity that has just occurred, everything suddenly becomes silent. John says, *"after these things I saw..."* four angels commanded to hold back the winds and raging activity on earth. Something momentous is about to happen in heaven—the Tribulation Saints are being drawn into the Throne Room, from under the altar where they have been waiting. Additionally, a carefully chosen group of 144,000 Jews is sealed away from persecution by the evil forces of the Antichrist and any further outpouring of God's wrath.

As this is accomplished, a great display of praise and worship erupts before the Throne of God. All of His children have been brought into His presence, and it is a time of glorious rejoicing. It is not the case on earth, however. This interlude between the breaking of the sixth and seventh seals has dire consequences on earth. The four angels John has seen are about to pour out further punishment upon a wicked world. They are stopped for a moment, however, until what has just been described is accomplished. They hold back the wind, but are not to harm the earth. Nevertheless, this action precipitates significant negative consequences on the wicked world below.

1. Following the great earthquake, a strange calm falls over the earth, and three visions are seen taking place simultaneously.
   a. Nature is stilled on earth,
   b. The sealing of the 144,000 takes place, and
   c. A host of palm-bearers surrounds the throne in heaven.
2. At this point, John sees four angels standing at the four corners of the earth ready to rain God's wrath upon it.
   a. There is a hesitation, however, just as there was in the time of Moses (Ex. 11:7).
   b. The final outpouring cannot take place until the multitudes of Tribulation Saints, who were martyred during the breaking of the first six seals, are removed from under the altar, and the 144,000 are sealed.
3. An angel of the Lord, carrying a seal, tells the four angels not to hurt either the earth, or the sea, or the trees, until the mark, or seal of the "living God," has been placed upon the head of each righteous servant from the tribes of Israel (Ex. 12:13).
4. During this time of sealing, nature stands still.
   a. The wind and breezes stop.
      (1) This results in the air becoming totally polluted on earth.
      (2) Breathing itself becomes a struggle.
   b. The tides cease, because there are no winds.
      (1) The oceans, lakes, and rivers become stagnant and contaminated.
      (2) All that lives within them die.
   c. No rain falls to cleanse the earth.
   d. The peoples of the world are stunned by what is happening.

THE 144,000 (REV. 7:4-8)

As seen in other instances thus far, there is little unanimity relative to who comprises this group of 144,000. Some followers of opposing points of view are so adamant in their beliefs that agreement has become almost impossible. Even many self-professed Christians have become so disturbed by the confusion that they have accepted erroneous conclusions. The scriptures clearly state, however, that these are a carefully selected assemblage of men from the twelve tribes of Israel, who are chosen to carry out God's singular purpose of spreading the gospel to the Jewish nation—something they would not generally accept from Gentiles.

There is a difference between Jews being in relationship with God, following their own will, and being outright disobedient to His law. They have vacillated back and forth in this respect throughout their history. When they have gone their own way and turned their back on God, He has had to discipline them. He is a just and jealous God and cannot condone rebellious behavior. Despite this, God loves them, but He must withhold His blessings when they are out of relationship with Him. It is not a matter of accepting Jesus Christ as their Messiah. God-fearing Jews were not promised they would go to heaven; they were promised they would live in their land <u>forever</u>, with King David as their ruler. Jews, on the other hand, who accept Jesus as the Messiah become a part of the body of Christ. It is the responsibility of the 144,000 to spread this gospel to their own.

The significance of the impact of differing interpretations, therefore, once again points to the importance of considering <u>all</u> of God's Word, not merely certain verses that support a particular point of view. Understanding comes through the Holy Spirit from the One who is the Way and the Truth. Unless one uses discernment and seeks the truth, a belief system can be built around a false premise.

1. There are differences of opinion concerning who makes up this limited number of 144,000.
    a. Some believe the number is merely symbolic of, and represents, all of the redeemed throughout the ages.
    b. Others consider them to be the reclaimed from the nation of Israel and the saved Gentiles, who are a part of the true Israel.
    c. Both are interpreted as representative of all who recognize Jesus Christ as Lord.
2. <u>These</u> points of view presume, therefore, that the Church goes through the Tribulation and is" Raptured" only when Christ returns to do battle with Satan and the armies of the world.
    a. They postulate that all believers are to suffer from the hand of the Antichrist until the end.

b. The Word says, however, that these believers—the 144,000—are protected from "God's Wrath," which is to be only the very last events to occur.
   c. These interpretations create many questions and very few answers.
3. The scriptures are clearer than that, however, and to read something into them other than what is actually stated is taking a risk of adding to, or subtracting from, the Word (Rev. 22:18).
   a. The text specifically says that these are 12,000 Jews (holy men) from each of the tribes of Israel, who come to accept Jesus as the Messiah.
      (1) They are the "first fruits" of Israel. (Rev. 14:4)
      (2) How they come back to God and to the Lord is not described in Revelation, however.
   b. The following are the twelve tribes and what each means:
   Judah - praise of God or confessions
   Reuben - viewing the Son
   Gad - a company
   Asher - blessed
   Nephtali - striving with
   Manasseh - forgetfulness
   Simeon - hearing and obeying
   Levi - joining or cleaving to
   Issachar - reward
   Zabulun - home or dwelling place
   Joseph - added (½ the tribe of Ephraim & ½ the tribe of Manasseh)
   Benjamin - son of old age
   Dan (the Lost Tribe) is left out - They turned to idolatry (Deut. 29:18-21).
   Dan was restored at the end, because they repented, and God is faithful to keep His word. God restores His own.
   Ephriam and Manasseh (sons of Joseph) were also left out.
   c. If you put these meanings together, this group is described as:
   "Confessors or praisers of God, looking upon the Son, a band of blessed ones, wrestling with forgetfulness, hearing and obeying the word, cleaving unto the reward of a shelter and home, an addition, sons of the day of God's right hand, begotten at the end of the age."
   d. It is difficult to justify that these are any other than Israelites who have accepted Jesus as their Messiah. They are placed on Mt. Zion for protection, during the tribulation that is to come.
      (1) God has a plan to restore Israel (Is. 27:12-13).

    (2) Though more Jews will be saved later, at this particular time, He seals the initial 144,000.
  e. During the tribulation period, these men proclaim God's Word, and the Antichrist is not able touch them.
    (1) It is their job to preach the gospel to the Jewish nation in an attempt to open their eyes, for not one is to be lost (Amos 9:9).
    (2) This initial group finds safety, at first in Palestine and later on Mt. Zion.
    (3) Satan is <u>never</u> allowed to take Mt. Zion.

THE SCENE IN HEAVEN (REV. 7:9-17)

As previously stated, the great multitude that John sees before the Throne, wearing white robes and waving palm branches, are those from every tribe and nation who, over the ages, have elected to follow God's Word. In addition to these are the Saints who are martyred during the first three and a half years of the Tribulation Period. They are the Gentiles, or professed Christians, who failed to be ready at the moment of the Rapture. They gave their hearts and lives to Christ only after the blowing of the trumpet. When asked, John does not know who these people are, because they are on earth when his visions first begin.

During the last days of life on earth as we know it, there will be no protection from the outpouring of pain and torment that befalls mankind. Only the 144,000 will have that—everyone else will be forced to make a choice between accepting Jesus in service to God or following the wicked ways of the Antichrist and the world. If one chooses the former, he or she will be physically put to death, but saved from the second, or spiritual death. If one chooses the latter, however, the outcome will be an eternity separated from God and an eternity of pain and torment. The impact of waiting to make such a decision could result in missing the Rapture and enduring the alternative.

1. John sees a great multitude in heaven, dressed in white robes, praising God and waving palm branches.
   a. These are numbered beyond count and are from every tribe and nation.
   b. They are Gentiles, who were found lacking, or were sinners, at the time of the Rapture of the Church.
   c. For their earlier resistance, they were required to suffer the thirst, famine, and persecution of the tribulation, resulting from the opening of the first six seals.
   d. These Tribulation Saints repented, however, and came to the Lord during the previous three and a half years, accepting Christ as their true Savior.

  e. They were martyred for their faithfulness to the Word, and thus earned garments washed white by the blood of the Lamb, but they have had to wait under the altar until the appointed time before becoming a part of the Bride.
  f. God is a merciful God and desires that all should come to Him and be saved, and He now comforts and cares for those who come to Him the hard way.
  g. The time of waiting is over, however, and they too are now before the throne, worshipping God their Father and the Lamb.
  h. They are given palm branches to denote their victory.
   (1) As Jesus was given palm branches by the multitudes upon His triumphal entry into Jerusalem, before His crucifixion; He now gives them palm branches.
   (2) There is a detailed description of this in the Apocryphal Book of *2 Ezdras* 2:42.
  i. As Creator of the universe, He who entered Bethlehem on the night of His birth on the back of a donkey, lived His life on earth possessing nothing.
   (1) The week before His death, which would save mankind, He rode into Jerusalem on a borrowed donkey.
   (2) This was a man of peace and humility.
  j. But this time, John will see Jesus ride out of heaven to Jerusalem on a mighty steed, as a Warrior, Judge, and King.
   (1) This time He comes to restore the world and do battle with the ultimate Evil One.
   (2) He returns to earth as LORD OF LORDS and KING OF KINGS.
  k. Another great praise service, therefore, erupts before the throne of the Lord God Almighty.
   (1) Even the angels, who surround the throne, and the elders and the living creatures, are on their faces saying, "*Amen, blessing and glory and wisdom and thanksgiving and honor and power and might, be to our God forever and ever. Amen*" (Rev.7:12).
   (2) Jesus is their Shepherd, and because He has been their constant companion throughout their suffering, they are particularly close to Him now.
2. When asked by one of the elders if he knows who these people are, John indicates that he does not recognize them, because he has been in heaven and unaware of what has been occurring on the earth.
  a. The elder tells him that these are the Tribulation Saints, and why they are here.
  b. This leaves little room for doubt, as to who this group is.

CHAPTER 7
Sounding of the Trumpets

REVELATION 8:1-12

ALL THAT JOHN HAS VIEWED thus far has taken place over a period of nearly seven years in earthly time—three and a half years leading up to the Rapture and three and a half years since. As a result of the opening of the first six seals, those left behind have suffered the effects of war, famine, physical torture, disease, and fear of personal attack from the Antichrist and his followers—both natural and supernatural. The earth and heavens have been polluted and ravaged, or changed in ways we would never imagine. Where there was once an illusion of peace and safety, everyone and everything has been catapulted into a state of utter chaos. All occurs as Jesus—one-by-one—breaks the seals of the scroll He holds.

God's people have overcome, however, and been translated into the presence of God. The final act of war against sin and the powers of darkness is nearly at hand. It is almost time for Jesus to ride out of heaven with the Saints and carry out the final destruction of sin and the one that has held the world in bondage for so long. Adam and Eve gave up their birthright to the Author of Lies, but his reign is finally about to end. The final battle between good and evil will soon take place and Christ reclaim the earth with the Title Deed. However, there are a few things yet to take place, but victory-in-Jesus is assured, and there is hope for all who choose to be a part of it.

BREAKING OF THE SEVENTH SEAL (REV. 8:1)

With the breaking of the seventh seal, a strange thing occurs. Only in heaven, another period of silence, lasting about half an hour, takes place. Prior to this, the great throne room was resounding with celebration, song, and praise. There was joyful adoration of the heavenly Father and Son, and then suddenly everything becomes still. As we have seen at other times, there is again speculation about the reason for this. Some of the interpretations are actually quite plausible, and may even be accurate. The Word itself, however, does not specifically say why this occurs. All we know for certain is that it does. To assume anything else is to put one's own spin on a particular point of view. The Scriptures are adamant that we not add to or subtract from the Word. We are simply to accept what it says—anything more is strictly opinion.

1. As the seventh and final seal is broken, a great silence suddenly falls over heaven for what John estimates to be *"about half an hour."*
   a. This is the climax of the ages—*"The Day of the Lord"* has arrived.
   b. There are many broad interpretations as to what this silence represents.
      (1) One view is that it is an indication of a final rest for God's people who have just experienced the events of the first six seals.
      (2) Another explanation is that the silence is a result of stunned fear of what is yet to take place.
      (3) Some also believe that the silence occurs so that the prayers of the ages may be heard.
   c. Upon careful examination, however, only the facts that are actually written are clear.
      (1) The silence is in heaven,
      (2) It is a result of the opening of the last seal,
      (3) It lasts for about half an hour,
      (4) And to infer more is to make the scriptures say what one might like them to say.
2. As the last seal is broken, the Title Deed to the earth is completely opened.
   a. Satan must now legally relinquish his hold upon mankind.
   b. We see him refuse, however, and only increase his efforts to retain possession of the earth.
   c. Jesus is now forced to physically remove him and his followers.
   d. All of this is to fulfill God's plan (Prov. 16: 4).
   e. The wicked will now be punished without mercy, and the earth will be purged to cleanse it of all that is not acceptable to God (Is. 13:9-11).

PREPARATION FOR THE TRUMPETS (REV. 8:2-5)

Before Christ rides forth into battle, however, seven angels are given trumpets. Each will sequentially blow its trumpet and affect further action upon a particular part of creation. The end is near, but not yet over. Another Angel—probably Christ—steps forth first. He takes a golden censer, or bowl, filled with prayers from the Saints, from under the altar, and presents it to His Father. The prayers of centuries are about to be answered. He also fills a censer with fire from a second altar, and pours it down upon the earth. This is the final outpouring of God's Wrath upon a wicked world. This is announced by means of thunder, lightning, and an earthquake, emanating from the Throne.

1. Seven angels, *"who stand in the presence of God,"* are given the assignment of carrying out the last expressions of wrath (Rev. 8:6).
   a. They are intelligent, high ranking angels, and they are about to finish the desolation of a doomed man and earth.
   b. Each is given a trumpet—an instrument used to announce happenings of great importance.
      (1) They will sound their trumpets one at a time, and each will affect a different part of creation.
      (2) These effects are orderly and progressive.
      (3) The angels prepare for and plan their actions.
      (4) Trumpets were commonly used in John's time for many purposes.
         (a) They called the people into battle or to worship (Num. 10:5-10),
         (b) They proclaimed great celebrations (Num. 10:10), and
         (c) They preceded persons of royalty and occurrences of great note.
         (d) They would now declare that the forces of heaven were moving.
         (e) They indicate that the wicked are about to be overcome.
      (5) A silence, followed by the sounding of trumpets, is reminiscent of the march around Jericho.
         (a) For six days the people marched around the city in silence.
         (b) On the seventh day, they marched around seven times and the trumpets were blasted.
         (c) The walls fell and the city was overcome (Heb. 11:30).
2. *"Another angel"* appears before the trumpets are sounded (Rev. 8:3-5).
   a. While this may be one of the archangels such as Gabriel, there is some evidence that it might also be Christ Himself.
   b. He is called an angel at various points throughout the scriptures (Rev. 1:1; 10:1-3; 14:14).
   c. The description of the place of this vision is reminiscent of the Tabernacle.
      (1) It is in the presence of God.
      (2) Though it does not say there are two altars (the altar of prayer and the altar of burnt offerings), this was the case in the Tabernacle, and two actions do take place here.

  (3) Christ (the angel), as High Priest, has the position and authority to carry out what is to occur next.
 d. As our intercessor before the Father, He holds a golden censer filled with our prayers mixed with incense.
  (1) The prayers are "*given to Him*" (Christ) by <u>all</u> the saints, and only <u>through</u> Him can they reach the Father.
  (2) These are the prayers of all the ages. "*Thy will...*" is finally about to be done "*on earth as it is in heaven*," and "*Lord, come quickly*" (Matt. 6:10) (Rev. 22:7, 12, 20).
  (3) They have been stored for this day.
  (4) This is the reason we are to pray without ceasing (1 Thess. 15:17)
  (5) These prayers are a vital part of the process of reclamation.
 e. After the prayers, like incense, are given to the Father, the "angel" fills another censer with fire from the other altar and casts it onto the earth.
  (1) Jesus has the power and authority to pour out this wrath upon mankind.
  (2) He launches both judgment and destruction of evil onto earth, as well as its restoration.
  (3) Out of this fire from the altar of God comes the damnation of the wicked.
 f. Heaven again announces this with thunder, lightning, voices, and an earthquake.
 g. For those who have denied the Word, the Truth, and Jesus Christ, and all that is evil in and on the earth, <u>the total judgment of God is now unleashed</u>.

SOUNDING OF THE TRUMPETS (REV. 8:6 - 9:21)

As just described, the sounding of each trumpet triggers more action against a different part of the earth. The first trumpet sends hail and fire; the second, something like a burning mountain; and the third, a burning star falling to the earth. These particular incidents produce a specific reaction within the land, the oceans, as well as the rivers and streams. The fourth trumpet, however, elicits a response in the heavens—with the moon, the stars, and planets.

1. With the <u>sounding of the first trumpet</u> comes hail and fire mingled with blood (Rev. 8:7).
 a. This is reminiscent of what once occurred in Egypt (Ex. 9:18-26).
 b. The storm of hail and fire is so great that it burns a part of the earth, but not all, as in Egypt.

    c. The entire earth is affected and the land is purged.
       (1) One third of the earth is burned.
       (2) One third of the trees burned.
       (3) All of the green grass is burned.
       (4) It is not random; God chooses what third needs restoring.
    d. One third is a significant number.
       (1) 3 persons in one = the Trinity
       (2) $\frac{1}{3}$ = 1 person in 3 forms—the Unholy Trinity (Satan, the Antichrist, the False Prophet)
       (3) There is always a counterfeit to whatever God creates.
    e. Some strongly believe that what is described in these scriptures is not what is actually meant, but symbolic of something entirely different.
       (1) If that is so, how do we ever know what to believe is truth in the Word?
       (2) Many things are symbolic in the Bible, but in most cases, they are indicated to be so, in order to avoid misunderstanding.
       (3) Confusion only results from reading other meanings into God's Word.
       (4) Man, not God, turns the Word into a riddle.
2. With the <u>sounding of the second trumpet</u>, something <u>like</u> a great burning mountain is cast into the sea (Rev. 8:8-9).
    a. This is one of those places where symbols are used, and we are told it is such by the reference to the fact that it is <u>like</u> a mountain.
       (1) "Like" indicates that this is symbolic rather than literal.
       (2) It is not likely that a literal mountain is cast into the sea, but something the size of a mountain.
       (3) It is possible that a mountainous, fiery mass falls from the sky.
       (4) The image is more meteoric than volcanic, but that too is a possibility.
    b. The result is that a third of the ocean is turned to blood.
       (1) This is reminiscent of when Moses smote the Nile (Ex. 7:19-21).
       (2) It also turned to blood.
    c. This action causes a third of the living things of the sea to die and one third of the ships on the sea to be destroyed.
       (1) Such an occurrence would affect life throughout the world.
       (2) Food would be further diminished and shipping brought to a standstill.
3. At the <u>sounding of the third trumpet</u>, a great burning star, or comet, falls out of the sky or heavens, and is absorbed by the earth and the water in it (Rev. 8:10-11).
    a. It is physically possible for such a meteoric phenomenon to penetrate the earth and contaminate springs, rivers, and lakes, as well as make the water bitter like absinthe.

  b. This star, called Wormwood, is mentioned a number of times throughout the Bible, as a judgment on the non-believing (Jer. 9:15; 23:15) (Deut. 29:18).
  c. Wormwood is an "herb," which causes convulsions, paralysis, and death, just as the water in one third of the rivers and springs cause men to die.
  d. Again, man has given various interpretations to this occurrence.
    (1) Though it has been proposed, there is no support for the fact that this is "the church," or Christ, or an apostate teacher, etc.
    (2) The Word indicates when symbolism is being used, and it does not suggest that in this instance.
 4. With the <u>sounding of the fourth trumpet</u>, the heavens are impacted (Rev. 8:12).
  a. To this point, the land, the seas, rivers, and springs have been purged.
    (1) In each case, man has experienced disaster, suffering, and death.
    (2) Life around the world is in chaos.
  b. Activity in the heavenly bodies now intensifies.
    (1) One third of the sun, one third of the moon, and one third of the stars are destroyed (Is.13:10-11) (Joel 2:31) (Matt. 24:29).
    (2) This affects the seasons, the growth of things, and temperatures.
    (3) When the sun does shine, it is so intensely hot that it burns the very skin of people, and when it does not shine, they freeze.
    (4) It continues day after day without relief.
    (5) This is a dark time of suffering and hopelessness—a great punishment of the wicked and unrepentant.
    (6) God has done this before in Egypt, when darkness fell during the plagues.
  c. Men have tried to attach obscure meanings to this phenomenon.
    (1) There is even an attempt to relate it to historical people, places, or events.
    (2) This is pure imagination, however, and unsupported by the Word.

A Heavenly Proclamation (Rev. 8:13)

Before the last three trumpets sound, John notices an eagle flying across the sky saying, "*Woe! Woe! Woe...*" Whether this is actually a bird with the capabilities of speech, or one of the Saints sent to proclaim a warning of more great punishments and judgments yet to come, is unclear. We have a merciful God, and it is His desire to give mankind every chance to repent and be saved from the Final Judgment. Unfortunately, most at this time will not accept the offer.
 1. Three trumpets have yet to sound, and they will bring about even greater judgments.

2. Before that happens, however, John sees an eagle flying through the heavens saying, "*Woe, woe, woe, to the dwellers on the earth...,*" for there is more to come with the blowing of the final three trumpets (Rev. 8:13).
    a. This three-fold proclamation signifies total and ultimate judgment.
        (1) It is Jewish custom to emphasize things by repeating an expletive twice, i.e. "*Verily, verily...*" or "*Woe! Woe to you...*" (Ezek. 16:23).
        (2) <u>This</u> pronouncement is even stronger, however, to the extreme.
        (3) Any Hebrew would know that "*Woe, woe, woe...*" meant that something, as bad as it can get, is about to take place.
    b. Repeatedly, Jesus calls His saints eagles—those who are vigilant, watchful, and ready for Him and to do His bidding.
    c. Both the eagle and the saints are strong, and that strength lifts them heavenward.
    d. This eagle has a voice and is in the heavens, thus supporting the fact that it is very possibly a saint, and not some historical person or event, as some interpretations propose.
3. In giving the world this last warning before the final judgment trumpets sound, God again shows mercy to any who hear and seek salvation.
    a. He is a merciful God.
    b. He takes no pleasure in death—even of the wicked.
4. One would think the evil of the world would repent, but many do not.

THE TRUMPETS AND THE SPIRIT WORLD
(REV. 9:1-12, 13-21, 11:15-19)

The last three trumpets bring action against the supernatural world of Satan and the Antichrist. At the sounding of the fifth trumpet, Satan is given the keys to the abyss, and allowed to release the vilest of his demons, against the world. Like locusts, they attack mankind for five months, and during that time men will want to die, but, as mentioned earlier, death will be removed for a period and not be an option. People will have to suffer and endure the will of the Evil One. This is a representation of the first "*Woe.*"

1. At the <u>sounding of the fifth trumpet,</u> judgment moves beyond the material world into the supernatural (Rev. 9:1-12).
    a. The heavens are reclaimed.
        (1) The Prince of the Air (Satan) is banished permanently <u>to the earth</u>.

- (2) He still has power over mankind on the earth, but only as much as he is allowed.
- b. John sees "a fallen star."
  - (1) It is hard to mistake the meaning of this image.
  - (2) Satan and his angels fell once, from heaven to the air above the earth (Is. 14:12) (Luke 10:18).
  - (3) They now fall again, to the earth itself.
  - (4) Satan's power and dominion continues to diminish.
    - (a) Our prayers help to keep his power in check and from increasing.
    - (b) Again, this is one of the reasons we are told to pray, *"without ceasing..."*
    - (c) We have been given the power of spiritual warfare, as referred to in Luke 10:19, *"...authority to tread on snakes and scorpions..."*
  - (5) It is a fair assumption, therefore, that this "fallen star" is symbolic of Satan, and in this scene, he <u>is given</u> the key to the abyss.
  - (6) In other words, he is permitted to open the pit, or hell, and let loose the most malevolent of the demonic spirits imprisoned there.
    - (a) Some evil spirits have been loosed to torment mankind for ages; i.e. Legion, but the very worst of these beings have been restrained in the abyss until this time.
    - (b) There are those who believe that hell is merely a condition of the less exalted, as contrasted to the heavenly place of the godly.
    - (c) It is not interpreted as literally under the earth, but rather the underworld with respect to its position in creation.
    - (d) Others are a little more literal, or less symbolic in their interpretation.
    - (e) In either case, there are evil spirits (demons) on earth even now, but the worst have been held captive in the abyss until this point.
    - (f) God <u>uses</u> this evil to bring further judgment upon a wicked world.
- c. The people remaining on the earth at this time, who have aligned themselves with Satan—as the Antichrist—are now allowed, by God, to experience what Satan's kingdom is really like.
- d. He is permitted, again by God, to set free his strongest forces of evil upon the world.
  - (1) Prior to this time, the key that Satan is given has kept the full fury of evil in check.
  - (2) Things could actually have been worse than they have been to date.

e. Out of the pit pours smoke and darkness sufficient to darken the sun (Rev. 9:2).
   (1) From the smoke come living beings <u>likened</u> to locusts (Ex. 10:1) (Joel 1:2-2:11).
       (a) They have the ability to devour everything in their path.
       (b) Some see this as a symbol of the power of a great army to attack suddenly and wipe out everything.
       (c) They come out of the sky and leave utter destruction.
       (d) This explains the interpretation of some that, in today's world, these are planes or helicopters used in warfare.
   (2) These "locusts" have the power to torture and torment man, but not to kill him.
   (3) They are also not allowed to harm the grass or any green thing, or any of mankind who have the seal of God on their foreheads.
f. These beings are horrible to behold—part horse, part man, part lion, and part scorpion.
   (1) They have wings and, when in flight, sound like horses and chariots.
   (2) They have teeth that bite, but do not consume.
   (3) They have a tail like a scorpion that stings and does not kill, but causes excruciating pain.
   (4) They have long Medusa-like hair and breastplates, which some believe are symbolic of uninhibited, unrestrained, barbaric armies, which attack with ferocious might.
   (5) They infest the entire earth, and attack everything in every place.
g. Over these beings is a "king," or general (one of Satan's high-ranking angels), whose name is Abaddon, or Apollyon, which means "destroyer."
h. The duration of this plague is "five months" (Rev. 9:5).
   (1) This time period is reminiscent of the fact that the flood lasted five months.
       (a) It is a time of purification.
       (b) All that has been corrupted is being destroyed.
   (2) This is an eternity to those experiencing it and there is no relief.
   (3) The anguish of these days is beyond description.
   (4) One of the greatest torments for man is to desire to die and be unable to do so.

(5) Death would be a welcome relief from the agony inflicted by these demons.
(6) *"Men seek after death, and are unable to find it"* (Rev. 9:6).
(7) Although death would be preferable to what is being experienced with this plague, it is not an option.
    i. In spite of all of the evidence of God's power, however, people continue to deny Him.
2. Scholars have tried to make an allegory of this vision, but such interpretations are pure speculation.
    a. John said that what he saw was "in the Day of the Lord."
    b. It is not truth, if these things occurred in the past.
    c. If the Word is truth, then it has to be truth all of the time.
    d. These things seem impossible, but man lives between the forces of good (above) and the forces of evil (below), and *"all things are possible"* for God (Matt. 19:26).
3. Thus ends the first "Woe."

The Impact on Satan's Realm

Following the blare of the fifth trumpet, Satan is further removed from the heavens. He is now cast down to abide <u>on</u> the earth. He is allowed to go unchecked, but only by God's will. Demon and idol worship become the norm, and mankind is predominantly heathen or pagan. Every evil vice becomes both desirable and acceptable. There is no moral code left, as depravity and corruption go unrestrained.

By this time, even Satan's followers begin to experience who Satan truly is. As he sets free his most evil forces to cause a plague that lasts for five months, it will not matter to him upon whom it falls. He has no concern for any of mankind. They are merely his pawns.

1. This is a period of great demon-worship.
    a. There are many interpretations of what demons are.
    b. Some believe "fallen angels."
    c. More believe they are souls or spirits of the wicked dead—unholy spiritual beings that belong to the evil kingdom.
    d. They generally are assigned to interfere in the affairs of man.
    e. Satan is "The Devil," but demons are also often called devils.
    f. They attempt to control man's physical actions, overpowering the "will."

2. Man has always tried to find ways to communicate with these beings or spirits.
   a. Familiar spirits, oracles, soothsayers, channelers, etc. have been common tools throughout history.
   b. We are specifically told, however, not to have anything to do with them (Lev. 19:31).
   c. Today, this interaction is called "spiritism," and even in some cases "spiritualism."
      (1) It is designed to add wisdom, offer comfort, and dictate faith in place of Christian teachings.
      (2) The Word warns that this will become particularly popular in the end times.
      (3) It is the basis of the New Age Movement and will become the prevailing religion during the last days.
3. This will also be a time of great idolatry.
   a. Much worship of idols of gold and silver, etc. will become the norm.
   b. Man has a need to elevate and worship something, and with the rejection of Christ and His teachings, idol worship will fill that need.
4. Man will return to heathen ways.
   a. Murder, the use of drugs that increase wicked actions, and the indulgence in sexual and sensual behavior will be rampant.
   b. Morality and honesty will cease to have value.

THE SIXTH TRUMPET (REV. 9:13-21)

By this time, everyone left on earth is there by his or her own choice. They have denied Christ and accepted the ways of the world. Therefore, Satan is allowed to do with mankind as he chooses. They belong to him, but he has no love for them. They are merely pawns in his final efforts to survive the inescapable—total annihilation and being cast into the Lake of Fire forever.

At the sounding of the sixth trumpet, the living creatures from around the throne, tell the sixth angel to set loose four demons to kill one third of mankind. With them are 200 million supernatural forces that go forth—to kill by fire and smoke. They have come from the pit of hell and bring fire and brimstone with them. Though precipitated by Satan's powers of darkness, the outpouring of this death and destruction upon the wicked world is by the command of heaven. God is still on the Throne, and He is ever in control. There is never anything beyond His oversight. He created mankind and this world, and He will restore it according to His plans.

1. At the <u>sounding of the sixth trumpet</u>, the living beings with horns, which are standing around the altar of God, speak with one voice (in unison) to the <u>sixth angel</u> (Rev. 9:13-21).
    a. He is told to loose four other angels (demons) to go out and kill one third of mankind.
        (1) These four "angels" have been bound until this day and hour, so they are not heavenly angels.
        (2) They are loosed to carry out their evil deeds and kill one third of mankind.
            (a) Because all who are left on earth at this time are there by their own choice, no one is worthy of escaping the attacks of these demons.
            (b) Those remaining have chosen to follow the ways of evil, and now they get a taste of what it is like to experience the consequences.
            (c) Satan has no love of mankind, so none will elude his assaults.
            (d) This is a part of God's judgment, and all things are created for His purpose—even evil things (Prov. 16:4).
            (e) Satan is <u>allowed</u> to have his diabolical way with mankind, so he can never say that, if he could have just had his way, he would have been victorious.
        (3) Prior to this time, these beings have been bound for our mercy, until the appointed time of judgment. That time is at hand.
    b. These four "angels" have been bound near the River Euphrates.
        (1) This is the Middle Eastern area of Babylon—Iraq.
        (2) It is where the first murder took place—Cain and Abel.
        (3) It is also the location of other judgments; i.e. the fall of man, the flood, Sodom and Gomorrah.
        (4) Repeatedly, it has been the center of Satan's earthly power and control, and he will return to this location in the last days.
    c. As the four "angels" are loosed, 200 million supernatural, fiery horses are sent out to bring death.
        (1) Fire, smoke, and sulfur (3 plagues) come out of their mouths.
        (2) These forces from hell burn and suffocate one third of mankind.
        (3) The horses kill with their fiery breath and torment and injure with tails like snakes.
    d. This horrific scene was prophesied and described in Joel 2:3-10.
    e. Despite the fact that God spares two thirds of mankind, those who experience the wrath of God and torment of Satan still do not repent.

      f.   These events have been planned for this particular hour, day, month, and year.
- (1) Unlike before the Rapture, when no times were given, times are now very specific.
- (2) Although the Word says no one shall know the time of Christ's coming, if you believe in a Pre-Tribulation Rapture, you can almost predict it, once these events begin to take place.

2. Those who take a symbolic approach to the interpretation of these events see them as evidence of some great, nuclear holocaust.
   a. The "angels" loose hosts of beings (human and 200,000,000 in number), and some believe they represent an army—probably of Chinese or eastern origin.
   b. An army of this size is possible today, and with our technology, it could easily be mobilized.
   c. Such an army would kill with fire, smoke, and destruction.
   d. This speaks to some, of a nuclear war.
   e. It is not likely, however, that the Bible would say, "Woe, woe, woe; the Chinese are coming."
   f. Not knowing what the future holds, John describes these as supernatural beings.

THE LITTLE BOOK/SCROLL (REV. 10:1-11)

A mighty angel now comes out of heaven and yet again there is dispute over who this is. Based on the description of this being, however, it is safe to say that again it is Christ Jesus—particularly, since He is holding the scroll that was given to Him to open. As He steps out of heaven, He plants one foot on the land and one foot on the sea, finally claiming it as His own. He then declares in a powerful voice that more judgments are yet to come. This is confirmed by the thunders and voices associated with the Throne of God. As John begins to write what they say, He is told to stop and not to write, because there are some mysteries too holy to be revealed.

1. <u>Another</u> "mighty angel" appears, coming out of heaven (Rev. 10:1).
2. This is one more place where there are differences of opinion as to who this "angel" is.
   a. Angels are created beings, less than deity, and are not to be worshipped.
   b. One of their foremost functions is to act as messengers.
   c. All angels have power, but this angel is "mighty," which makes it "more than."

3. The word "angel" is also often used as a title of office based upon its function. In this case, it is very possible that again the angel is Jesus Christ, Himself.
   a. He has appeared in many forms before; i.e. lion, lamb, also as an angel (Rev. 8:3-5).
   b. Again, He is described in all His divinity.
      (1) He is clothed in a cloud—clouds repeatedly covered the divine nature of God.
         (a) The word itself means weighty or heavy.
         (b) The Shekinah Glory, which surrounds Him, reflects on the weightiness, or importance of God's nature and holiness.
      (2) The, not a rainbow is on His head.
         (a) This rainbow was seen earlier around the throne of God.
         (b) It belongs to God, not angels.
         (c) It is a sign of mercy in the midst of judgment—God's covenant with man.
      (3) His face is described as the sun, which is common when describing God/Jesus.
      (4) His feet are as pillars of fire, as depicted in Rev 1.
   c. Also, in the hand of this mighty angel is the opened book or scroll; i.e. the one, which has been slowly opened throughout this vision (Ezek. 2:9).
      (1) This too would tend to identify the *angel* as Jesus, the Lion/Lamb, who takes the book in Chapter 5, opens the seals, and begins the judgments of the last days.
      (2) This Angel of the Lord is claiming the earth and has the title deed as His authority.
         (a) Jesus is filing His papers in heaven, in order to go forth and reclaim what is legally His. He purchased it on the cross.
         (b) Satan's time is up.
   d. The angel, Christ, sets His feet upon the sea and the land, taking possession of the earth and claiming it as His own.
      (1) Often throughout the Bible, setting one's feet in a place indicates taking possession of it (Deut. 11:24).
      (2) This claims dominion over, and ownership of, a land by such an action.
   e. Only Jesus, not the angels, has that right or authority.
4. In this show of power and authority, He speaks in a great voice.
   a. This is the voice of a mighty judge, not an angel, and foretells more judgments to come (Ps. 29:4) (Is. 42:13).

    b. At His cry, the seven thunders utter their voices in sympathy and agreement with what is yet to be.
       (1) In Chapter 4, John mentions these thunders going out from the throne with voices.
       (2) These are judgment thunders associated with the throne of God, and they number seven—just like the seven torches, seven spirits of God, seven seals, seven angels, seven trumpets, seven vials.
    c. No mere angel could initiate response from these thunders.
5. As previously instructed in the beginning, John begins to write what he hears the thunders say, but this time a voice out of heaven tells him not to write it.
    a. What the voices in the thunder say is still a mystery.
    b. It is God's strategy, but not yet to be known.
    c. Some things are too holy to be revealed.
    d. Man will know only as these events actually take place.

NO MORE DELAY (REV. 10:5-11)

Because of God's mercy, and the fact that He is long-suffering, He has put off the events of the last days for thousands and thousands of years. He has done so in order to give a lost world time to accept Him and His son as Lord and Savior. Nevertheless, He will compel no one to make a choice against his or her own will. Time is up, however, and because He is a just God, there will be no more delay. The Day of Judgment is at hand.

Before the last acts, however, John is made a participant in the drama. He is told to take a book from the angel and *"eat it."* This is probably not the Title Dead to the earth we have seen previously, but a book of God's Word. He is told that it will be both sweet and bitter, as is the Word of God to those who take it to heart. The promises and hope of the Bible are sweet, but the warnings of what will happen to a wicked people are bitter. As a representative of all Christians throughout the ages, John is obedient to the command, and is then to pass on to future generations what he has experienced and been shown.

1. The angel raises His hand and swears, by God Almighty, that there will be no more delay (Rev. 10:5-6).
    a. The plea of the souls under the altar of "How long?" has been answered.
    b. This oath can be trusted as truth.
    c. It is the same scene as observed in Dan. 12:7.
       (1) The man in linen swears that after *"...a time (1 yr.), times (2 yrs.), and a half a time... (one half year),"* the end would come (Dan. 12:5-7).

        (2) This three and a half years, follows the period during which the Jews made a covenant with the Antichrist.
        (3) It refers to the period during which the Two Witnesses preach to the Jews.
        (4) When that is finished, the final day is at hand.
    d. Because of God's mercy, "the last days" and end times which are throughout the Bible, have been repeatedly delayed in order for man to come to Christ before the end.
    e. It is why no one has known the day or time. Only God knows.
        (1) Had the events of this book already occurred (1st century), we would not be here today.
        (2) They cannot take place until <u>all</u>, who will come to the Lord, have done so (Hos. 3:4-5).
        (3) Only God knows when that has been accomplished.
    f. The Great Mystery of God is now to be fulfilled.
2. At this point, John moves from just being an observer to becoming a participant.
    a. He is called into action by a voice from heaven to take the book from the hand of the angel, who stands on the land and the sea (Rev. 10:8).
    b. He asks the angel for the book, and the angel says, *"Take, and eat,"* which John does, both for himself and as a representative of the Church and all Believers.
        (1) John acts as a representative of all the saints.
        (2) By giving this promised gift to John, the angel gives it to all of His own.
        (3) *"...the meek shall inherit the earth..."* (Matt. 5:5).
    c. Ezekiel and Jeremiah were also told to eat of the Word (Ezek. 3:3) (Jer. 15:16)
        (1) The Word of God is intended as our food (Matt. 4:4).
        (2) We are to get it into our blood.
        (3) Only in this way can we truly live the Word.
        (4) It is to be devoured in mind and spirit.
        (5) That which is a part of one's inner self can then be shared with others.
    d. This little book is the instrument of man's redemption, direct from God through Jesus Christ—the inheritance that is to be given to mankind.
    e. Man is the intended benefactor of all that was, is, and is yet to come.
    f. This knowledge is encompassed in the book that John is given.
        (1) Man is to consume it, draw life from it, and be strengthened by it.
        (2) God's Word and plan are sweet to him who accepts and consumes it, but will also be bitter, and, as it is fulfilled, bring pain.

g. John is told to continue to prophesy (after this prophetic vision) among the nations that they might be prepared.
   (1) This Word is intended for all Christians who read it—even today.
   (2) The work is not yet finished.
h. The statement concerning "*...prophesying again concerning many peoples and nations and tongues and kings*" (Rev. 10:11) may also refer to the fact that John will soon tell this story of the events of the last days <u>again,</u> from the perspective of the peoples on the earth.

CHAPTER 8
Dealing with the Nation of Israel

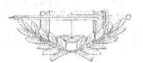

GENERAL COMMENTS

BEFORE CONSIDERING THE SOUNDING OF the seventh trumpet, however, it would be useful to take a moment to reflect on what has just occurred in preparation for the next step in God's strategy to recapture His creation from the world of sin. Christ Jesus has just stepped down to reclaim the earth and the seas, which legally became His when He paid the price on the cross. Satan has spent eons convincing individuals of their own self-sufficiency—that they know what is best for themselves, as well as everyone and everything else. As a result, the world has become increasingly perverted and corrupt. Under the delusions of the Great Deceiver, all that mankind has actually managed to accomplish is to destroy the greatest gift ever given—the gift of eternal life.

Jesus is nearly ready to restore that gift and physically take possession of what rightly belongs to Him. Nevertheless, are <u>we</u> ready? Have God's people made that final choice to accept His will and be obedient to the Word? Today, most of the world knows there is a God of all creation, but all still do not know Jesus is their Messiah or personal Savior. Fortunately, it is not too late. It is actually we who hold back that moment when the regeneration process can begin. Our individual choices are the deciding factor between life and death—physical and spiritual. Out of love, God has not yet released His final outpouring of Wrath, in order that mankind should have just a little more time to choose between Him and the Father of Lies. God has placed great power in our hands, but we can only handle it through obedience and His grace.

Since the Rapture, and before the sounding of the seventh and last trumpet, John recognizes that God has been dealing primarily with the Gentiles. So far, despite all of their persecution, many have accepted the teachings of Christ and willingly died for their newfound faith. As a consequence, however, they have had to suffer the effects of the opening of the first six seals—as well as the attacks of the Antichrist. Many originally thought they would be taken up in the Rapture for their "good deeds" and "professed" allegiance to God and Jesus Christ, but because they were only nominal Christians that compromised their beliefs, they were not true Christians. Others actually recognized the truth and turned to Christ in the midst of the persecution. In either case, these are individuals whom Satan, in the person of the Antichrist, desired to eliminate because they presented obstacles to his cause of destroying God's people. Now, however, all of the Overcomers, who will have accepted Christ and been martyred for their faith and testimony, have gone into the presence of their Heavenly Father. Any left on the earth by this time are there by their own choosing and comprise the wicked nations that are under the influence of the Antichrist—whether they realize it or not. They may believe they are free agents and in control of their own destinies, but actually, they are merely puppets of the Great Deceiver.

From this point forward, not only will God pour out His wrath on the wicked of the world, but He will begin to deal with the nation of Israel and allow the Antichrist to shift his attention to the chosen people of God. This is the beginning of the period of the Tribulation called Daniel's Seventieth Week. The Jews are a stiff-necked race. They have a long history of dedication and commitment to God and His Commandments, but then a gradual drift toward an attitude of self-sufficiency and indulgence. They begin to rely on their own will and an acceptance of an idolatrous world. This has caused God to resort to strong discipline and chastisement of His people until they repent and return again to a position of obedience and faithfulness. They have repeated this cycle over and over again since His covenant with Abraham.

Unfortunately, in the last days, it will take the persecution of the Antichrist, as well as severe, prophetic words and acts on the part of Two Witnesses, to open their eyes to the error of their ways. God is patient, but He is also a God of justice. Without repentance and an acceptance of His truth that Jesus Christ is their long-awaited Messiah, there will be more devastating times ahead for His Chosen people.

Israel's History Prophesied

Before moving on with the account of John's vision, it is important to have at least a cursory understanding of Daniel's prophecy about the "seventy sevens" and the length of Israel's history as a nation. Without this, it is difficult to grasp the significance of the Seventieth Week. This is an amazing example of just how specific God's Word is and yet remains consistent and accurate over time. This prophecy is revealed in both the Old and New Testaments (Dan. 9:24-27; Neh. 2:1-8; Matt. 24:1-25:46). Combined, they provide the clearest outline of Israel's history, as well as a detailed analysis of the timeline of events leading to the end times. Although it is complex and subject to countless interpretations, we are provided an outstanding illustration of literal prophecy and the consistency within God's Word. Scripture supports and interprets scripture. It does not contradict itself (2

Pet. 1:20-21). In most respects, Daniel himself did not understand the meaning of what he was told, but he was faithful to record God's revelation as it was given. Its meaning was further interpreted later.

From the dispensational pre-millennialist perspective, the Second Coming of Jesus Christ is preceded by a seven-year period known as the Great Tribulation—the events of which John has been describing through his visions. According to this view of the end times, the nation of Israel will be saved and granted God's promise to them for eternity. We see that their reward differs from that of the Gentiles in that they will dwell in their land forever, with David as their regent king, rather than in the New Heaven, as promised to the Saints.

We are told in Daniel just how long it will take to redeem and deliver God's people from the wicked world and their own sinful natures. This is described in great detail and allows one to actually calculate the end of days and Christ's Second Coming. Analyzing the information carefully reveals again the defensibility of literal prophecy and the consistency of God's Word.

1. Seventy weeks, or 490 years (Dan. 9:24-27), are decreed as the time needed to save the nation of Israel and rebuild the eternal Holy City.
    a. Six major events must take place during this period of time:
        (1) To finish transgression—break their tendency toward apostasy and restore them spiritually,
        (2) To put an end to sin—bring them to a point of repentance,
        (3) To atone for wickedness—accept Christ's death as the sacrificial payment for their sin,
        (4) To bring in everlasting righteousness—acknowledge Jesus Christ, at the Second Coming, as the King of Kings and Lord of Lords,
        (5) To seal up vision and prophecy—recognize that with the end of the New Testament there will be no more added to the written word of the Bible, and
        (6) To anoint the Most Holy—dedicate the temple of the New Jerusalem.
    b. Though there are other variations in interpretations of these requirements, they all add up to the same conclusion—atonement, forgiveness, judgment, and spiritual restoration.
2. According to Hebrew culture and tradition, the seventy sevens, or 490 years, are calculated in the following way:
    a. 1 week = 7 years
    b. 70 weeks = 490 years (70 x 7 = 490)—until the Kingdom of God begins.
    c. The Hebrew calendar has 360 days/yr.

3. When does this 490 years begin and how is it calculated?
   a. In Nehemiah 2:1-8, King Artaxerxes of Babylonia grants Nehemiah his request to return to Jerusalem to rebuild the City after its captivity and destruction.
      (1) This occurs in 444 B.C. and the King not only decrees it, but provides the resources to make it happen.
      (2) This marks the beginning of the 490 years of Israel as a nation.
      (3) It follows Nehemiah's prayer to God that the King would accept his plea and give him favor.
      (4) God answers the prayers of a righteous man.
   b. The 490 years are divided into three parts.
      (1) 7 wks. x 7 years = 49 yrs.—The time in which Nehemiah oversaw the rebuilding of the wall around Jerusalem and ordered the building of houses for every ten persons.
      (2) 62 wks. x 7 yrs. = 434 yrs.—The years until Jesus, the Messiah is born.
         (a) In Daniel 9:25, we are told, *"From the issuing of the decree to restore and rebuild Jerusalem until Messiah the Prince, there will be seven weeks and sixty two weeks...after the sixty two weeks, the Messiah will be cut off..."*—crucified.
         (b) 444 B.C. + 69 wks., or 434 yrs., = 33 A.D.
         (c) Amazing!
      (3) 1 wk. = 7 yrs.—The Tribulation Period or Daniel's Seventieth Week
   c. Thus, 49 yrs. + 434 yrs. + 7 yrs. = 490 years
4. Because the years between the death and resurrection of Jesus Christ and the beginning of the Tribulation Period make up the Age of the Gentiles, the prophetic clock for the nation of Israel stops.
   a. This period is not counted in the 490 year calculations.
   b. It is not known how many years it will take for all Gentiles who would be saved to be saved, so the beginning date of Daniel's Seventieth Week is a mystery that only God knows.
   c. Once it begins again, it will be seven years until the Second Coming of Jesus Christ.
5. During the Seventieth Week:
   a. There will be a three and one half year covenant signed between Israel and the Antichrist.
   b. At the end of that time—the middle of the seven year period—Satan will reveal his true nature and there will be *"... a stop to sacrifice and grain offering; and on the wing of abominations will come one who makes desolate, even to complete destruction..."* (Dan. 9:27).
   c. The second three and one half years will be called Jacobs Trouble.

RESTORATION OF THE TEMPLE (REV. 11:1-2)

With all of the Gentile children of God gone, the Antichrist reveals his true nature—he begins his plan to annihilate the Jews. Whether they are Jews by race or by religion, they are still God's chosen people and an irritant to the one who wishes to be revered above all gods. Before this plan is put into action, however, John is given a measuring rod and told to measure the temple, the altar where sacrifices are made, and the number of worshipers. He is not to measure the outer court, as only non-believers will be there. Because the temple, in reality, has been destroyed by Rome at this point, the Jews have been scattered, and left without a focal point for their religious ceremonies and observances. They are like a ship without a destination. In the last days, however, the temple will be rebuilt—most likely during the time of peace and safety before the Rapture of the Church.

Considering all that will take place during the first half of the tribulation, building anything like a temple will be unlikely. Therefore, the command that John measure the temple, the altar, and the worshippers therein is not unreasonable. It reflects that the Jews have been practicing their religion in the temple, but no longer measure up. God too measures the value, worth, and character of the temple, the people, and their worship, and as so often in their past, they fall short of His expectations for His chosen ones. Because all creation belongs to God, He Himself gives the unsaved Gentiles the authority to trample on the Holy City, as a part of His judgment of the Jews for turning their backs on His Son and followers.

Although the temple does not exist at the time of John's vision, it will in the last days. Consequently, the Jews are particularly vulnerable to the perverted influence and attacks of Satan and the unbelieving Gentile nations. Because God is a loving God, however, and is always in control, this will only be for a specified time—time, times, and a half a time, or three and a half years. The Man of Lawlessness will take his seat in the temple and declare himself God. In the second half of the Tribulation, he will destroy the temple again. Simultaneously, the Holy City will be trampled upon by the Gentiles.

1. John is told to take a rod and measure the temple and altar of God, and count all who are worshipping in it. He is not to measure the outer court, however, which was reserved for the Gentiles (Rev. 1:1).
    a. Because the only remaining Gentiles left on earth by this time all belong to the Antichrist, the outer court is excluded from this measurement.
    b. The "*fullness of the Gentiles*" has been completed—the Saints are gone, but "*the time of the Gentiles*"—those wicked ones still remaining—is at hand (Luke 21:24) (Rev. 11:2).
        (1) Those who <u>would</u> worship God have been removed at this point.

(2) At the bidding of the Antichrist, the unsaved nations now focus on destroying the Jews.
  c. The image of a measuring rod depicts a setting aside of some place, or group, for a particular purpose.
     (1) It can be a special benefit or a special fury.
     (2) The purpose can be either God's judgment or for His preservation.
  d. The measuring of the temple is for the purpose of protecting it and those who worship in it.
     (1) These are the remnant of the Jewish nation that is faithful to their covenant with God.
     (2) Some believe those being protected are the elect of the Christian Church, but that is not consistent with what is herein described.
     (3) Those rebellious Jews, and pagan nations, must still suffer God's judgment and wrath.
  e. In order for the temple to be measured, it seems reasonable that it must first be rebuilt.
     (1) Rebuilding is not likely to occur during the turmoil of the tribulation period.
     (2) That means it will probably have to occur during a time of peace and prosperity—before the Rapture.
     (3) This image, however, could refer to a measuring of the spiritual temple within man, but that too is highly speculative.
  f. Anything outside of these measurements is not acknowledged by God and is considered defiled.
2. The "holy city"—Jerusalem—is to be trodden under foot, <u>except for</u> the protected areas in the inner courts.
  a. The city of Jerusalem will be overrun by the people and nations of the world.
  b. They will be sent by Satan to wipe out the Jews and partake of the spoils.
  c. This is only for a time, however.

CHAPTER 9
The Two Witnesses

REVELATION 11:1-13

NO MATTER HOW MUCH GOD loves his stiff-necked, chosen people, repeatedly throughout history He has had to discipline them severely, in order to bring them back into a righteous relationship with Him. One generation they are obedient and submissive to His Word and will, and the next, rebellious and living by their own wicked code. Only when they follow His law is He able to bless them in the manner He so desires. This time is another example of His need to use the stern, parental hand of a good and loving Father to reach their minds and hearts.

THE TWO WITNESSES (REV. 11:3-14)

Two Witnesses are His way to get their attention and yet mercifully attempt to save them from both themselves and the efforts of the Antichrist to eradicate them as a race. To accomplish this end, He sends two of their own to prophesy and give testimony to what lies ahead. In his vision, John hears the Mighty Angel—Jesus Christ—say, *"I will give <u>my</u> two witnesses power, and they shall prophesy for 1,260 days..."* That is forty two months, or three and a half years—a period called Jacob's Trouble. This is the length of time it will take to bring the Jews wholly back to their God and convince them that Jesus Christ is their long-awaited Messiah.

John does not say who these two prophets are, because he does not actually see them. He is in heaven and they are on the earth. He is given a description of them, however, and again, there is not agreement as to whom these two men are—or even if they are truly men at all, or merely symbolic images of some institution or cause. Nevertheless, all we have are John's words, and to read more into them than is written is to construct our own account of their identity. Nevertheless, we are told that these are two men—Old Testament prophets—who are given the authority to operate in the power of the Holy Spirit, to expose the evil works of the Antichrist, and spread the gospel of Jesus Christ among the Jews. It is their temporary assignment to reveal the sin of God's chosen people and warn them of the punishment to come for their wickedness and rebellion against Christ. The purpose, however, is to prepare them for their final deliverance into God's promise of an eternity in their own land, with David as their King. For that to happen, however, they must repent and accept the divine truths of God's Word.

As we look at what these two witnesses do during their ministry, in order to convince the Jews of who they are and what God wants of them, we see that they perform many signs and wonders reminiscent of those done by Moses and Elijah. They bring down plagues upon the people, turn water into blood, call fire down from heaven, and stop the rains from falling for three and a half years. These are the two most influential men in the history of the Jews, and God kept their bodies upon their physical death for use at a later time. Elijah was prophesied to return in the last days, and Moses would again lead his people out of captivity. They are not gentle in the delivery of their message, because they understand the Jewish mentality. It requires Jews speaking to Jews, in power and authority, to change their minds and opinions. These Two Witnesses speak with both. To reach other conclusions about whom and what these messengers represent is one's own prerogative, but careful consideration of the Word is strongly advised.

1. In the midst of these times, God uses two of His anointed ones to communicate hope and salvation to the Jewish nation.
   a. In preparation for their promised restoration as a nation, three things must happen to the Jews:
      (1) They must return to the land. (That has partially occurred today.)
      (2) They must return to God, and
      (3) They must accept Jesus as their Messiah.
   b. The witnesses come to remind the Jews of the Old Testament prophecies (Hos. 3:5) (Zech. 12:10).
   c. John does not actually see these witnesses, as he is in heaven.
      (1) He is only told about them.
      (2) Their <u>confirmed</u> identity, therefore, is not absolute.
   d. Because of this uncertainty, again there is not agreement as to who these two witnesses are.
      (1) Some believe they are symbolically the institutions that will preach the gospel during the last days.
         (a) The Christian Church
         (b) Converted Jews

(2) The interpretation of <u>this</u> teaching is that they are two specific persons.
    (a) They are explicit men, who bear witness to God's judgment.
    (b) They are prophets, and they are wearing sackcloth (Zech. 3:4) (Is. 20:20).
2. We are told that, for 42 months—1,260 days, or three and one half years—two witnesses will be sent by God, with a divine commission.
   a. The angel, Jesus Christ, even describes them.
     (1) We have here another indication that this angel is Jesus, because He says, *"<u>I</u> will grant authority to <u>my</u> two witnesses..."* (Rev. 11:3).
     (2) They would, therefore, not belong to ordinary angels.
     (3) They are persons/men.
     (4) They are dressed in sackcloth, denoting calamity and judgment, because they are mourning over the condition of their people.
     (5) They come in power and with great authority to perform signs and miracles.
     (6) In the Old Testament, they are called olive trees and lampstands—anointed ones standing by the Lord (Zech. 4:3).
     (7) No one can harm these men during the period of their ministry.
       (a) Fire issues from their mouths, and they kill any who would injure them (2 Kin. 1:10, 12).
       (b) They have the power to prevent rain from falling during these days (1 Kin. 17:1) (James 5:17).
       (c) They turn the waters into blood (Ex. 7:17).
       (d) They are able to call plagues of judgment upon the earth.
   b. These witnesses represent the word of <u>the prophets</u> and <u>the law</u> in Jewish history.
     (1) For Jews, this carries the highest of authority.
     (2) They believe in that which comes from the law and through the prophets.
     (3) This power is familiar, and they listen to what the Witnesses say.
3. What is their commission?
   a. The Two Witnesses are given an assignment to return to earth in living form, during the end times, and testify to the events of God's Word.
   b. They are messengers from God sent to wander through the streets of Jerusalem, prophesying and preaching the gospel <u>to the Jews</u>, but not in a typical Christian fashion of love and compassion. Their approach is different.
     (1) Their ways are harsh, but their purpose is one of mercy.

   (2) They are to save as many Jews from the clutches of the Antichrist as possible.
  c. They unmask Satan's evil works, teach the scriptures, demand obedience to God, point out ways of escape from the coming damnation, insist upon repentance of sin, and attempt to turn men from darkness to light.
  d. They witness for Christ, the Judge, not Christ, the Lamb.
  e. These witnesses have been sent from heaven—they are Saints.
   (1) But they come as men who can be killed, for their bodies have not been resurrected.
   (2) There are two persons who have previously done miracles, such as here described, and whose bodies Satan could never claim.
4. Based upon all the information given about these personages, it is the interpretation of <u>this</u> teaching that these two witnesses are Elijah and Moses (Luke 24:44-49).
  a. God retained possession of both their bodies.
  b. Places of burial were never found on this earth, because God had a use for their bodies.
   (1) They acted as witnesses on the Mt. of Transfiguration and at Christ's resurrection from the grave.
   (2) These prophets still had roles to play, even after their life on earth.
  c. Elijah never died, but was *"taken up in a whirlwind"* (2 Kin. 2:11)
   (1) He was a rough and solitary man, who was a thorn in the side of many.
   (2) He spoke with great force and was not easily ignored.
   (3) It was foretold that he would return to earth to preach before the final *"Day of the Lord"* (Mal. 4:5).
   (4) Some thought he had returned in the person of John the Baptist (Luke 1:17).
   (5) Even Jesus said Elijah would come again and restore all things.
   (6) He was also able during his life to hold back the rain for three and a half years, as happens at this time (James 5:17).
   (7) He was the ultimate prophet.
   (8) Because the Jews still wait for his coming, they will recognize him at this point.
  d. Moses died, but Satan could not claim his body, because God had further use of it also (Deut. 34:6).
   (1) Unlike Elijah, he was a meek, learned man, but he too acted with great power.

(2) As during his life, Moses brings plagues upon the land and turns the water to blood.
  (3) He brought "the law" to God's people.
5. Nevertheless, because the Word says "*...and he was not, for God took him...,*" some believe Enoch could have been one of the two Witnesses rather than Moses. Possibly (Gen. 5:24) (Heb.11:5).

CONDITIONS OF THE TIMES

And what is the reaction of the Antichrist and the nations during these three and a half years? Obviously, the Two Witnesses cause great commotion and bring about further torment to those who rebel against Jesus and God's will. Jesus is the Messiah that was prophesied in the Old Testament, but the Jews not only rejected Him during His life, but they also had Him put to death. Although He came to save all sinners, regardless of nation, tribe, or tongue, all who refuse His gifts are destined for judgment and eternal condemnation. This is a sinful time into which the Two Witnesses come, but God kept them for this very day. They serve Him well, and their reward will be great.

The ministry of the Two Witnesses is harsh, and they are understandably feared and hated by the ungodly. The Antichrist is furious. Many are brought to Christ, the Messiah, as a result of their preaching, and they cause great damage and turmoil, as a consequence of the plagues they bring upon the earth. The Antichrist must be rid of them at all cost. Many actually attempt to kill the Two Witnesses, but for three and a half years, they are supernaturally protected from any harm. They are invincible until their assignment is completed—only then, in God's time, does He allow them to be put to death. Once more, they serve His purpose well.

1. This is a period of great evil.
   a. The Antichrist has had a covenant with Israel for three and a half years, but he now breaks it and takes possession of the temple area.
   b. This is the time of the "abomination of desolation" predicted by Daniel and Christ (Dan. 9:27; 11:31; 12:11) (Matt. 24:15).
   c. The wicked Gentiles overrun the temple.
   d. The Witnesses plague Satan and the unbelievers for another three and one half years.
   e. Satan sets loose all his forces to torment the earth and the holy ones, and still is unable to overcome God's protection.

    f. The Witnesses are immortal until their mission is completed.
2. In God's good time, however, He allows the Beast (Satan) to overpower the Witnesses and kill them (Rev. 11:7).
    a. In his perverse way, Satan has them crucified, as was their Lord.
       (1) It is his way of mocking them and their mission.
       (2) <u>He</u> believes he has been victorious this time.
       (3) He does not realize this is only possible by God's will.
    b. The Witnesses are denied burial and left for three and a half days on the street, in the "great city"—Jerusalem—for all to see.
       (1) This is long enough to prove to the world that they are truly dead.
       (2) Even criminals were buried, so the denial of burial shows how horrible their treatment is—how important these men must be.
       (3) Satan wants everyone left to see and know that <u>he</u> has killed these men, and that <u>he</u> is the victorious one.
       (4) Besides, he lost his prey once before through burial and will not make that mistake again.
       (5) The result is that all who remain rejoice and celebrate at this seeming victory.
       (6) Today, with satellite TV, it is possible for the entire world to see such events as they occur.
    c. At the end of three and one half days, a voice out of heaven says, *"Come up here"* (Rev. 11:12).
       (1) With all cameras rolling, the Witnesses stand up and face the throngs.
       (2) This also will be seen by the entire world, with lots of reruns and instant replay.
       (3) The reaction is one of total disbelief, fear, and horror.
       (4) Their work completed, the Witnesses ascend in a cloud to finally be crowned as princes in heaven.
    d. At this point, another great earthquake takes place, and a tenth of the city falls—7,000 men die (Rev. 11:13).
    e. The Jews who remain finally acknowledge God and give Him the glory.
       (1) They have been blinded to the person of Jesus Christ as their Messiah to this point, but finally the scales fall from their eyes and they understand and believe.

(2) God's plan is fulfilled.
  (a) Because the Jews rejected Christ, the gospel was taken to the Gentiles that they might be saved.
  (b) That accomplished, the Word is again taken to the Jews, and they too ultimately accept the Truth (Is. 45:17).
  (c) They return, in whole, to their God.
  (d) As He returns to rule and reign over the earth, they acknowledge Jesus as their long-awaited Messiah.
  (e) <u>All</u> of <u>God's</u> people have now been saved.
3. Thus ends the second "*Woe.*" The first being the release of additional demonic forces from the abyss, into the world (Rev. 11:14).

CHAPTER 10
The Seventh Trumpet

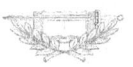

THE SOUNDING OF THE SEVENTH TRUMPET (REV. 11:15-19)

THE FINAL DAY OF THE Lord has come. The temple in heaven, after which the temple on earth was designed, opens revealing The Ark of the Covenant, containing the Ten Commandments, manna, and Aaron's rod. This is the most sacred of all artifacts, and was kept in the Holy of Holies—the innermost part of the temple where God communed with His people. Missing since Nebuchadnessar destroyed the temple and took the people into captivity in Babylon, the Ark here appears in the heavenly temple. As the seventh trumpet sounds, Christ returns, and the final battle is fought to overcome sin. The Day of Judgment is at hand. A new government will be established and a restored heaven and earth given back to the Heavenly Father and Creator. All heaven rejoices as thunder, lightning, and hailstones rain down on the wicked still remaining on the earth. Lastly, a great earthquake takes place, and *"it is finished."*

1. At the <u>sounding of the seventh trumpet</u>, the return of Christ becomes a reality (Rev. 11:15).
    a. All heaven raise their voices, because the world is now the Lord's, and He will reign over it forever and ever.
        (1) This is the third of the heavenly praises.
        (2) They praised Him as the Creator (Rev. 4:10-11).
        (3) They praised Him as the Redeemer (Rev. 5:8-10).
        (4) They now praise Him as the King and Judge (Rev. 11:17).
    b. *"Thy kingdom come, Thy will be done"* is finally to be accomplished, exactly as in heaven (Matt. 6:10).
        (1) The prayers of the martyrs will now be answered (Rev. 6:9-11).
        (2) Sin shall be overcome.
        (3) As when the Lamb took "the book," the twenty-four elders again rejoice and fall on their faces in worship and thanksgiving.

    c. All the world—those who have denied Him—see Him and are enraged.
    d. The third and last "*Woe*" shall now begin.
       (1) Jesus, the Conqueror, comes to pour out His full wrath and destroy those who destroy the earth.
       (2) They must now realize that all they have been told about the Lord is true.
       (3) Also, all that the Antichrist has told them is false.
    e. The government of the world is about to change.
    f. This is the time when all unbelievers who have died will also be raised and judged for their works.
       (1) Many of the sinful died without being punished.
       (2) When the Day of Judgment arrives, however, none shall escape answering for their actions.
    g. Additionally, the prophets, the saints, and the godly will receive their rewards.
       (1) No good deed has been forgotten.
       (2) God's own will receive their mansions, thrones, and crowns.
       (3) What we do today determines what we will receive on "that day"—reward or punishment.
       (4) All who have ever been will be there on that day.
2. With the final overthrow of all sin, a mist lifts and the heavenly temple opens; the Ark of His Covenant—the symbol of all of God's promises—appears.
    a. There is lightning, thunder, hailstorms, and earthquakes, and the wicked who remain are scourged and punished.
    b. What they have sown, they now must reap.
3. The Jews missed their Messiah when He came as a Savior and Lamb.
4. Now He returns as the conquering king they expected the first time.
    a. This time they get it.
    b. They recognize Him.
    c. This is how Jesus gathers His own.
       (1) It was prophesied that <u>all</u> should be saved (Hos. 3:4-5).
       (2) It is finally a reality.
5. Israel will now get its inheritance.
    a. God's covenant with the Jews was made with Abraham and all of his descendants.
       (1) God would give them the land "*...from the river of Egypt to the great river, the Euphrates,*" "*as an everlasting possession*" (Gen. 15:18 & 17:8).
       (2) Throughout history, when the Jewish nation has been in covenant with God, they have had their land, and, when they have been out of covenant with Him, they have not.

(3) These are a stubborn people, and they have repeatedly been out of covenant, as they have been now for nearly 2,000 years.
  (4) God's promise is conditional upon their obedience.
  (5) It will take a mighty happening to bring them back permanently into a right relationship with Him, but He has said that <u>it will</u> occur.
  (6) At this point, it does.
 b. Their inheritance is to be the land, with David as their blessed king.
    (1) Jesus reigns as ruler over all the earth.
    (2) David rules as king of the Jews.
6. They have the same access to God and Jesus as the Saints, but it is different.
7. They are "...*the friends of the bridegroom*," not "*the Bride.*"

Thus ends the Events of the Last Days as told from a Heavenly Perspective.

PART IV
The Tribulation as Seen from Earth

CHAPTER 11

The Tribulation as Seen from Earth

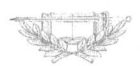

REVELATION 12:1-7

JOHN HAS FAITHFULLY RECOUNTED ALL that he has thus far seen and heard—beginning with the One through whom the revelation of the end-time events are given. This is followed by messages to seven churches in Asia Minor. He tells of being translated into the Throne Room of God and experiencing the awesomeness of that scene. Finally, he has written about the process that God utilizes to redeem mankind from a corrupt world. He describes actions initiated in heaven that result in intense suffering and tribulation on the earth. This is followed by an outpouring of God's wrath and judgment—all to save mankind from his or herself and the influence of Satan and his demonic forces.

Step-by-step, what will occur in the last days is revealed to an awestruck John. He recognizes that, despite the fact that this is a time of great devastation and chaos, it is tempered by God's love and mercy toward his beloved children. It is His desire that all should be saved. Nevertheless, He knows that will never happen. He, therefore, has provided a contingency plan to assure our eternal life with Him and His Son, Jesus Christ—if we so choose. Because He has given mankind a free will, our destiny is dependent upon the choices we make concerning whom to follow—a God of love that offers an eternity in a new and perfect heaven and earth, or Satan, the Deceiver and Father of Lies, who can only offer an eternity of torment in hell.

The unveiling of the end times, as revealed in the Book of Revelation, is seemingly complicated and confusing. That being the case, much debate and heated arguments often take place based on misunderstandings and misinterpretation of the Word. God's Word, from beginning to end, is all we authoritatively have—anything else is merely opinion and speculation. For this reason, meticulous and painstaking study of the scriptures, as a whole, is imperative to meaningful interpretation. Results must then be either accepted or rejected, based on a freedom of choice. *"Write What You See..."* provides a platform for that study.

As mentioned earlier, an understanding of the chronology of events is paramount to rightly interpreting the message of Jesus Christ concerning the consequences of what lies ahead and the impact of our choices on our eternal lives. What John has just recounted has been from the perspective of heaven, where all things have their beginning. Nevertheless, it is an incomplete picture. The Book of Revelation is not one, long, sequential chronology of events. If examined carefully, it is an initial telling of what is to come, from a heavenly perspective (Rev. 1-11), a retelling of the events from an earthly perspective (Rev. 12-16), and a third telling from the perspective of Satan from his demonic realm (Rev. 17-19). Together, along with references from Daniel, Matthew, Thessalonians, Joel, etc., they provide an increasingly detailed picture of what the Word says will take place in the final days.

Another significant bone-of-contention involving interpretation is an understanding of who and what the symbolized participants represent. There fails to be agreement, because these are not physical beings. They are representations of people, places, or things other than themselves. In some cases, they may be the result of images John uses to describe what he sees. In other cases, they may actually be what he sees, but symbolic of something not easily described. In either case, one must have an open mind and be willing to be led to the truth by the Holy Spirit.

We must remember that as John describes his visions, we now go back chronologically to the beginning of the previous timeline, before the Rapture and the beginning of the Tribulation Period. This time he sees the sequence of events, initiated in heaven, from an earthly perspective. The chronology is a repeat of what he has thus far seen, but the outcomes are viewed in expanded detail, and from the position of the earth and its inhabitants. This provides increased detail to what we have already been shown.

1. With Chapter 12, John's account of his visions of what is to occur in the last days, before the Second Coming of Jesus Christ, slips back to the time period described in Rev. 4:1.
   a. This time we are told what shall take place *"...after these things"*—following the Church Age—but from a different perspective.
   b. The events described thus far have been from the vantage point of heaven.
   c. John now sees the events of the final days, as they shall appear from an earthly perspective.
   d. Each telling adds detail to the previous one.
2. We also see further evidence that when the Bible intends for an image or event to be interpreted as a symbol rather than taken literally, it tells us so by calling it a "sign."

a. In prophetic style, signs are never used to describe events that have occurred in the past.
b. They are always used to depict the future.
c. Additionally, symbols are also never mixed with literal images.
d. Images are described either symbolically or literally.
   (1) A symbolic Woman (the Church) would never be described giving birth to a literal Child (Jesus.)
   (2) This would not follow prophetic writing style.
3. In John's next vision, the Word tells us that what is described is a "sign" or "wonder"— a symbol of something other than what is being described.

INTERPRETATIONS OF THE PARTICIPANTS (REV. 12:1-17)

One of the difficulties with interpreting the scriptures rightly is that people often tend to take verses out of context and place their own points of view onto them. Amazingly, if you study the Bible carefully, it soon becomes obvious that, despite the fact that it was written over a period of nearly 4000 years, by some 44 separate writers, the message and supportive details are consistent. This is because there was only one author—God. So, to take one verse, or group of verses, and apply a meaning without determining if it is consistent with similar references, one is in jeopardy of reaching a wrong conclusion. Only the Holy Spirit can reveal the truth, but one must be willing to consider the facts, as well as alternative points of view. This is particularly true of Chapter 12. It is almost entirely symbolic in nature and thus open to many interpretations.

For there to be a clear understanding of who does what to whom, it is imperative that one arrive at a reasonable and biblically sound conclusion about who the players are, or represent. Because they are not specific personages, and the fact that John had no way of knowing what things might be like when the end times actually come to pass, he used symbolic images and prophetic language that the people of his day would understand— hopefully it would make sense to future generations. For this reason, the description of the players presents an opportunity for varying explanations. Who is the woman about to give birth to a child? Who does the child represent? And what is the Great Red Dragon that bears no resemblance to anything most people could relate to.

Without an agreed-upon conclusion, however, it does not lead to a meaningful understanding of John's vision, nor provide a platform upon which individuals can discuss a shared outlook. Jesus Christ is the truth, and we are told that if we seek the truth, we will find it through the guidance of the Holy Spirit. This is how we must approach any and all scriptural language.

1. John sees a Woman about to give birth to a Child, and there are many interpretations of who and what this woman and child represent.
    a. The visions John sees next are now viewed from earth.
    b. He is no longer in the dwelling place of God, but on the earth where Satan reigns.
2. The Catholic view of this Woman is that she is the Virgin Mary, and the child is Jesus.
    a. If this were the case, because John knew Mary, he would have recognized her and identified her as such.
    b. Mary, however, has already died by this time and would not be used prophetically to represent someone or something in the future.
    c. She will not return to earth until the last trumpet is sounded and she returns with Christ.
    d. Nor is she persecuted for three and a half years during the "last days."
    e. Also, if this is supposed to be Jesus, He, as this Child, was not snatched from the earth upon His birth.
    f. He, in fact, ascended following His resurrection—by His own power and choice.
3. Another interpretation of this symbolic vision is that the Woman represents the nation of Israel, and the Child is the Messiah.
    a. Because of the reference to the symbolism of the moon and stars, this is a very common interpretation, reminiscent of Joseph's dream of the rebirth of Israel (Is. 66:7).
    b. The Messiah is thought to have come out of the pain of Israel.
    c. In John's vision, the Dragon (Satan) is waiting to devour the child as soon as it is born.
    d. This is not defensible, as the Jews (Israel), not Satan, killed their Messiah.
4. The historic point of view is that this is the New Testament Church and Jesus.
    a. While this may be closer, it still is not justifiable.
    b. The Church does not give birth to Jesus; in fact, it is the other way around.
5. A further prospect is that this is the heavenly <u>idea</u> of the Church.
    a. It reaches into Gal. 4:22—the story of the slave woman (Hagar) and the free woman (Sarah), who give birth to Ishmael and Isaac.
    b. The free woman gives birth because of a promise.
    c. According to this interpretation, the Church is the free woman, and Jesus is the promise.
    d. She represents the Mother of Israel.

e. It takes a long stretch to make this connection, however.
6. Further interpretations are that this is:
   a. The Roman Church,
   b. The emperor Constantine, or the state, under his rule.
7. None of these views, plus many more, come out of the Church, however, or exist <u>before</u> the return of Jesus Christ.
   a. Either one believes that John's vision is of the events of the "last day," as the Word says they are, or one denies that the Word is accurate or true.
   b. Most disagreements result from a difference of opinion over what is meant by "the last days."
      (1) If one takes the stand that it refers to the last days of the sacrificial system of Redemption, and before the destruction of the temple in 70 A.D., the conclusion will be vastly different than if one means the last days before the Second Coming of Jesus Christ.
      (2) Without an agreement of terms, there can be no agreement in interpretation.
8. The explanation of <u>this</u> teaching is that we are seeing the organized Church (the Woman) and the Raptured Saints (the Child).
   a. The Woman represents the visible, historic Church (the organization), and the Child represents the Saints—the Philadelphia Church—the fruit of the Church destined to inherit God's promises.
   b. The child John sees is delivered in "the last days," at the sounding of the mighty trumpet—the Rapture.

THE WOMAN (REV. 12:1-2)

John's attention is now drawn to the heavens above the earth. Observing his visions at this point, from an earthly perspective, he sees the image of a Woman appear in the sky. Beautiful beyond description and clothed in the sun and moon, with a crown of seven stars on her head, she is regal to the utmost. Hermeneutically, it is not uncommon for a woman to be considered a sign or representative of an important idea or entity. In the Book of Revelation alone, we see Jezebel as a false religion, the harlot as an apostate church, and the Bride of Christ as believers promised to rule and reign with Jesus over the New Heaven and New Earth. Additionally, the woman John sees is pregnant with child.

Who or what do these two signs represent, and how can we be certain we rightly identify them? In this particular case, there can be reasonable explanations for various views. One of the most common is that the woman represents the nation of Israel, waiting on the birth of her Child—the Messiah. According to this belief, she suffers the agony of a long and painful pregnancy with many false labors. Her description is reminiscent of Jacob's dream, dressed in the sun and moon, with a crown of twelve stars—the tribes of Israel. The belief is that out of her comes Jesus, the long-awaited Messiah. Being a long-standing interpretation, this tends to be a widely accepted and little disputed conviction.

Nevertheless, if one compares this concept with numerous other scriptural accounts throughout the Bible, it becomes obvious that there are details that are not consistent. Upon careful consideration of biblical evidence from across the scriptures, it is the conclusion of <u>this</u> writing that the Woman is the organized Church and the Child symbolizes the true believers that are taken up in the Rapture. While the child, whom the woman carries, may originally have been from a Jewish heritage, it does not generally come out of the nation of Israel. The majority of believers, at the time that John has his visions, are Gentiles, and the labor pains suffered by the woman result from the growth and increase of the body of Christ, as the Church grows. This woman is given power and authority over darkness, and her crown represents not only the twelve tribes, but the twelve apostles—the patriarchs. Upon careful analysis, these are attributes of the organized church. Additionally, at the moment of birth, the child is snatched away, *"in the twinkling of an eye,"* and the woman is left powerless, and vulnerable to what lies ahead.

God is still in control, however, and cares about His own. He sends her into the desert for 1,260 days, or three and a half years of tribulation mixed with mercy. She and her later children—the Tribulation Saints—are tormented and tortured by Satan and his evil forces. Nevertheless, they are cared for until the last of the Gentiles, who would be saved, are taken to their Father in Heaven.

1. This Woman is clothed in the light of the sun, and is magnificently arrayed with a crown of stars (Rev. 12:1).
    a. She stands on the moon, like the empress of the night.
        (1) She has dominion over the darkness, denoting ultimate victory over Satan and the powers of his kingdom.
        (2) These are the characteristics of the Church and its <u>potential</u> authority.
        (3) True believers are victors over the forces of darkness.
    b. She appears royally dressed and of high rank.
        (1) The Church holds this royal position.
        (2) It is intended one day to rule and reign over the nations along with the King of Kings (Rev. 2:26-27).
        (3) Her crown with gems of 12 stars is representative of the 12 tribes, the 12 apostles, or the patriarchs.

2. In all her glory, the Woman also cries out and travails to give birth (Rev. 12:2).
   a. She, like the Church, knows the pain of giving birth.
   b. That pain comes from the attempt to multiply, increase, and give-up its young.
      (1) In the last days, the time comes for the birth and completion of that which has been promised through the ages.
      (2) This is a representation of the Rapture of the "true church"—true believers, or saints.
   c. The Woman has the light, however, only until she gives birth, and then the light passes to the Child.

THE CHILD (REV. 12:4-5)

The interpretation that the Child is the Messiah is not based on prophetic form—you do not mix symbolic (the nation of Israel) with literal (Jesus, the Messiah) images. There also fails to be consistency in fact. Neither Jesus Christ, nor the Messiah, for whom the Jews await, was whisked away upon His birth. He was neither taken out of the nation of Israel nor the Church immediately upon His arrival. Actually, the Church came out Jesus, and the Saints came out of the Church. Finally, His death and resurrection were thirty-three years later, by the power of God—not an attack of evil forces. Therefore, it is the consensus of <u>this</u> teaching that when John sees the child caught up in the power of Jesus Christ, in order to protect him—the Saints, or true believers—from the tribulation of the last days, this is symbolic of the Rapture. As these two personages are the only ones in dispute at this time, one must again take the responsibility upon him or herself to carefully search the scriptures and make a determination of what is most consistent with the sum total of God's Word.

1. If the Woman is a symbol, then we must also be dealing with a "sign" or symbol of something other than a literal child, since symbolic and literal images are never mixed.
2. The Woman gives birth to a Child, which is referred to as male.
   a. Male characteristics are exemplary of the strength, courage, and perseverance of the Saints, and stereotypical of males.
   b. We must remember that the word <u>male</u> that is used is actually neuter in gender and refers to male <u>or</u> female.
      (1) These are the true 'sons or daughters' of God (Gal. 3:23-26).
      (2) Jesus alludes to this when He said, "*Blessed are the peacemakers, for they shall be called <u>sons of God</u>*" (Matt. 5:9).

  (3) This reference is to male and/or female.
- c. The birth (the Rapture) occurs when the trumpet sounds and the Lord descends from heaven to resurrect the *"dead in Christ"* and translates those believers who remain, into the promised glory with Him (1 Thess. 4:16-18) (Is. 26:19).

3. In John's vision, the child, when born, is immediately caught up into heaven to insure its safety (Rev. 12:5).
   - a. The Greek word used to describe this action is *harpazo*—seized, caught up (by force).
     - (1) Some say this is Jesus, but He was not taken back to heaven immediately upon His birth.
     - (2) He did "ascend" into heaven later, but He was not snatched away for His protection.
     - (3) His departure into heaven came only following His resurrection.
     - (4) The Greek word used in that case is *anabaino*—to arise or go up.
     - (5) The word *harpazo*, not *anabaino*, is also used in 1 Thess. 4:16-18 to describe the *"catching up... of the dead in Christ, and those... who still remain...."*
     - (6) It is, therefore, reasonable to infer that the "taking" of the child is referring to the same event as that which happens with the Rapture of the Saints.
     - (7) Prophetic imagery and hermeneutics (textural interpretation) must be consistent.
   - b. The interpretation of <u>this</u> teaching is that this "taking up" is symbolic of the Rapture (1 Cor. 15:51-52) (1 Thess. 4:16-18).
     - (1) Satan obviously needs to prevent the Rapture of the Church, because when the groom comes for His bride, Satan's days are literally numbered.
     - (2) He, therefore, lies in wait for the Child in order to destroy him (Rev. 13:4).
     - (3) We are told he fails, however, and the Child is whisked away.
   - c. With the removal of the Child, the Woman then becomes powerless and is persecuted by the Antichrist for three and a half years.
     - (1) She and her later offspring—the Tribulation Saints, or those who come to Christ during the tribulation of the next three and a half— spend that period running from the Antichrist and his pawns.
       - (a) Satan and the Antichrist are furious that they could not get their hands on the Child.
       - (b) Their efforts must, therefore, shift to those who are still remaining.

(2) At the end of this time, those Saints, martyred during this period, are taken from under the altar to be with Christ.
    d. It is, therefore, the true believers, who exist within the Church and whom only God knows, that constitute the Child.
        (1) Jesus does not come for the entire organized Church—only those who hear and recognize His voice.
        (2) There are those who call themselves Christians, but about whom Jesus says, *"Depart from Me; I never knew you..."* (Matt. 7:23-25).
    e. The true believers, for whom He will come, are the <u>invisible</u> Church, and only He will know them.
    f. Those who come to Him after the Rapture must endure much pain and suffering before being taken to Christ.
4. This Child is to reign with authority and power over the entire world.
    a. Such total authority never belonged to the Nation of Israel nor any other alternate.
    b. This is the repeated promise of the Word for the Saints (Rev. 2:26-27).
    c. No hardship or trial of this life is too great to bear, when one contemplates all that God has prepared for us.

THE GREAT RED DRAGON (REV. 12:3-4)

Though there is much debate relative to what or whom the woman and child represent, there appears to be little doubt that the "Great Red Dragon," which John also sees in the sky, is none other than the Devil—Satan himself. More fearsome than one could imagine, this frightful serpent is depicted primarily in mythological terms. Like the legendary hydra, it has seven heads with seven crowns. Each represents a world government over which Satan has had control. Based on this image, one might surmise the Dragon to be of high position or royal origin. At one time, Satan, originally known as Lucifer, was actually one of God's highest creations. He became prideful, however, and desired to be equal to his Creator and higher than man. Because of this rebellious nature, he even convinced a third of the heavenly angels to turn their backs on heaven and follow him, resulting in their expulsion from the Throne Room of God. Recreated as a Serpent, Satan became a Liar, the Deceiver, the Ruler of Demons and Darkness. Because of God's judgment, the Dragon was relegated to merely a tormentor of mankind and a dictator over world governments and their rulers. This does not make him a happy being.

Through Satan, sin entered the world, and through him, it has enveloped every aspect of life on earth. He is representative of evil personified, and it is not surprising that, with his mighty tail, he sweeps a third of the stars—his demonic angels, to the earth. This is prophetic of their final fall into the Pit of Hell that is yet to come.

John sees this Dragon standing before the woman, just waiting to devour the child to which she is about to give birth. By divine intervention, however, and for its protection, the child is immediately snatched up into heaven at the moment of its delivery. It is no longer present for the Dragon to claim or destroy.

1. In John's vision, before the Woman, there stands a "Great Red Dragon" (Rev. 12:3).
    a. This too is described as a sign or symbol.
    b. Again, the Word tells us when something is not literal.
2. The image is of a "great red dragon" waiting to devour the child (not the Woman), when it is born.
    a. It has seven heads and a crown upon each head.
        (1) These heads represent the world governments or empires, which Satan has controlled to that time: Egypt, Assyria, Babylon, Medo-Persia, Greece, and Rome.
        (2) The crowns symbolize the kings who ruled them.
    b. It also has 10 horns, out of which another will come.
        (1) They signify the nations that arise out of the Roman Empire.
        (2) The horns are the same as the toes, which Daniel saw in his vision (Dan. 2:42-44).
    c. The Dragon has a huge tail that trails across a third of the stars in the heavens.
        (1) Some interpret the tail as false prophecy, deception, and lies.
            (a) The tail is an instrument, or function of Satan, to deceive the nations.
            (b) It is his favorite weapon.
        (2) As this is a sign, it is also possible to interpret these stars as fallen angels.
        (3) Satan uses his army to torment, persecute, and deceive.
3. Satan, the Dragon, is evil and the antithesis, or opposite, of God, who is all-good.
    a. At one time, he was the greatest of God's creations—perfect and beautiful (Is. 14:12).
        (1) No one but God and Jesus was higher than Satan.
        (2) He, originally called Lucifer, had everything, and yet he still desired more—to "...*be like the Most High*" (Is. 14:14).
        (3) It was his wish to be <u>above</u>, or on the same level as, the throne and those who sat upon it (Is. 14:13).
        (4) His own arrogance resulted in his downfall (Is. 14:15).
    b. Now, Satan is a murderer—seeking whom he may devour (Jn 8:44).

c. He is a destroyer of both bodies and souls.
  d. He has had a hand in every evil thing that has ever occurred.
     (1) God intended from the beginning of time for there to be a Bride for Christ, and mankind was to be that Bride.
     (2) It was for that reason that our names were written in the *Book of Life* before time began.
     (3) Man was created to be that Bride, and Satan hates him/her with all his being for that privilege.
     (4) With the creation of man, Satan saw his position move one step lower, and he was outraged.
     (5) Since that time, he has done everything in his power to destroy humanity.
  e. When Jesus first came to redeem us, died, and rose again, He reclaimed man and the earth as His.
     (1) As "prince of the air," Satan has had power over man's life. Nevertheless, Jesus shall return again to take His Bride away, and take the earth back from Satan and his wicked cohorts.
     (2) The Dragon must do everything he can, therefore, to prevent or forestall that from happening.
     (3) When it does occur, his reign will finally come to an end.
4. By coming against mankind, Satan <u>enables</u> the Plan of God to be carried out.
  a. Through his persecution, man is forced to make a choice between obedience to God or the Power of Darkness.
  b. There is no virtue in being good, if there is no choice to be bad.
  c. Without Satan, this choice would not exist.
  d. Persecution makes one strong and an Overcomer.
  e. Our purpose for being is to give glory to God and be victorious over Satan.
  f. That requires action on our part.
5. Satan knows his days are numbered, and he must continue to intensify his works.
6. Throughout history, he has attempted to destroy what God has created, and it will be his mission until the very end.

THE WAR IN HEAVEN (REV. 12:7-12)

Although he was able to cause Adam and Eve to fall into a state of sin, Satan has known that one day God would restore mankind to a position of righteousness. For that reason, he has done everything in his power to prevent that from happening. He has lied, tortured, and murdered throughout history to increase sin and ensure man's destruction by evil. Satan is fully aware that as time passes, his existence and reign shortens. Consequently, he continually ramps up his efforts to prevent the events of the last days. He is even willing to go into battle with God's heavenly army.

In order to forestall the Rapture of God's Saints, Satan wages war against God's angels, with Michael, the Archangel, as their Commander. This conflict between good and evil is not in the physical realm, however, nor between physical beings. It is a spiritual war with Satan as the Accuser of the Brethren. It is his desire to prevent God from seeing His children as worthy of being taken out of the tribulation of the last days. Nevertheless, because we could never be worthy, God looks at all true believers through the righteousness of Jesus Christ. Satan cannot outdo that, and once again he loses the battle. This time he is cast out of the heavens above earth—where he has been called Prince of the Air—down to earth. This is yet one step closer to his ultimate destination—Hell. The war is ended. Satan loses his prey once again, and the Rapture of the Saints takes place. All heaven rejoices.

1. Satan understands that, with the removal of the Church, his day will soon be at an end, and he will be destroyed once and for all. He must, therefore, do whatever it takes to prevent this from happening.
   a. He is even willing to risk war with heavenly forces, in order to keep us from going to God, as promised in the Word.
   b. Satan goes into battle in the heavens, therefore, to destroy any powers of protection over the Church.
   c. The result is a battle of wits between good and evil—heaven and hell.
      (1) Our very lives are about the cosmic battle being waged between the powers of light and darkness.
      (2) This world is not our home; it is but a battleground.
      (3) Mankind has the choice to align with one side or the other.
      (4) Our purpose is to stand firm against Satan, so that we might spend eternity with God.
      (5) We are to overcome Satan, on his own ground, and be conformed into Christ's likeness.
      (6) This battle is the story of the Bible.
2. John continues to relate what he sees and has been instructed to write.
   a. Various interpretations have been assigned to this particular battle, which takes place on a spiritual plane, and again they are not consistent.
      (1) One is that it represents the moral conflicts, which have occurred throughout history <u>within</u> the Church.

(2) Another is that it is the war between pagan Rome and the Christian Church.
(3) And yet another, the general conflict between good and evil.
   b. In context, however, this account is still prophetic of the end times and the events yet to occur.
3. The Occasion of the War (Rev. 12:7)
   a. The birth of the Child (the Rapture) is the event that Satan and his "angels" have been attempting to prevent throughout the ages.
   b. The closer it comes, the greater the efforts to stop it.
   c. The last intense moves are what cause a great conflict between heaven and Satan.
   d. The participants are:
      (1) Michael and the heavenly hosts—angels.
         (a) He is the chief archangel and has authority over all others.
         (b) He is the guardian prince of the people of Israel—the defender of God's people (Dan. 12:1).
         (c) Some say he represents Christ at this time.
         (d) The general (Michael) fights the battle <u>for</u> his king (Christ.)
      (2) Satan and his angels, or hoards of demons, are the adversary.
         (a) He is the prince of darkness and rules his agents of wickedness.
         (b) His "angels" were not created evil, but by their own free choice rebelled against God, causing them to be cast out of heaven.
   e. Because these are all spiritual beings, this is a spiritual war, rather than a physical one.
      (1) There is no killing or bloodshed in this battle.
      (2) This is a war of the minds, intellect, and reason.
4. How is this war fought?
   a. Satan is the great deceiver, accuser, and liar, and this is the method he uses in his attacks (Rev. 12:10).
   b. He accuses God's plan and His people of being without virtue and unholy (Zech. 3).
      (1) He points out the unworthiness of the saints for the glory they are promised.
      (2) He is the *"accuser of the brethren,"* and keeps track of all of our misdeeds to use against us.
      (3) He expounds upon our sinfulness, which we cannot deny.

(4) We are not judged for our unrighteousness, however, but for the righteousness of our Savior in whom we believe.
  (5) Satan refuses to accept that the atonement, or the shed blood of Jesus Christ, makes all of his accusations false (Rev. 12:11).
 c. It is Satan's jealousy, arrogance, and pride that cause him to believe he can win such a war.
 d. In a courtroom scene, his every argument is met and proved unfounded (Dan. 7:9).
  (1) He can deceive man, but not the *Ancient of Days*.
  (2) God's plan is perfect, and Satan unwittingly plays a vital role in it.
  (3) Throughout the ages, Satan and his attacks against mankind have forced us to make a choice between good and evil—God and Satan.
  (4) That choice determines either our salvation or eternal condemnation.
  (5) Satan is an instrument of God's grace, and merely assures his own downfall.
5. He, therefore, loses this war (Rev. 12:8).
 a. Satan is overcome, proven false, and a destroyer of good.
 b. His original revolt began in heaven, and the final victory over evil takes place there.
 c. As a result, he and his demonic forces are cast out of the heavens <u>onto</u> the earth.
 d. Not only does he fail to prevent the Saints from being taken up in the Rapture, he confines himself to the earth, and can only exert what is left of his power on that plane.
6. All of the hosts of heaven rejoice at this victory (Rev. 12:12).
 a. The accuser has been overcome.
 b. The Judgment of the Saints has been made, and they are found worthy.
 c. Satan has no further power or authority over them.
 d. The Rapture <u>is not stopped</u>, and the Child is whisked into heaven out of the Dragon's reach.

THOSE LEFT BEHIND (REV. 12:13-17)

Having failed to destroy the Child, Satan turns his attention to the Woman and those who have been left behind. The Woman finds herself greatly weakened by having lost the power and strength of the Child, however, and without the protection, faithfulness, and unceasing prayers of the light that has sustained her, she is now vulnerable to the renewed efforts of Satan to exterminate her and those who missed the Rapture. This is Satan's last ditch effort to exercise his control over the undecided.

God has promised He will never leave us, nor forsake us, and once more He proves His faithfulness. In her weakness, God picks up the Woman on *"wings of eagles"* and carries her into a place in the desert prepared for her care. For three and a half years, she and *"the remainder of her seed"* will be pursued and persecuted by Satan and his evil forces. Overwhelmed by what seems like a never-ending river of torment and anguish, God sends some relief either through supernatural occurrences or the aid of some people who offer the refugees protection or assistance. As a consequence, even brief periods of rest are a blessing. Despite her weakness, however, the Lord's strength enables the Woman and her children—the Tribulation Saints—to persevere and overcome. Though ultimately martyred for their newfound faith, they too will be taken to their Father in Heaven and become part of the Bride of Christ.

1. Though the Child is taken out of the world, the Woman, and those found unworthy at the time of the Rapture are still left on the earth.
    a. This is "the visible church."
    b. She is now greatly weakened by the birth of the man-child, however.
    c. Her other offspring are grieved and in shock at being left behind.
        (1) These are those who called themselves "Christians," but in their hearts were not—the Laodicean Church.
        (2) That, which they had been so certain of, did not take place.
        (3) It is a bitter pill to swallow.
        (4) They must now <u>unlearn</u> their mistaken philosophies and learn the truths they had ignored or denounced.
        (5) Only then can they become true believers.
        (6) For their earlier resistance to God's Word, they must now endure the persecution of the Antichrist. It is part of the consequences they must suffer for their resistance to truth.
2. Enraged at failing to destroy the Woman and the Child, Satan turns his wrath toward these new believers (Rev. 12:12).
    a. His hatred toward God's people has always resulted in his greatest efforts of destruction directed toward them.
    b. He is, therefore, determined to destroy any and all of those still on the earth.
    c. They, not the wicked, are his focus.
    d. We are talking about "Christians" at this point.
    e. Satan knows his days are numbered, so he must increase his evil attacks upon these Gentiles for fear of losing them too. Jews will be dealt with later.

3. The Woman and her children—the Tribulation Saints—flee into the wilderness to a place that God has prepared.
    a. The wilderness represents the evil world controlled by Satan.
    b. Even in these days, however, they are not without God's mercy.
    c. As in earlier times, the Woman is born up *"...as on the wings of eagles,"* so that she might go into the wilderness (Sinai) for protection (Ex. 19:4) (Deut. 32:11-12).
    d. This is the way the Israelites were saved from persecution in the days of Moses.
    e. They are also nourished by God, as they were once before in the wilderness (Ex. 16:11-15).
    f. In this manner, they are protected and sustained for three and a half years.
4. Satan's persecution is so severe that, without the prayers of the Saints who were Raptured, they cannot survive.
    a. All who now refuse to worship the Dragon, and accept his mark, are not allowed to buy or sell.
    b. The absence of the mark required by the Antichrist makes them easily identifiable, and when they are found, they are killed.
    c. A great system is put into place to identify and locate these people.
5. Satan wishes to destroy this small tribe and continually has them pursued
    a. He sends *"water like a river"* to carry the Woman away (Rev. 12:15).
        (1) As a sign or symbol, this river could be an expedition of soldiers sent to wipe out the refugees.
        (2) These forces are directed by Satan to accomplish his will.
    b. God provides a way, however, for His people to withstand Satan's attack.
        (1) Possibly the earth opens and devours the enemy.
        (2) A natural phenomenon of this type could swallow up and wipe out the attackers.
        (3) This would be reminiscent of the dividing of the Red Sea for the Hebrew children, as they came out of Egypt (Ex. 14:16).
        (4) The "earth" could also refer to other individuals on the earth who help the Woman and her offspring to survive, at least for a time.
            (a) These would be "good people," but not necessarily believers.
            (b) Such individuals would reflect those who deny any need for Jesus, because they feel they are self-sufficient and good, moral people without Him.
    c. The continued opening of the seals, however, distracts Satan and scatters his attention.

CHAPTER 12
Daniel's Prophetic Dreams

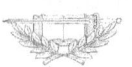

SIMILARITIES IN END-TIME PROPHECIES

THERE IS A VERY OUT-SPOKEN position that the Book of Revelation is purely an allegory depicting universal truths. This speculation asserts that, considering the desolate environment in which John was being held captive and, as a consequence of the severe living conditions he was forced to endure, it would be understandable that, while meditating one day, he might have a bizarre flight of fantasy about events of the last days. Being a man of God, John was familiar with Old Testament prophecy about end times, as well as Christ's promises that He would go to prepare a place for His people, but return one-day to gather them to rule and reign with Him for eternity. Much is said in the scriptures about the judgments of mankind for his sin and ungodliness, as well as the rewards intended for those who accept Jesus Christ as their Lord and Savior. Considering his age and situation, John might well have had such topics on his mind, but the assumption that what he experienced was simply imagined or a daydream is not supported by scripture. The Word is either true, or a well-constructed fabrication designed to lead people astray.

Based on the details of his visions, however, it is difficult for true believers to rationalize that there is not some guiding force behind the innumerable references throughout the Bible concerning the last days. Granted, teachings were handed down from generation to generation, and many written into biblical texts. Learned Rabbis even read these to the people in Temple. Though details were generally vague at best, upon careful examination of such prophetic accounts, not only are they similar in content, but they seem to build upon one another to enhance clarity.

As we look at the scriptures today, it is almost inconceivable that over thousands of years, many accounts of the last days—recorded by so many different people—could be so consistent in both description and language. Yet, the message is generally the same—there will be cataclysmic occurrences in the heavens, economic and environmental disasters, wars between peoples, and unexplainable signs and wonders in the last days. It is difficult to chalk these similarities up to mere coincidence. The most striking example of likenesses between prophecies is based on the visions experienced by Daniel, in the Old Testament, and John's visions in the Book of Revelation. Though their perspective and directives are different, many of the details of what they saw and heard are consistently similar. They also foretell the same outcome—a plan of redemption for the Gentiles and the establishment of a Messianic kingdom on earth, for the nation of Israel.

Like the Book of Revelation, the book of Daniel is also considered apocalyptic in format. It too reveals mysteries of the future through a chronological description of what lies ahead relative to the involvement of the Gentiles and the nation of Israel, both at that time and in later days. Daniel and John may have used different symbols to prophesy the future, but the similarities are remarkable. For instance, Daniel's four creatures reflecting different kingdoms culminate in a beast almost identical to the dragon seen by John, rising out of the sea. In both cases, they describe the dominance of the Beast/Dragon/Satan over the nations and their rulers throughout history. This is the prophetic message of both.

Daniel's First Vision (Dan. 2:1-45)

Although Daniel was a Jew, while held captive in Babylon after the destruction of Jerusalem in about 587 BC, he became known for his ability to interpret dreams. When King Nebuchadnezzar had a particularly disturbing one that none of his wise men could interpret, Daniel prayed for enlightenment, and was given a vision about its meaning. Prophetically, it outlined the systematic, future destruction of four great kingdoms of the Gentiles, leading to the final kingdom following the Second Coming of Jesus Christ.

1. King Nebuchadnezzar had a dream, which Daniel was asked to explain and interpret.
2. That dream was of a great statue, depicting four of seven kingdoms in prophecy, which would rise and fall. Daniel does not see Egypt or Assyria, because they were in the past (Dan. 2:19-28).
    a. Head of gold—Babylon with Nebuchadnezzar as king
    b. Breast and arms of silver—Medes and Persians
    c. Trunk and thighs of bronze—Greece
    d. Legs of iron—Roman Empire
    e. Feet and toes (part iron & part clay)—ten Nations coming out of the Roman Empire (some nations strong/some not)
    f. A Stone—Jesus, or the Kingdom of God

3. The image was standing, but a stone (cut without hands) falls, striking the feet of the statue, and the whole image collapses and is crushed.

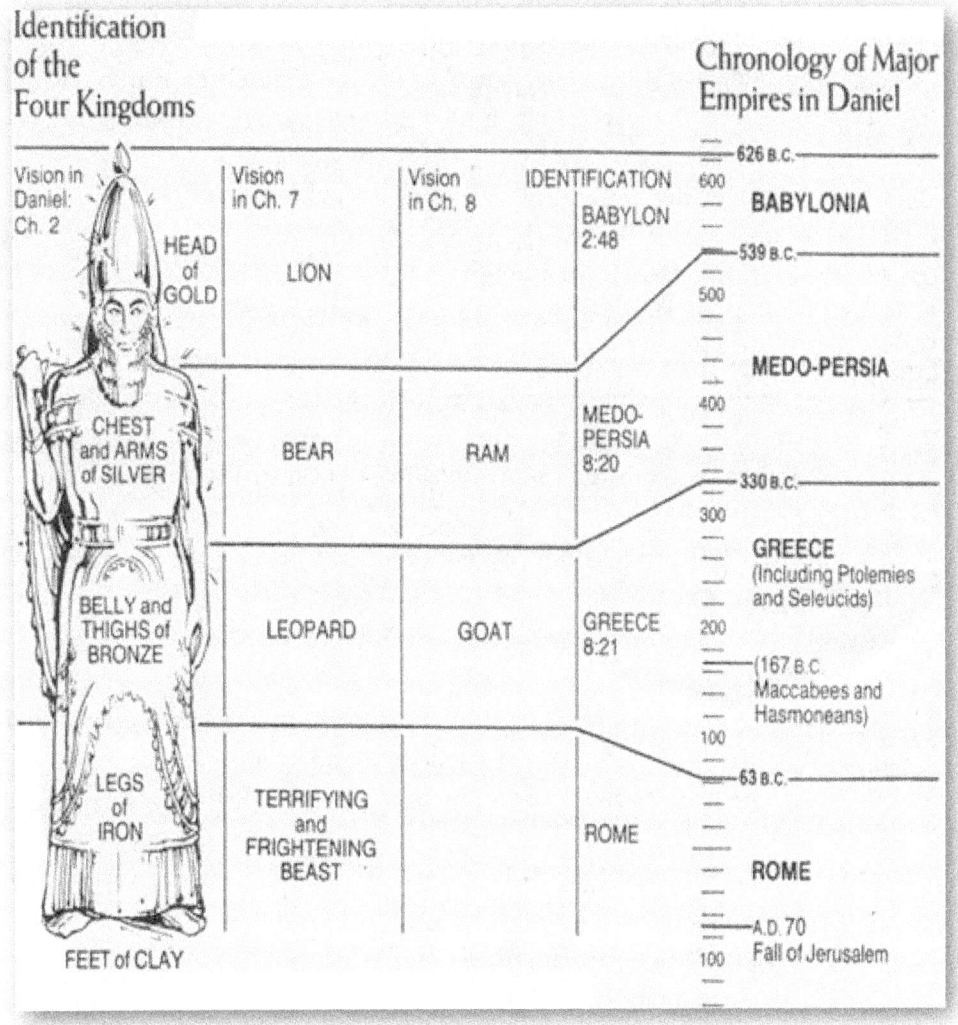

4. Daniel's interpretation of the dream was (Dan. 2:31-44):
   a. After Babylon, a kingdom inferior to it would come, but overtake it.
   b. Babylon was a magnificent city divided by the Euphrates River.
   c. To fortify it, great walls lined the river with locked iron gates, allowing entrance where the streets intersected.
   d. King Cyrus, of Medo-Persia (an inferior country), hoped that one day the gates would be left open so that he could invade the city.

(1) In preparation, he built a lake for the river to drain into, drying up the river.
(2) One night, a great feast took place, all became drunk, and the gates were accidentally left unlocked.
(3) The Medes and Persians moved in and completely captured the city.
(4) God enabled Cyrus to accomplish such a task (Is. 45:1-3).

e. During the feast, Babylon's King Belshazzar saw a sign—writing on the wall—warning him of his impending fall (*Dan. 5*).
(1) He died during the invasion, and his kingdom is lost because of his sin.
(2) The prophecy was fulfilled.

f. Today, the gold (Babylon), silver (Persia), and bronze (Greek) empires have disappeared; all that is left are the toes (the Roman Empire).
(1) While the Antichrist will <u>begin</u> with the Roman Empire, his empire will eventually include all the kingdoms of Daniel's vision, if it is accurate.
(2) This means that those empires are going to have to be revived again before the end.

g. The Roman Empire was never destroyed, but broke into pieces and divided into ten countries (toes).
(1) These ten countries have always existed, but have never come back together again as one unit.
(2) Current prophecy teaches that the Common Market—ten countries will unite and Europe will unify then the Antichrist will arise.
   (a) The world powers of today; however are not the players described by Daniel.
   (b) Prophecy teachers today consider the U.S., Russia, and China major players.
   (c) This is not according to scripture.
(3) Daniel says the Roman Empire will be a divided kingdom with the toughness of iron, and a man will appear who will loosely unite the kingdom, but they will <u>not</u> adhere to one another.
   (a) <u>They</u> will not produce the man, however.
   (b) The man will unite them only in the last kingdom.
(4) The entire statue will be put back together under the Little Horn—the Antichrist.
(5) According to Daniel's first vision, great things must still occur, before the last days can come and the Rapture take place.

THE SECOND VISION (DAN. 7:1-27)

A second vision, similar to the first, again foretells the progression of the fall of these four major kingdoms, including that of the Antichrist in the last days. The climax of this vision is of *"one like a Son of Man"*—Jesus' favorite name for Himself—returning with the clouds of heaven—the Saints. Despite the fact that Daniel recorded his vision hundreds of years before John, they could not have been more prophetically similar.

1. This vision is similar to the first. They both refer to the four kingdoms.
2. Daniel saw a great beast—Babylon with Nebuchadnezzar as king.
   a. It appears like a lion with wings.
   b. The wings are ripped off, however; it stands up like a man, and is given a human mind.
3. He also saw a second beast—Medo-Persia
   a. It is likened to a bear, raised on one side and with three ribs in its mouth.
   b. Babylon, Libya, and Egypt are the three ribs.
4. A third beast—Greece and Alexander the Great
   a. This is like a leopard with four wings and four heads.
   b. When Alexander died, Greece was given to his four generals.
   c. They divided the empire into four parts. The power of these empires was removed, but they remained for a time.
5. A fourth beast—The Roman Empire
   a. Terrifying and strong, with teeth like iron, the beast has claws of bronze and ten horns.
   b. This Empire would be split into ten nations that never would reunite as a single nation.
   c. A little horn—the Antichrist—would come from among the others and subdue three of the ten nations.
      (1) When this happens, the entire world will recognize his power.
      (2) Out of his mouth come boastful, blasphemous words.
      (3) He wages war against the Saints, and overpowers them—the Tribulation Saints—for three and a half years.

THE THIRD VISION (DAN. 8:1-27)

As mentioned previously, Daniel's first and second visions dealt with the prophetic governance of four, historical kingdoms of the Gentiles, from the period of Babylonian dominance to the end of days. His third vision, however, focused primarily on the period of

Persian and Greek supremacy relative to the impact on the nation of Israel and its deliverance. At the time of his vision of interplay between a ram and a goat, however, even Daniel had no understanding or interpretation of what he saw. Only when Gabriel sent a 'man' to explain that this was prophetic of what must occur leading toward the last days, did he grasp its meaning.

1. Daniel saw a ram in front of a canal—Medes and Persians.
    a. It had two horns, one longer than the other.
    b. It butted to the north, south, and west and was prideful.
    c. For a while, nothing challenged it.
2. A goat with a horn between its eyes, however, came from the west—Greece with Alexander the Great as leader (Dan. 11:3-4).
    a. It rushed and struck the ram and shattered its horn.
    b. The ram became powerless and was trampled by the goat.
    c. As the goat magnifies itself, its horn (Alexander) is broken, or defeated, and four more horns then appear—four generals.
    d. Out of one of the horns, a small horn grows to compare itself with the commander of hosts.

Consistency of the Scriptures

1. All of these visions describe the same scenarios.
    a. What is revealed is a history lesson, but for this teaching, it is not outlined in detail.
    b. Babylon is overcome by the Medes and Persians.
    c. The Medo-Persian Empire gives way to Greece.
    d. The Greek empire disappears as Rome arises.
    e. Rome divides, never to be reunited until the last kingdom of the Antichrist comes forth.
2. Daniel's visions are almost identical to John's visions of the kingdoms and the progression toward the rise of the Antichrist.
    a. More than anything else, they impress upon us the consistency of God's Word regardless of time or place.
    b. They are a confirmation of prophetic style in prophecy, regardless of when they occur.

CHAPTER 13

Rise of the Antichrist

SIGNS OF THE TIME (MATT. 24:3-44)

BEFORE RETURNING TO JOHN'S PROPHETIC visions, there are a few questions it would be important to ask. Based on scripture, could the Rapture take place today? Have all of the conditions, about which we are told musttt occur before Christ's return, been met? Are circumstances such that we could actually be approaching the end times today, rather than in another thousand plus/minus years? Only God knows the day or time, but He has given us signs to direct us toward our destination and through whatever lies ahead. Have we read those signs correctly, and most importantly, are we prepared?

It is God's desire that none should be left behind, but He has given us the freedom of choice to either follow His plan of salvation or that of the Great Deceiver—the Antichrist. Do we want our rewards now in this life, or are we willing to pay the price for eternal rewards? In order to make the best choices about whom and what to follow, it is imperative to understand the times in which we live. Scripture tells us that the times shall produce the man, and in order to recognize the primary players of the last days—Satan, the Antichrist, and the False Prophet—we must be sufficiently informed to recognize our Adversary. Only then can we appropriately respond to him and his deceiving lies. We must be prepared for what lies ahead.

Many throughout history have proclaimed that they were in the end times and the signs were right for the Second Coming of Jesus Christ. Some of the signs have been there, but they only pointed toward the sorrows that lie ahead. This is obvious since the world did nottt end in days past. As with any childbirth, the pains become more intense and frequent as the event approaches. This is what we are observing in this generation.

Each day we hear more about devastating, natural disasters around the world—floods, fires, earthquakes, droughts, hurricanes, tsunamis. Violence between family members, total strangers, and countries is rampant. The economy and political environment has become increas-ingly perverted and corrupt. Perhaps it has always been this way, but the technology of today keeps it continually in our face. Consequently, it has become more personal, and affects our individual responses and behaviors to a greater extent.

Jesus Himself told His disciples what to look for before His return at the end of the age (Matt. 24:3-35). He said there would be wars and rumors of wars. There would be famines and earthquakes. Brother would turn against brother. In addition, there would be those who would come in His name with lying signs and wonders to deceive the world into believing that they had the answers to all the problems of the day. Alternatively, as little gods, we could even have the answers within ourselves. These lying signs and wonders, despite the lack of proof or evidence, will actually convince many, even the elect. Out of this time of chaos, a world leader will come on the scene to create a new world order that responds to the times. As a result of his actions, things will turn around and <u>appear</u> to be better than ever before. This will be the man for whom the world has been waiting, and who will create the illusion of peace and safety.

Scripture has told of this man and that he will be the very opposite of what he appears. He will be the Anti-Christ, and only true believers will be prepared to recognize him. He will be considered a savior, but his power will be from Satan. However, God will actually allow its release, according to <u>His</u> perfect plan. Then, the Rapture will take place.

1. There are many interpretations concerning <u>when</u> the Antichrist will appear and the Rapture take place.
    a. Some people believe the Rapture will occur <u>before</u> the Antichrist's reign of terror begins, (Pre-Trib.), simply because that is the order in which it is described in Revelation.
    b. Some believe it will happen midway through the Tribulation (Mid-Trib.).
    c. Others have concluded that it will occur just before Christ returns to do battle with Satan and his demonic forces (Post-Trib.).
    d. Only God knows *"...the day or time,"* however (Matt. 24:36).
    e. The only thing that is truly important is that we be prepared.
2. All men are a product of their times, and the Antichrist is no exception.
    a. Failure to identify the times leads to the conflicts between prophetic interpretations.
    b. The Word says to look for the times, and the man will come out of them.
    c. Misinterpretation comes from looking for him when the signs do not exist.
3. With the coming of the Antichrist, there will be an acceleration in the fulfillment of prophecy.
    a. Much of prophecy deals with end-time events—the days before the Second Coming of Jesus Christ.

    b. Every detail of prophecy concerning the Antichrist <u>must</u> be fulfilled, or the scriptures are not reliable.
        (1) This has not been the case in the past, when certain individuals have been thought to be the Antichrist.
        (2) In those instances, Christ did not return, and the end of time did not occur.
        (3) Examples of Antichrist <u>types</u> have been Nero, Alexander, Napoleon, Hitler, Nostradamus, etc.
4. There will be three occurrences, within one generation, which must take place just before the Rapture occurs (Matt. 24:34-37).
    a. A build-up to a world crisis based on great deception,
    b. A time of lying signs and satanic wonders, and
    c. Peace and safety, as in the Days of Noah.
5. These must all transpire before the Rapture can occur.
    a. These will be the times that will produce the Antichrist, and the Antichrist will impact the times.
    b. Second Thess. 2:3-7 says the Rapture will not take place until "the man of lawlessness is revealed."
        (1) The Holy Spirit restrains this lawlessness, but when the time is right, He will step out of the way, and God will allow the Antichrist full rein.
        (2) What will appear to be by the power of Satan will in fact be in accordance with God's perfect plan.
    c. It is imperative that we, therefore, know how to recognize the times, so that we will know when and how to identify the Antichrist when he steps forth.
    d. In this way, we can be ready, and the Son of Man shall not come like a thief, at an hour we do not expect (Luke 12:39-40).
    e. Jesus specifically tells us when to "...*look up for our redemption draws nigh...*" (Luke 21:28).

THE BUILD-UP TO A WORLD CRISIS

The first sign that we are moving into the end times is that the whole world will be in crisis—politically, economically, environmentally, and psychologically. There will seem to be no relief and no one capable of producing a discernible change. The world will be ripe for someone to step forward and take charge. One man will, but only those who are informed and spiritually alert will recognize him for who he truly is. He—the Antichrist—will institute changes that immediately begin to make life seem easier and better. Everyone, particularly world leaders, will be anxious and willing to do whatever he asks, because the rewards will be tangible. Every aspect of life will appear to be righted, and life will seem to be good. Like in the days of Noah, however, it will simply be just the calm before the storm (Matt. 24:38-39).

1. General world conditions
   a. Man will bring himself to the brink of world destruction.
   b. There will be wars, rumors of wars, and commotions everywhere.
      (1) There will be anarchy in the streets.
      (2) The justice system will become totally powerless, corrupt, and useless.
   c. The economy and political environment will be in utter chaos.
   d. This is not the tribulation, however. These are merely the moaning and groaning of labor pains leading to the birth of the Child—the Rapture of the true church.
   e. Only a significant person or event will be able to restore the order that must exist for a time.
   f. At this point, people will be ready to accept any answer, and the Antichrist will provide it.
2. This is the time when the Antichrist will come upon the scene.
   a. He will be <u>a man</u> such as the world has never seen.
      (1) He will have supernatural wisdom and intelligence that no one is able to surpass.
      (2) He will have the power, authority, and ability to bring economic and political order to a world in chaos.
      (3) This will be granted to him by Satan.
      (4) Everything he needs to create a new-world order will be in place.
   b. He will be able to accomplish <u>worldwide</u> what no man has been able to before, but it will be intended to serve Satan's end.
3. This man will single-handedly change a world in crisis into one of prosperity, peace, and seeming safety.
   a. He will establish a <u>world</u> common market—not the European Common Market.
      (1) Because of this common market, world free trade will become a reality.
      (2) Free trade will facilitate enormous economic growth.
      (3) In turn, it will bring about unbelievable prosperity.
      (4) Everyone will have jobs, amazing salaries, and everything they could want.
   b. The Antichrist will rule the political leaders of the world and be able to bring about what appears to be universal peace.

      (1) This peace will be both worldwide and local.
      (2) People will finally feel safe, secure, and happy.
      (3) No one will think of questioning the motives of this man.
      (4) He will be loved and revered by the masses.
      (5) This will be the most extraordinary man since Jesus, and he will be called a savior.
   c. Only those who know prophecy, however, will recognize this man as the Antichrist—the Vile One.
      (1) To deny that this man is anything but wonderful will be politically incorrect.
      (2) Such a point of view will bring great ridicule and persecution.
      (3) The Philadelphian Church will do this, however, and the world will hate them for it (Rev. 3:9).
   d. Even the visible Church—the false Laodicean churches—will herald the Antichrist and accept him as an advocate and hope.
      (1) Like the world, they too will become prosperous and see this man as the source.
      (2) The Church will also believe it has need for nothing, because of its wealth.
      (3) The *Spirit of Deception* will cause even the elect to be blinded to the identity of this man (Matt. 24:24) (Mark.13:22).
      (4) They will see him as a man of miracles, signs, and wonders.
      (5) Unfortunately, they will be <u>lying</u> signs and wonders.
   e. This man will be the Little Horn seen by Daniel, and he will not need to overpower with military force.
      (1) He will conquer by means of peace.
      (2) He will overwhelm with words of flattery and deception.
      (3) He will have riches and power to offer and all will seek after it—regardless of the ultimate price, which no one will consider.
      (4) This is exactly what biblical prophecy foretells.
4. Because this will be a period of great prosperity, many great cities will be rebuilt that are referred to in prophecy, but do not currently exist.
   a. Much attention is given in scripture to the destruction of certain of these centers, but for them to be destroyed in the last days, they must be rebuilt.
   b. Egypt, as a revived world power, will become incredibly powerful and set out to rule the world (Jer. 46:7-10).
      (1) It will be the "*King of the South.*"
      (2) The African nations will unify into a Federation and rule from Egypt.

        (3) A huge lake will be formed south of Aswan and support the growth of Egypt.
        (4) The Aswan Dam will make this possible.
    c. Babylon will be rebuilt to its original glory.
        (1) It will become a world capital of commerce, culture, and religion.
        (2) It will also be the center of the Antichrist's New World Religion.
    d. Tyre must also be rebuilt.
        (1) In Lebanon, it will be the Antichrist's political capital.
        (2) Satan is even called the *"King of Tyre"* (Ezek. 28:1-19).
    e. And finally, the Temple in Jerusalem will be rebuilt, to accommodate the prophetic events of the end times.
5. Such activity, growth, and development will have to take place during a time of prosperity and peace.
    a. It would never be possible later, when men and the world are in the throes of disaster, death, and persecution.
    b. Survival will be all anyone will be able to think about when that occurs.
    c. This restoration must take place, therefore, before the judgment process begins—before the Rapture of the true Church.

TIME OF GREAT DECEPTION (2 THESS. 2:1-4, 9-10)

This will be a time of great deception. Not all that glitters is gold. We are told in the scriptures to *"be not deceived,"* and yet the Father of Lies will convince a majority, even within the Church, that they should follow him. Any who resist or speak out against him will be ridiculed and scorned, though they speak the truth. Considering all of the prophetic information and warnings throughout the Bible, God obviously desires that we be prepared and able to recognize that, as prophecy is being fulfilled at a faster rate each day, the day of infamy is approaching at an increasing speed.

1. The *Spirit of Deception* will become the prevailing spirit within the world during this time.
    a. We are told repeatedly throughout scriptures to *"...be not deceived"* (2 Thess. 2:1-4).
    b. Jesus said many would come in His name in order to deceive.
        (1) There will be many false teachers, and they will all preach prophecy.
            (a) This will be a time of religious fervor and revival.
            (b) However, people will be told, and come to believe, that <u>they</u> are gods.

(c) Cult leaders will say that they are God or Christ.
(d) Many who come in the <u>name</u> of Christ, however, will not have Him in them—the Laodiceans.
(e) Many will also fall away because they become so deceived and confused.
(2) All who do not have a <u>real</u> love for the Church and the Truth will be deceived—even the elect (Matt. 24:24).
(a) Those that do know Christ and speak out against false prophets and false teachings will be scorned.
(b) Those false teachers will preach feel-good, get-rich doctrines that entice the uninformed "Christians" and set the groundwork for demonic deception.
(c) Those who deny such teachings as unscriptural will be considered unloving, bigots, and narrow-minded, if they say there is but one Christ and one way to salvation.
(d) In the last days, it will be crucial for God's people to stay together, encourage one another, and hold their ground, so they may endure (Heb. 10:25; 10:36-38).
2. The Antichrist will use this confusion and provide false truths.
3. Where Christ is the embodiment of truth, the Antichrist will be the embodiment of lies and deception.
4. Satan will cause this deception to occur, so he can bring forth <u>his</u> man.

THREE GREAT CRISES FOR THE JEWS AND ISRAEL

During the Pre-tribulation days, the primary focus of the Evil One will be on the true, Gentile believers. They will be those who fight him daily with their ceaseless prayers, their spreading of the gospel among unbelievers, and their godly ways. They are a threat to him and his plan of destruction of mankind, and it is his desire to destroy them and prevent the occurrence of the Rapture. When his battle to accomplish this is lost, however, he will turn his attention toward annihilating God's other chosen people—the Jews. Initially, he, in the person of the Antichrist, will act as an advocate and benefactor of their cause. The Jews will believe they have a mutually beneficial covenant with this world leader, but it will all be a façade. When the time is right, the Antichrist will do an about-face, and set out to eradicate these people as a race.

Though the Jews have currently reclaimed the nation of Israel, the first crisis of the end times is that they will again be removed from their land and driven into all parts of the world. The second crisis will be that God will provide a standard, or symbol, around which the Jews can rally, in order to re-establish their faithfulness to God and return to their land. This sign could even be a conveniently rediscovered Ark of the Covenant.

Because the Antichrist cannot overpower the Jews, when they are in covenant with God, the third crisis is that he must again entice them into believing in their own self-importance and ability to prosper by their own efforts. As a part of this deception, he will enter into a seven-year peace treaty with Jewish leaders, and, for three and a half years, the Jews will consider this one more sign of their ability to act on their own behalf. This will be the point at which the Two Witnesses come onto the scene to convict them of their blindness and sinful ways.

1. Once the true believers are gone, Satan will turn his attention to the Jewish nation.
    a. He will seek to destroy the Jews.
    b. He will launch new attacks against them.
2. World War I freed Palestine from the Turks and made it available to the Jews.
3. World War II, and Hitler's persecution of the Jews, caused them to return in part back to the land and Israel.
4. Because they do not fully return to God, however, the <u>first crisis</u> of this period will be that they will again be removed from their land.
    a. This is in accordance with God's covenant with them.
        (1) The land will be theirs only when they are in obedience to Him (Deut. 4:1, 27).
        (2) It is their rebellion that separates them from God and His blessings.
    b. Only the persecution by the Antichrist will again turn them back to God (Ezek. 36:3-5).
5. Because of worsening world conditions, the Jews will be blamed for the problems of the world, and they will be hated everywhere.
    a. The Antichrist will propose a solution, however.
        (1) The Jews will be driven from all parts of the world into the desert again.
        (2) Every nation will send them to Egypt (now a great power) "in ships" to die (Deut. 28:68).
        (3) Because every nation has seen all the "good" the Antichrist has done, and wishes to continue to prosper, they will participate in this plan to exterminate the Jews.
        (4) They will be blackmailed into compliance.
        (5) The persecution of this day will be greater even than what was experienced by the Jews under Hitler.

b. Why are God's Chosen Ones persecuted so?
   (1) God's covenant with Abraham, and the Jews, was:
      (a) He would multiply them and give them the promised land/Israel (Gen. 15:18).
      (b) They were to worship Him, however, as the one true God.
   (2) Throughout history, when the Jews have turned from God, He has taken the land from them, or taken them out of the land; when they returned to Him, He kept His promise and returned them to their land.
      (a) They were warned what disobedience would bring (Deut. 28:36).
      (b) They are a stiff-necked people, but God never stops loving them.
   (3) Satan knows Christ will return to be King of the Jews and establish His kingdom.
      (a) He must, therefore, kill <u>all</u> Jews, in order to thwart prophecy and stop it from being fulfilled.
      (b) He uses all of his powers to accomplish this end.
   (4) If we know prophecy, we should recognize the Antichrist, partly because of his treatment of the Jews.
   (5) If we speak out against this, however, no one will listen, for this is a man of miracles.
   (6) We will be persecuted as sympathizers.
   (7) This time of persecution will become so bad, however, that the Jews will repent again, and in His mercy, God will provide an escape.
c. The <u>second crisis</u> to affect the future of the Jews is that God will raise a standard that will appear in Ethiopia, and the Jews will rally around it (Is. 11:11-15; 18:1-7).
   (1) It will be a type, or may actually be, the Ark of the Covenant rediscovered. Under its power, the Jews will again march out of Egypt.
   (2) Without a weapon, they shall be victorious, and none will come against them.
   (3) Even the Red Sea will again dry up for them to cross, as in the time of Moses.
   (4) They will return to their land and customs, and the standard will again rest on Mt. Zion.
      (a) Israel and Judah will be reunited.
      (b) <u>All</u> of Palestine will be reclaimed this time.
      (c) They will have their temple, which will have been rebuilt.
      (d) They will be prosperous and at peace, <u>for a time</u>.

(5) It was God's promise that <u>all</u> of the nation of Israel would be returned to the land.
  (a) He would gather them from all of the places to which they have been scattered, and return them to their own land (Ezek. 20:34-38; 34:11-13; 37:21-22).
  (b) Satan's efforts are merely a part of God's plan.
d. Egypt will then fall from power again and be severely punished by God, because of its part in the plan to destroy the Jews (Ezek. 29:12).
e. This will <u>begin</u> to take place <u>before</u> the Rapture.

6. A <u>third crisis</u> must then occur to fully restore the Jewish commitment to God and cause them to acknowledge Christ as their Messiah.
  a. Because the Antichrist cannot fight against the Jews, when they are in covenant with God, his approach is to turn them back to sin once more.
   (1) As in the past, their faithfulness to God does not last.
   (2) Satan convinces them that they have been victorious because of their <u>own</u> efforts.
   (3) They elevate themselves and turn again to the ways of the flesh.
   (4) Even idolatry will become rampant.
   (5) When he—the Antichrist—gets them out of covenant with God, he signs a "peace treaty" with them for seven years Dan. 9:27.
   (6) Though this covenant is only with a few leaders, the protection of the Lord leaves them, and the Jews are again at the mercy of the Antichrist.
   (7) He is able to scatter them yet once more and remove their blessing.
   (8) Three and a half years into the treaty, however, the Antichrist will reveal his true, satanic self.
      (a) His persecution will take on renewed strength and power.
      (b) This time he will bring the armies of the world against the Jews.
  b. Half way through the seven years, the Two Witnesses will begin to preach to the Jews, in order to open their eyes to the truth (Rev. 11:3-14).
   (1) They bring plagues on the wicked.
   (2) They attempt to show their people what is truly happening.

CHAPTER 14

The Rapture

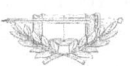

RAPTURE (1 COR. 15:52; 1 THESS. 4:16-18; REV. 12:2-5)

AS WE SAW EARLIER FROM a heavenly perspective, Satan, often referred to as the Devil, is so presumptuous as to actually go into a war of wits with Michael and the hosts of heaven. His intent is to demean the Saints before the throne of God. It has been his mission—since he was expelled from heaven for his own sinful desire to be equal to, or above, the Godhead—to destroy human beings before their Creator. Satan has always considered mankind to be his greatest competitor for such a high status, and in a spiritual battle of words, he seeks to undermine those who follow God's commandments and accept Jesus as Lord and Savior. The purpose is to prevent God's plan of redemption to draw His children to Himself for eternity.

As a part of Satan's strategy, he expounds upon the sins of man over the ages. Utilizing such weapons as lies, slander, and deception, he actually believes he can change the tide of prophecy. God, however, is fully aware of mankind's failures, and, in His mercy, He judges His own through the righteousness of Jesus Christ rather than based on their own best efforts. Not surprisingly, Satan fails to accomplish his goal and he, along with his minions, are cast out of the heavens onto the earth, where his power is even further diminished.

At this point, Satan, as the Great Red Dragon, is forced to watch the Woman—the Church—give birth to the Child—true believers in Jesus Christ—as they are snatched out of his grasp. All he can do is rage and torment those who are left behind. The Rapture, which he has so desperately desired to prevent since man's fall from grace, takes place, and he is powerless to stop it.

There are many, even within the Church, who do not believe in a Rapture, because it is not specifically named in the Bible, but for that matter, neither is the Trinity. Others argue about when it will occur. For this reason, it is important that one carefully examine all relative scriptures throughout the Bible, to determine whether the pieces actually fit together to create a defensible conclusion or not. As with any other decisions, however, this is a choice left up to the individual, at the leading of the Holy Spirit.

1. One of the greatest disputes in biblical interpretation is whether the Bible actually teaches that there is such an event as the Rapture.
    a. As mentioned earlier, while the word itself does not appear in the scriptures, it is a Latin translation of the Greek word *harpazo*—to seize or catch up by force.
    b. There are many Christians who do not believe in a Rapture at all.
    c. There are others who believe in a pre- or mid-Tribulation Rapture.
    d. Yet others believe such an event will only take place at the end of the Great Tribulation, as Christ returns to do battle with the remaining ungodly nations and to rule and reign over a new world.
    e. There is also an interpretation that such events are merely symbolic of the Roman custom of a victorious, returning general and his army.
        (1) That army would return home and send a message of their victory ahead into the city.
        (2) They would then wait outside the city walls, while the people prepared for their victorious entry.
            (a) An arch of triumph would be constructed.
            (b) The city would be decorated and a great feast prepared.
            (c) Then, only the <u>citizens</u> of the city would go out to meet the army and march back into the city with them, while all others looked on.
            (d) These citizens would participate in the victorious entrance of a conquering body.
2. The interpretation of the scriptures in <u>this</u> teaching, however, is that there will be a pre-Tribulation Rapture of God's Saints.

THE FIRST PRONG OF THE FIRST RESURRECTION (1 THESS. 4:16-18)

Scripture tells us that the moment the Saints are snatched out of the reach of the Evil One, the Lord Himself will step down out of heaven, and with a loud command and the sound of a trumpet, call first the dead in Christ—those who died believing in Him—and then those still alive. They will meet Him in the air and live with Him forever. Any who are not ready, because of their life choices, will only hear thunder and be left behind. Throughout history, God has protected His own from an outpouring of His wrath upon a sinful world. He is not about to do less when the time comes for the release of His final Great Wrath.

1. The *"taking up"* of the Saints is said to occur *"...in the twinkling of an eye"* (1 Cor. 15:52).

a. First go those who have already died, and then those who are yet alive (1 Thess. 4:16-18).
　　b. These are true believers who were promised protection from the last days.
2. Jesus tells us to pray that we might be found worthy to escape the persecution that is yet to come (Luke 21:36).
　　a. If this were not possible, He would not have told us so.
　　b. He says He will keep us from "that day" of God's wrath (Rom. 5:8-9) (1 Thess. 1:10; 5:9).
　　c. The Word tells us that the true Christians will be taken out and gathered to Christ (Matt. 24:31).
　　d. Also, if we are not taken <u>to</u> Him, we cannot come back <u>with</u> Him.
3. As was foretold, the Rapture, which this event has been called, will be heralded by a shout and the sound of a trumpet (1 Thess. 4:16).
　　a. Those that are believers, and are ready, will hear and recognize the call and be taken unto the Lord.
　　b. Those that do not believe, or are not prepared, will only hear thunder and be left behind.
　　c. Even among the dead, some graves will open and others will remain undisturbed.
　　d. True believers are to be removed from the last outpouring of God's <u>full wrath</u> upon the ungodly.
　　　　(1) He has protected His people in the past and will be faithful to His word again.
　　　　(2) Noah and his family were removed, and then God sent His punishment upon the wicked world.
　　　　(3) Lot and his family were taken out of Sodom and Gomorrah before He poured out His wrath upon those sinful cities.
　　　　(4) Why would God promise to protect His Church, and then do any less than He has done in the past?
　　　　(5) If He is in fact *"honest and true,"* He will do exactly as He promises
4. We are also told that the Rapture will come *"...when we least expect it"* (Matt. 24:44).
　　a. This will be an extraordinary event and will attract great attention.
　　　　(1) If the Rapture occurs <u>before</u> the Tribulation, the loss of Christians will be highly noticeable and a great loss.
　　　　(2) If it were to take place in the midst of the Tribulation, when many people are already dying or disappearing, such an event would go unnoticed for all the commotion and horror that is occurring throughout the world.

(3) By that time, everyone would wish to be removed from what is happening.
(4) Midway through this period, things will be in such chaos, and so many people dying, that if many vanish, few people would really notice or care.
   b. If the Rapture occurs just as Christ returns, God will not have kept His word that He will keep us from His day of wrath.

THE DAYS OF NOAH (MATT. 24:37-44)

Though no one knows the day or time of Christ's return, we are told it will come as in the Days of Noah. Everyone will be doing well and feeling safe and at peace. This would seem reasonable during a period in which the Antichrist restores peace and prosperity to a world that has been in chaos. Though it will be based on lies and deception, people will be living their daily lives as if all were well. For this reason, an event such as the Rapture—when people around the world suddenly disappear—will cause great shock and anxiety for those who are left in a state of confusion and pandemonium. Many will begin to recall prophecies of the last days and start to question the times and their own beliefs.

1. Christ said He would come at a time "*...just like in the days of Noah*" (Matt. 24:37).
   a. We are not given many details concerning those times in the Genesis account.
   b. Revelation, however, expands upon what we know about those days.
      (1) It was a time of prosperity, peace, and safety.
      (2) People were eating, drinking, marrying, and having a good time.
      (3) There was a false sense of security, and no one was prepared for the destruction that was about to come in the form of a flood.
      (4) Such will be the conditions when Christ comes again to take His own (1 Thess. 5:3).
      (5) The Antichrist will restore such order, peace, and safety to a world man has nearly destroyed, <u>then</u> Christ said He would return for His saints.
   c. Once the final days begin, there will be <u>no</u> peace or safety anywhere until the battle is over.
      (1) A mid or post-tribulation interpretation is, therefore, not consistent with the scriptures.
      (2) To believe otherwise is to doubt the truth of the Word.
2. In the last days, these same conditions will exist.
   a. When there is world crisis, people look for Christ to return, but He will not (Matt. 24:44).
   b. Scripture tells us that He will come like a thief in the night (1 Thess. 5:2-6).

(1) If read carefully, however, this is only the case for unbelievers.
(2) God wants us to be prepared for "that day" and is a primary reason why John is given this revelation—so that we might recognize the times and be ready.
3. The greatest test for the Church will be staying focused and alert, even when times are easier.
    a. The parable of the virgins is an example of the times (Matt. 25:1-13).
        (1) Those who are prepared, informed, and watchful go with the Bridegroom into the wedding—the Philadelphian Church.
        (2) Those that become inattentive and run out of oil—the Holy Spirit—will miss out.
    b. During good times, God does not seem to be needed every moment just to survive.
    c. It will be easy to fall into sin, as noted in 1 John 2:16.
        (1) This is not just the sin of the world but the system of sin established by the Evil One.
            (a) The sin of the flesh,
            (b) The sin of the eyes, and
            (c) The sin of the ego, or pride.
        (2) It is rebellion against God's Word and will.
        (3) And the wages, or consequences, of sin is death.
4. This will also be a time of great apostasy.
    a. It will be partly due to the great deception, and
    b. Partly because of the enormous prosperity of the times.
5. This is equally true within the Church.
    a. The Laodicean Church will be the predominant church in these days.
        (1) It is self-sufficient and self-centered.
        (2) It is rich and without need.
    b. This is the visible church that will be left behind.
6. *"Mockers of the Word"* will be rampant (2 Pet. 3:3-4).
    a. Many will laugh at prophecy and say, *"Where is the promise of His coming?"*
    b. The Second Coming will become a joke, and the very beliefs of Christians will be tested.
    c. Even the Church will begin to doubt.
7. New Age beliefs will become Truth to many.
    a. Man will see himself as saved by his own efforts.
    b. He will magnify himself.

c. Idolatry will become commonplace.
   d. Angels will be exalted and worshipped.
   e. This will be the New World Religion of Babylon.

Summary to Date

1. All that has been described to this point must occur before, or at the time of the Rapture.
   a. The war in heaven is fought and Satan and his forces cast down to the earth.
   b. The Woman gives birth, the Rapture takes place, and the Woman and her other offspring flee into the desert.
2. Earlier, John saw the Great Red Dragon.
   a. This creature is identified as Satan, himself.
   b. His intent from "the fall" has been to destroy mankind.
   c. He is the antithesis of God.
   d. He is the destroyer, deceiver, and source of all sin.
   e. He is a spirit, and as such must use man to accomplish his vile deeds.
      (1) If we would only refuse to carry out his bidding, much of the evil in the world would never take place.
      (2) Satan controls man's behavior in order to achieve his goals.
      (3) He can only be stopped when we say "No" to him.
3. Such is the condition of the times as John's vision continues.

CHAPTER 15
The Participants

REVELATION 13: 1-18 - 14:1-5

IN ORDER TO FULLY COMPREHEND the rationale and methods used to persecute God's children during the end times, it is necessary to understand the individuals responsible for their oppression. Who are they? What are their characteristics? What are their motivations and objectives? Only then is it possible to grasp the lengths to which they will go to accomplish their purpose.

John has already shown us God the Father on His throne, the Son, in the image of a Lamb that was slain, and all the hosts of heaven. He has also identified the Woman, representing the Church, who gives birth to the Child—the Saints taken up in the Rapture. All of these make up the company of God—the Creator of all that is good. Everything that occurs during the last days is according to prophecy and God's perfect plan. Difficult and painful as it may be, it is motivated by His love and desire to save us from Satan and our own sinful natures.

There is also a band of adversaries, however. Who are they, and how do they go about challenging prophecy and confounding God's plan? This is where we pick up John's account of his vision. The Dragon—Satan—has already been introduced. He is a spiritual being who corrupts mankind and all creation for his own perverted purposes. However, in order to carry out his agenda, he needs physical hands and feet to accomplish his vile deeds. To this end, he sends the Beast from out of the sea—the Antichrist—and another Beast from within the earth—the False Prophet—to do his bidding. These represent men who act on his behalf in the physical world. Additionally, any men or women who can be enticed to become followers of their cause are a part of those used to bring pain and destruction upon the world.

This demonic threesome—Satan, the Antichrist, and the False Prophet—compose an unholy counterfeit of the Trinity made up of God the Father, Jesus the Son, and the Holy Spirit. Satan cannot create, but that does not prevent him from duplicating whenever possible. All of these participants are the forces of good and evil that do battle over the souls of man in the last days.

THE BEAST FROM THE SEA (REV. 13:1-8)

At this point, John sees a Beast stepping out of the sea, and because of the use of prophetic language, it is obvious that this beast, with all of its attributes, is a sign or symbol of something other than what it appears. Much like the Dragon, it is described as *like* a mythical beast, similar to the one seen by Daniel in the Old Testament. The Beast John describes has seven heads, which represent seven historical kingdoms. At the time that Daniel saw the beast, three—Samaria, Egypt, and Assyria—had already passed as world leaders. Babylon was then in control, and the rule of Medo-Persia, Greece, and Rome had not yet come. As time approaches, before the return of Jesus Christ and His kingdom, which nation will be dominant is not clear, but with Babylon at the center of the seven heads, it could well be restored and become the political and economic capital of the Antichrist. Scriptures are not specific, however, and since only God has the full picture from beginning to end, we have to accept that some conclusions may be speculative rather than definitive.

Accepting that the Dragon and Beast are symbols, and that symbols are never mixed with real images, the sea would necessarily be a symbol also. It is, therefore, a reasonable assumption that the Beast is the Antichrist and the sea from which it rises represent the masses of people out of the Middle East. Though the Dragon and Beast are similar in appearance and have the same characteristics and purposes, the Beast represents a man, and he is intended to become a primary world leader. His assignment is to bring about the annihilation of God's people and take over all of the world governments that come under his rule. He acts as Satan's emissary, but in fact, he is merely one more component of God's plan. Nothing takes place outside of His control.

The Antichrist does not act on his own, however. His power and authority are granted to him by the Dragon (Satan). He is given power to make war against every tribe and nation, and as Daniel prophesied, this world ruler would *"devour the whole earth... crushing it."* For three and a half years, he will ravage the Gentile nations, and though he may overcome the Saints, most of whom will be martyred, they can be secure that their faithfulness will ensure God's eternal blessings. Those who choose to worship evil will be condemned to pain and suffering in the everlasting presence of their god.

1. John has already seen a "Dragon" standing on the seashore, and now he sees *"the Beast emerge from out of the sea"* (Rev. 13:1).
   a. The description of this Beast is similar to Daniel's vision in Dan. 7:3-7.
      (1) He saw four beasts representing four successive empires:
         (a) a lion with wings = Babylon
         (b) a bear with three ribs in his mouth = Medo-Persia

(c) a leopard with four wings and four heads = Greece
(d) a beast with iron teeth and ten horns = Roman Empire.
  (2) The Beast John sees incorporates the evil of all of the above four creatures into one beast, with its characteristics described in reverse order (Rev. 13:2).
    (a) It looks like a leopard.
    (b) Its feet are like a bear.
    (c) It has the mouth of a lion.
  (3) Daniel was looking forward into the future; John is recounting what has already occurred.
  (4) Evil is the same, however, regardless of the perspective.
  (5) This vile Dragon from the sea is also described in Job 41:1-34, as a leviathan (a beast) that cannot be subdued by man with typical methods or weapons.
 b. This too is a satanic being empowered by Satan himself.
 c. Only God has power over this demon of the deep.
2. Coming from out of the sea, the Beast is a symbolic representation of the Antichrist.
 a. He is a <u>man</u> through whom Satan will accomplish his last acts.
 b. The sea represents the masses, out of which the man will come.
 c. The time has finally arrived when God steps aside to allow Satan to have his final way (1 Thess. 2:7).
 d. In spite of appearances, God, not Satan, is still in control.
3. The Dragon (Satan) gives the Antichrist (the Beast) a throne and great power and authority over all people and nations of the world.
 a. As this supernatural power is granted to him by the Evil One, no man will be able to come against him.
 b. He will gain power over the leaders and rulers of all the political systems of the world.
 c. He will make war as he wishes and destroy with unbelievable strength.
   (1) He will control buying and selling, because he controls all governing bodies.
   (2) He is called *"that man of sin," "the Raiser of Taxes"* (2 Thess. 2:3-10) (Dan. 11:20).
     (a) As in the days of Christ's birth, he will put a world tax on everyone to further his kingdom.
     (b) Because he controls the governments of the world, he will be able to do whatever he wishes, and none will escape his influence.

d. This "man" will gather every tribe and nation under his control to oppose the final coming of Jesus Christ.
   e. His will be a worldwide kingdom—the first since Rome and the last before the kingdom of Christ.
   f. The Antichrist, as seen at this point, however, is Satan's instrument—but only until he is finished with him.

THE ANTICHRIST RESURRECTED (REV. 13:3; 17:8, 11)

This man will become so awesome, so influential, and unbelievably charismatic that for three and a half years only God's elect will recognize his true identity. The world will bask in his lying signs and wonders, and participate in the vast rewards offered for accepting his dominance over every aspect of life. Because of his charisma, a vast majority of the world will actually worship him, but this does not please Satan. The very entity he released to carry out his plan and purpose is suddenly reveling in the praise and worship he himself always coveted. The one he empowered is now experiencing all that he ever desired.

Unexpectedly, an unexplainable, supernatural phenomenon takes place. *"He who was, is not, and yet is."* Somehow, the Antichrist appears to die, is supernaturally revived, and then lives again. Obviously, God would never raise evil from the dead, so it has to be through the demonic power of Satan. As he never does anything unless it serves his own, perverted purpose, he takes over the body of the Antichrist for himself. This is so he can personally, and physically, rule and reign over the earth. His true nature surfaces, however, and his behavior does an about face. For the next three and a half years, he will kill and destroy anyone or anything that gets in his way of being considered a god to be obeyed and followed. Unfortunately, there will always be those who are willing to do what is most expedient and profitable for themselves.

1. The whole world will be in awe of the Beast.
   a. He will be attractive, charismatic, and unbelievably influential.
      (1) Everyone will want to follow him and share in the power and prosperity he has to offer.
      (2) He will bring such political, commercial, economic, cultural, and religious success that he will be undeniable.
      (3) Under his 'reign', all the greatness, learning, elegance, art, and religion of the Assyrian, Egyptian, Babylonian, Persian, Greek, and Roman empires will be restored to an even greater extent.

      b. Because of his greatness, he himself will be worshipped as a god by all whose names are <u>not</u> written in the *Book of Life*.
         (1) By this time, it will be clear to everyone, whom they are worshipping—God or Satan.
         (2) Only God's own will <u>not</u> worship this powerful being.
            (a) God has known us since before time began (2 Tim. 1:9).
            (b) We have been saved since that time, because the Lamb was slain before *"the foundation of the world..."* (Rev. 13:8).
            (c) He knows who will choose Him over Satan, and He is merciful.
2. The Beast will rule for 42 months—three and a half years (Rev. 13:5).
3. One of the heads of this Beast, however, will seem to be fatally wounded, but recover (*Rev.*13:3).
      a. As a consequence of this mortal wound, the Antichrist will appear to die, but somehow live again.
      b. Some type of diabolic procedure will be performed to provide a revived or duplicate body for Satan himself to inhabit.
      c. This will make it appear that it is the Antichrist that has been resurrected.
      d. A possible explanation of this in today's world is that he lives as a powerful leader for three and a half years; dies at the direction of Satan himself; and then, through some supernatural resuscitation or genetic engineering, is regenerated or cloned, using his DNA to create a duplicate body to be inhabited by Satan for the last three and a half years.
         (1) Because John has no way of knowing what life will be like in the last days, he does not try to explain what he sees—he only describes his vision.
         (2) God alone will provide the means, when the time is right.
      e. *"He was, and is not, and yet is"* (Rev. 17:8).
         (1) Satan will then take over this body, which the world will believe is the resurrected Antichrist.
         (2) Since before the creation, Satan has desired to be worshipped.
         (3) In order to be personally reverenced by man, however, he must exist in human form.
         (4) We are told, therefore, that the Antichrist will be slain, but his fatal wound will heal, and the whole world will be amazed (Rev. 13:3).
            (a) He who *"was and is not..."* is of the seventh head, but is also an eighth (Rev. 17:11).
            (b) The resurrection of the Antichrist creates an eighth head.

    (c) Through some chicanery, Satan will "become" the Antichrist, and his <u>true</u> nature will come forth.
  f. The power of <u>this</u> man will cause him to destroy anyone and anything that stands in his way, or goes against him.
   (1) Even those who follow and worship him are for his purpose and at his mercy.
   (2) He will blaspheme God and His tabernacle.
   (3) He will be so convincing that he will persuade the world that those who die by his hand are deserving of their fate.
   (4) He will defame their very memory.
4. Rev. 13:9 & 10 are then written to those who come to accept the Lord, live, and die during this time.
  a. As in the letters to the Churches, He says, *"He who has an ear, let him hear"* (Rev. 13:9).
  b. He speaks to the Tribulation Saints.
  c. Christ tells them that those who have lead them into captivity, shall go into captivity.
  d. Those that kill by the sword shall be killed.
  e. This will <u>not</u> be a time to resist and expect to survive.
  f. It will be a time of greater suffering than God's people have ever known.
  g. Evil will appear to rule, but God will overrule, and the unjust and evil <u>will</u> ultimately be judged.
  h. The Overcomers may not survive Satan's persecution, but because of their faithfulness, they will be victorious.

THE FALSE PROPHET (REV. 13:11-18)

What we have seen in the first Beast is a mighty, political figure. This is a man who will rule the governments of the world and control the economic and commercial aspects of everyday life. Wealth and power will be his weapons of domination.

  The Beast from out of the earth, however, is also given great power and authority by the Dragon, but his dominion will be over man's mind and spiritual life. He will perform great signs and wonders on behalf of the Antichrist, in order to convince the people that it is the Antichrist, not God, they should bow down and worship. As the third person of the unholy trinity, he will control the belief systems of the world. Humanism, idolatry, occultism, mysticism, and even witchcraft will become central to this new world religion.

  It is highly feasible that this False Prophet will enter the stage as a miracle-working religious leader or celebrity of the times—very likely a man who professes to receive messages from God. People who do not have God as their source of strength and guidance are always looking for answers to life's trials and mysteries, and unfortunately this makes them an easy prey to deceiving spirits. Jesus warned that in the last days there would be false christs and deceivers who would come in His name, and we must stay alert to their appearance (Matt. 24:24).

As a spokesperson and champion of the Antichrist, the Beast from out of the earth will become the leader of the new world religion. Recognized for all of his miracles, it will be easy for him to manipulate the minds and beliefs of people, who are already under the satanic influence of the Antichrist. The False Prophet's primary purpose for being will be to make the Antichrist appear god-like in nature and deed. To accomplish his assignment as supporter and spiritual advocate, he will go so far as to make an image of the Antichrist and seemingly breathe life into it. This idol, which will be placed in the Temple itself, will have a voice and command that all who do not worship him as divine should be slain. With modern-day technology, this could be accomplished in many ways, but, since only God can create life, the voice most likely will emanate from a demonic spirit empowered by Satan.

At the same time, the False Prophet has the power and authority to command that all persons have a mark of the Beast—666—branded on their right hand or forehead. This will be a sign of their allegiance to the Antichrist. As the economic system collapses and scarcity becomes the norm, people will do whatever it takes to provide for their families. The 666 will allow them to buy and sell the goods they need to survive. Without understanding the ramifications of taking the mark, to the unbeliever, it will seem to be an easy solution to a dire situation. Anyone without the sign will be quickly recognized and subject to death. If you do not know the Word of God, you will be easily deceived.

1. John sees *"another beast come out of the earth,"* with two horns like a lamb (Rev.13:11).
    a. Because this beast appears gentler, it represents the spiritual or religious element of the world, during the end times.
        (1) It has both natural and supernatural qualities.
        (2) The two horns represent two aspects of pagan worship—the worship of nature (Mother Earth) and/or the worship of the supernatural (occultism).
        (3) This "man" will combine them into one world religion.
        (4) It will satisfy man's need for something greater than himself in which to believe.
2. This beast represents the False Prophet—the spiritual leader and third person of the Unholy Trinity.

a. This counterpart is a mirror image of the holy trinity.
   God   -   Satan
   Jesus   -   Antichrist
   Holy Spirit -   False Prophet
b. The False Prophet speaks as for the Dragon.
c. He has the authority of the first Beast, that had been fatally wounded, and he commands the entire world to worship him.
d. Like the Holy Spirit, who presses us to worship Jesus, the False Prophet takes no honor to himself, but gives it to the Antichrist (Rev. 13:12).
e. This beast is also given great power by the Dragon to do miracles, signs, and wonders (2 Thess. 2:9) (Matt. 24:24).
   (1) These powers are from Satan and thus evil, though they appear good.
   (2) Their purpose is to deceive.
   (3) He even has an image, or statue, of *"the Vile One"* made and places it in the temple.
       (a) By Satan's power, the False Prophet breathes life into the image and causes it to speak (Rev. 13:14-15).
       (b) This is the *"abomination of desolation"* found in Matt. 24:15 and 2 Thess. 2:4.
   (4) The False Prophet convinces the people to worship the image of the Beast, who has been fatally wounded, and to take his mark —666—upon their right hand or forehead.
   (5) Because we are told that this is the *"number of the man,"* we cannot be referring to a philosophy or system of government, as some profess.
   (6) The Antichrist is a <u>man</u>, and those who do not worship him are killed.
f. As the False Prophet is intended to die and be bodily *"cast into the Lake of Fire,"* he too must be a man (Rev. 19:20).
   (1) He is the head of, or embodiment of, the false religion.
   (2) He will represent the new, universal, world religion.
       (a) It will be man-centered, occultic, idolatrous, and demonic.
       (b) It is against this that the Two Witnesses will preach.

THE LAMB AND THE 144,000 (REV. 7:4-8; 14:1-5)

What we saw in Rev. 7:4-8, from the heavenly perspective, was an unexpected interlude in the midst of great disasters falling upon the earth. This sudden calm was commanded by an angel from heaven, in order to allow for the sealing of a group of carefully chosen, Jewish men. By a mark ordered by God, they are protected from persecution by the evil forces of the Antichrist, as well as any further outpouring of His wrath upon the sinful world.

Now from the earthly perspective, John sees this 144,000 protected Jews standing on Mt. Zion in Jerusalem along with the Lamb—Jesus. As mentioned earlier, there is little agreement about who these 144,000 are, but the scriptures are very specific about them being undefiled, Jewish men from the twelve tribes of Israel. As the Lamb is with them— His and His Father's name written on their foreheads—they have obviously accepted Jesus as their Messiah. He, therefore, is their protection, as they go out to preach and witness to other Jews about what still lies ahead. This they do for 70 weeks, or three and a half years.

John then hears a voice like thunder mixed with the music of harps. With that as a background, the 144,000 sing a new song that praises God for redeeming them from the earth. Simultaneously, he has heard the Tribulation Saints sing their own song of deliverance before the throne of God.

1. John now sees the Lamb (Jesus) standing on Mt. Zion with the 144,000 men who have His and His Father's name written on their foreheads.
   a. Mt. Zion is in Jerusalem and is the place that is designated for their safety (Heb. 12:22-24).
   b. In some cases, this is interpreted as the inner chambers of heaven, and is symbolic of Christ in heaven.
2. As mentioned earlier, there are differing views as to who these 144,000 are.
   a. The Idealist view is that this scene reveals Christ in the New Jerusalem, after it descends from heaven.
      (1) With him are 144,000 Tribulation Saints seen earlier in Rev.7:4.
      (2) The mark on their foreheads separates them from the followers of the Antichrist, who also carry his sign upon them.
      (3) They represent <u>a portion</u> of all the redeemed.
      (4) These are called the first fruits—the first installment—because they are from the first harvest.
      (5) The second harvest reaps even greater numbers.
   b. Another viewpoint is that these are those who stayed faithful to their covenant with God.
      (1) They have not been corrupted, or prostituted their place as the Bride of Christ.
      (2) They remained chaste and do not succumb to the seduction of the Antichrist.
      (3) This interpretation asserts that the first fruits are the best, or the elect.

      c. The Jehovah's Witnesses believe they are the 144,000.
         (1) Because they do not recognize Jesus as God, however, He does not hold an equal position with God.
         (2) They would, therefore, never wear the name of Jesus, and His Father, on their foreheads.
      d. The scriptures specifically say, however, that the 144,000 are <u>Jewish men,</u> who are sealed from persecution (Rev. 7:4).
         (1) These are the first fruit of the Jewish nation.
            (a) They have come to understand God's plan for them and have accepted Jesus as their Messiah.
            (b) Because they are the <u>first</u> fruits, obviously more will come.
         (2) As we were told in Chapter 7, these are men, and they are spiritually and physically pure and chaste—undefiled by the times.
         (3) They are blameless and can tell nothing but the truth.
         (4) The mark that they wear is in contrast to the mark of Satan, which the unbelievers have on their foreheads.
         (5) While they are in the enviable position of <u>following</u> the Lamb wherever He goes, by this time we are even closer—we are <u>with</u> the Lamb (Rev.14:4).
            (a) We must remember that the Bride has already been made complete.
            (b) The Rapture has taken place, and the Saints are in heaven <u>with</u> the Lamb.
         (6) It is the responsibility of this group to go out, preach, and witness to the Jews, in order to bring them to understand and accept Jesus as the Messiah.
            (a) Jews do not generally preach to Gentiles, or try to convert them to Judaism.
            (b) Their ministry is to Israel.
            (c) Only the disciples went into the <u>world</u> to preach the gospel.
            (d) That was another of God's miracles, because this is not the nature of Jews, which the disciples were.
3. During this period, God does deal with the Jews—Daniel's Seventieth Week.
   a. In Dan. 9:24 the things that are left for the last week, and must be accomplished before the end, are enumerated. They must:
      (1) Finish their transgression, or their life of unbelief,
      (2) Make an end to sin,
      (3) Make atonement for iniquity,
      (4) Bring in everlasting righteousness,

(5) Seal up vision and prophecy, and
(6) Anoint the holy place.
    b. These tasks are given to Israel, and the 144,000 are involved in their accomplishment.
        (1) This will take 70 weeks.
        (2) Some of the tasks have been completed and some are still to be done.
4. All interpretations agree that this group (the 144,000) joins in a magnificent worship service.
    a. They have their own 'new' song that only they can sing—a song of deliverance (Rev. 14:3).
    b. Such celebrations, and new songs, always occur following a victory for God.
    c. At the same time that the elders and living ones have their specific song, the tribulation saints have theirs.
    d. Each, because of their unique experience and relationship with God, has a song and praises, which fit together to honor God.
    e. We were created to praise God; it is our primary purpose, and if we do not sing our particular song of praise, it will go unsung.

CHAPTER 16
The Harvest and God's Mercy

REVELATION 14:6 - 15:1-4

AS MENTIONED EARLIER, THERE HAVE been prophetic accounts of a climactic end of life on this planet, as we currently know it, since almost the beginning of recorded history. Every culture has appeared to anticipate some horrific end to mankind and the universe. With this being the case, why has no such event occurred to-date, when it has been foretold as being so imminent? Despite the fact that there have been many dates predicted to be <u>the</u> last day, they obviously have not been true. We are still here. Unfortunately, certain men have claimed to be granted specific foreknowledge of this event, and have managed to cause great confusion and anxiety about when and what to expect. Scriptures, however, say that only God knows the exact day or time, and any claims to the contrary are false.

If one searches God's Word and seeks to understand, it quickly becomes evident that, in spite of the trials and tribulations of daily life and our reactions to them, He already knows that mankind has a sinful nature. In our own strength, we repeatedly stumble and fall. His love is endless, however, and He desires that none should be lost to the Enemy. For that reason, all have been granted an opportunity to be saved and spend eternity with God and the Lamb. Because humanity is flawed and been perverted by the Evil One, without God's intervention, we are doomed to everlasting judgment. God knows this, so He has given His children the gift of free will, in order to choose whom to follow, what to believe, and how to live. In that way, mankind is allowed the capacity to elect how and where to spend eternity.

God knows the name of every man, woman, and child that will live with Him and His Son forever in the new heaven and new earth. In His infinite love and mercy, He has held back the outpouring of His wrath until each one has answered His call. He alone will know when the last person has chosen to accept Jesus Christ as the Messiah—Lord and Savior. Then, and only then, will He release the final judgment upon this sinful world.

The Horsemen and Angels (Rev. 6:1-8; 14:6-20)

John's prophetic vision began in heaven from which all things originate. However, he is now viewing the events of the last days from the perspective of earth. Because the chronology of his account is demonstrated through the retelling of what he sees three different times—from heaven, from earth, and from Satan's domain—it becomes apparent that there is a direct correlation between the events described in each version. Each telling provides greater detail to the picture that is being revealed.

With the opening of the first seal, a horseman is released to preach the gospel around the world. This continues until all who choose to be saved from eternal damnation are saved. On earth, what John sees is a messenger in the form of an angel, flying across the sky. It is spreading God's Word among the nations, and as mentioned before, this is most likely Jesus Himself. Who better knows and understands the Word of God?

The second angel John sees in the sky corresponds to the second horseman sent out from heaven. This is a time of great wars and conflict between men, and this angel announces the fall of Babylon. It has become the political, economic, cultural, and religious center of the Antichrist's domain, but it is not impervious to God's destructive power. It will be destroyed, just as Satan orders the destruction of so much of God's creation.

A third angel, corresponding to the third horseman, releases famine across the earth, and warns men to avoid taking the mark of the beast, in order to acquire the food and goods needed to survive. Such an act will result in spiritual death that will last forever in the pit of hell. For the Saints, however, not taking the mark will result in their physical death, but ensure the salvation of their eternal destiny.

At this point in John's vision, he hears a voice from heaven proclaiming the second beatitude presented in the Book of Revelation. It declares that the state of one's soul at the time of death will determine his or her eternal life. This proclamation demonstrates that God, in all his mercy, is still giving mankind an opportunity to elect his own destiny. We cannot say, "The devil made me do it," as we maintain a free will to the very end.

1. Comparison of Chapters 14 an 6.
    a. John sees angels going out to preach and proclaim God's messages to the world (Rev.14:6).
        (1) These angels, as seen from earth, are the horsemen we saw from the heavenly perspective, described in Chapter 6.
        (2) They go forth with the breaking of the seals.
    b. The <u>first angel</u>, like the <u>first horseman</u>, goes about spreading the gospel to <u>all</u> peoples (Rev. 14:1; 6:2).

(1) Some people today believe that this preaching will be sent across the world by Christian television and satellite.
   (a) Considering the fact that the Antichrist will be killing all who call themselves Christians, however, it seems unlikely that this broadcasting could occur without his knowledge and a violent reaction on his part.
   (b) Such a view waters down the way in which God is able to accomplish His works.
(2) Since the Church has been removed at this point, this duty is given to heavenly messengers
(3) The message is *"...the hour of judgment has come..."* (Rev.14:7).
(4) With the beginning of the tribulation and a time of judgment, there is one last word of grace and mercy to an apostate world.
(5) There is still time to come to the Lord, before the hour of final judgment begins.
(6) The world is told to worship the God who created all of the very things that are about to be destroyed—earth, sea, and springs (Ex. 20:11) (Ps. 146:6).
(7) Bible teachings always link the preaching of the gospel with creation and the Creator.
   (a) The world is to *"Fear God...and worship Him who created..."* (Rev. 14:7).
   (b) This always disturbs Satan, because he is <u>unable</u> to create, so it is clear who the world is told to worship.
   (c) To confound this issue, Satan has tried to convince man that the heaven and earth, and all that is in it, were not created.
   (d) Evolution is his explanation of how the earth and man came into being, as we know them today.
(8) The underlying theme of the Bible is that one day <u>all</u> will be judged, and man is responsible to God for how he lives his life.
(9) The only reason for the postponement of the end throughout history has been to give man an opportunity to be prepared.
(10) When people fail to take advantage of God's mercy, or do not understand His delay, they will have to suffer the consequences, and have no one to blame but themselves.
(11) God is faithful to forgive <u>any</u> sin for which man repents, not because of who we are, but because of who <u>He</u> is.
(12) This is a last warning and call to repentance.

    c. In the time of great wars, which the <u>second horseman</u> announces, the <u>second angel</u> tells of the fall of Babylon (Rev. 14:8; 6:3).
       (1) Babylon has reached its pinnacle by this time, and the world has turned to it and its teachings.
       (2) All the nations accept its ways.
       (3) This angel proclaims its fall.
       (4) God has ordained this, and though it still stands when John sees it, its fall is assured.
       (5) Satan's crown jewel shall be destroyed.
    d. The <u>third horseman</u> releases the great famines that shall result from the constant warring, and the <u>third angel</u> warns against taking the mark of the Beast to survive in this time of scarcity
       (1) All who <u>do</u> take the mark shall be judged and tormented in hell (Rev. 14:9; 6:5).
       (2) This mark will allow people to buy, sell, and exist in this perverse society.
          (a) Any who do not take the sign will be immediately identifiable and put to death.
          (b) Only the most committed will be able to hold out against the persecution of the Antichrist.
       (3) If God's own—the Tribulation Saints—hold fast to their faith, however, they will overcome, though they be persecuted and killed.
       (4) The torment they suffer will last for but a short time, but the torment of hell will last forever.
          (a) Hell is not just a separation from God.
          (b) It is a <u>place</u>, and because God is everywhere, those condemned to eternal fire and brimstone will see Him even from there.
          (c) This will be part of their punishment, because they had a choice.
          (d) They will <u>see</u> Him, but be ever separated from Him.
2. At this point, John hears a voice that says, *"Write. Blessed are the dead who die in the Lord… they will rest in their labor, for their deeds will follow them"* (Rev. 14:13).
    a. This is the second, and perhaps most significant beatitude of Revelation.
       (1) It is enough to justify the placement of this Book in the Bible.
       (2) It indicates that the state of our soul at the time of our death reflects our eternal state.
       (3) If we do not die "in the Lord," we die in a state of sin, which dictates our eternal life or experience.

    b. The fact that we shall find rest in the midst of our labors could well indicate that we continue to do God's work forever—be messengers, rule and reign, etc.
3. It says that our deeds will follow us, thus implying that there are different levels of attainment in heaven based upon our deeds.
    a. Some believe there are no differences in placement in heaven, but that is not borne out in scripture.
    b. There will be those in heaven who have lived godly lives dedicated to service and commitment to God.
    c. Some will just squeak through—just in time.
       (1) We must remember that our salvation is based upon faith, not works.
       (2) Though a believer's deeds for God during life may have been minimal, it is our acceptance of Jesus Christ as Lord and Savior that will save us.
       (3) Thus, there are different positions of existence in heaven, and our deeds affect our rewards—crowns, place of authority, prestige, etc.
       (4) The Word says, *"In my house are many rooms..."* (John 14:2).
       (5) It is far better to be in the kingdom of God, however, regardless of placement, than not.

THE HARVEST (REV. 14:14-20)

The time has come to separate those who have stayed faithful to their beliefs in God the Father and Jesus the Son, from those who have chosen to reject His salvation and stand with the Man of Sin. What John now sees is the preparation for the final judgment that will soon take place. As he scans the scene, he sees *"one like a son of man"* seated on a cloud, with a sickle in his hand. Although it looks like an angel, it is important to remember that Jesus appears as an angel numerous times. Knowing that His favorite name for Himself was *"son of man,"* John's description seems to confirm that this personage is most likely Jesus—about to carry out the judgment process.

    This is a time of harvest, and the Angel, Jesus, is prepared to separate the good from evil and send each to his or her just rewards. The Tribulation Saints—the wheat—are taken from under the altar, where they have waited for God's timing to call them into His presence before the Throne. The wicked and unrighteous of the earth—the grapes—are gathered and cast into the winepress of God's Wrath. In both cases, they are sent to their judgment. He who sits on the cloud carries out this action, as a voice from out of the temple commands Him to reap the harvest. The order is delivered by a messenger from God, telling Jesus that the time has come.

This separation of good from evil is evidenced as the fourth horseman—Death and Hades—goes out to collect the "dead in Christ," and the fourth angel directs *"Him who is on a cloud"* to harvest the wheat from among the living on earth. As the fifth seal is broken, a fifth angel, also directs the *"man on the cloud"* to gather the grapes—the unrighteous of the earth—and throw them into the winepress of God's Wrath. This process ends the period of God's judgment mixed with mercy. There will be no more chances for Gentiles to repent and be saved. What is left will be God's full Wrath upon the sinful of the earth.

1. John sees Jesus, *"one like a son of man,"* seated on a white cloud, with a sharp sickle in His hand (Rev. 14:14).
   a. The white cloud denotes the presence of God, and Jesus calls Himself the *"son of man"* (Dan. 7:13).
      (1) The sickle in His hand reflects His readiness to harvest His people.
      (2) Because it is sharp, the action will be swift and clean.
      (3) Only Jesus knows whom to reap into judgment and whom into salvation.
          (a) First comes the harvest of the just (wheat).
          (b) Next will come the harvest of the unjust (grapes).
   b. The <u>fourth horseman</u> of Chapter 6 is Death and Hades sent out to collect the "dead in Christ."
      (1) The <u>fourth angel</u> tells Him who sits on the cloud to take His sickle and reap the harvest.
      (2) *"...the time to reap has come, for the harvest of the earth is ripe"* (Rev. 14:15).
      (3) Some question how an angel could order Jesus Christ.
          (a) The angel, or saint, comes out of the temple and brings a message from God.
          (b) He is merely a messenger.
          (c) Even the Son of God did not know the time of His return (Matt. 24:36).
          (d) This is the revelation to Christ, by His Father, that the time for the final judgment and His return has come.
          (e) Everything in history moves toward this point.
      (4) He swings His sickle over the earth and reaps the harvest, for the time is ripe.
   c. With the breaking of the <u>fifth seal</u>, a <u>fifth angel</u> comes from the altar where the righteous were placed, and tells Him who sits on the cloud to gather the

clusters of grapes, or the unrighteous, and throw them into the winepress of God's Wrath (Joel 3:13) (Is. 63:3).
    (1) The wicked shall be trampled (judged), and their blood run bridle-high for 160 miles.
    (2) This is the approximate length of Israel from north to south, denoting the entire countryside.
    (3) Such action results in the splattering of the juice (blood) upon the white garments of Him who gives out the judgment (Rev. 19:13).
  d. There are those who believe this vision is merely symbolic of the totality of God's wrath.
2. Thus ends the Age of Grace and judgment mixed with mercy.
  a. There will be no more opportunity to repent and receive God's grace after this point.
  b. All of God's children have been called home, and now the sinful shall feel His full wrath.

CHAPTER 17

A Time of Praise

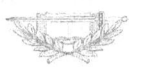

REVELATION 15:1-4

THE TIME OF HARVEST HAS passed. All who would be saved have been removed from the earth and taken out of any further persecution or tribulation. They have found their peace and rest, and they are blessed to have "died in Christ." They stayed faithful to Him in life, and *"their deeds follow them,"* granting them eternal rewards. In the First Prong of the First Resurrection, the Saints that were prepared were transported into the Throne Room of Heaven at the Rapture. In this Second Prong of the First Resurrection, the Tribulation Saints are removed from under the altar—where they must wait for God to avenge their persecution by the Antichrist. In His good time, they are made a part of the Bride that dwells in His presence in heaven. Simultaneously, 144,000 carefully selected Jews are sealed and placed on Mt. Zion for their protection from attack by the Beast and his followers.

Unless otherwise shielded, those that remain on the earth are there by their own choice. At this point in the narrative, the entire world knows who it is they have chosen to follow—God and His promise of eternal life or the Antichrist, who merely offers fulfillment of all earthly desires in this life. From the beginning, God granted His children the gift of freewill, but whether they use that gift wisely or not is up to each individual. The time of mercy is passed, and those who choose God are taken out of the world of sin. Those who elect to follow the Antichrist, or the ways of the flesh, are condemned to suffer the full impact of God's fury. There will be a settling of accounts and all will be rewarded according to their deeds. Seven angels are about to pour out seven plagues upon a rebellious and wicked world, and *"The wages of sin is death."*

Before this happens, however, at the midpoint in the chronological events leading up to the Second Coming of Jesus Christ, we get another glimpse of the joy and celebration that takes place in heaven when God's children are delivered out of the hands of the Enemy. This deliverance from the torment and tribulation of life precipitates a great demonstration of praise and worship to the Father and Son—all heaven rejoices. God's will is done. This display of joy is equally prophetic of the glory that is yet to come following the restoration of the earth to its original state of perfection.

1. Before describing the final outpouring of God's Wrath, John tells of another scene.
2. At this point in the account of the last days, Satan and the world believe that they have won the battle against God's own.
   a. The righteous have all been killed.
      (1) They were starved, persecuted, and tortured.
      (2) None of God's Tribulation Saints are left.
      (3) "He—Satan—has won," or so he believes.
3. From God's perspective, however, the saints are victorious—they have overcome and remained faithful.
4. There is great rejoicing before the Throne.
5. This elicits various interpretations.
   a. The symbolic view is that those who have been victorious are now standing beside a sea of glass mixed with fire.
      (1) They have harps in their hands, and they sing a song of deliverance.
      (2) This sea is interpreted as the ordeals and struggle (fire) of life, and now it is calm.
      (3) The journey is over and the faithful have arrived.
      (4) Those who have survived the trials now sing a song of praise to the God who brought them through.
      (5) This is similar to the song of Moses, which the Hebrews sang upon being delivered out of Egypt (Ex.15:1-18).
   b. The interpretation of <u>this</u> teaching is that the Second Prong of the First Resurrection has just taken place, and these are the victorious that have been taken from under the altar and now stand in heaven on the edge of a glassy sea.
      (1) The First Prong was the Rapture of those who were prepared.
      (2) The Second Prong is the harvest of the Tribulation Saints.
      (3) They <u>all</u> now stand before the throne of God and sing the song of Moses.
         (a) Their Deliverer is *"The Lord God, Almighty."*
         (b) This title is only used in the Book of Revelation, and it is used six times (Rev. 4:8; 11:17; 15:3; 16:7; 19:6; 21:22).
         (c) Revelation is the ultimate book of deliverance.
      (4) Despite what they have been through, there is no bitterness—no "Why me, God?"

(5) They worship the Lamb and rejoice, as we should in the face of adversity.
(6) God is more concerned with our holiness than with our happiness, thus we are to *"Consider it all joy...when you encounter various trials, knowing that the testing of your faith produces endurance"* (James 1:2-3).
(7) Everything that happens is a part of God's perfect plan, and He will never leave us or forsake us (Josh. 1:5).

c. These saints have felt the Dragon's wrath, and now they are free and safe from the wrath of God that is yet to fall.
d. At this point, all Gentiles who will respond to Jesus have done so, and they are safely with Him.
e. God has no further need to delay the outpouring of His Great Wrath.
(1) The 144,000 still on earth, who belong to Him, are sealed and protected from this final torment.
(2) Everyone else left on the earth is there by his or her own choice.
(3) The wicked world shall now feel God's sting.

CHAPTER 18

God's Timeline

SEQUENCE OF EVENTS *

ONE OF THE GREATEST CONFUSIONS of the Book of Revelation is the sequence of events and the time period over which they occur. The generally accepted interpretation is that it all covered a period of seven years—seven years of Tribulation. If you study the scriptures carefully, however, a somewhat different view emerges. It is the responsibility of the reader to examine the facts and reach his or her own conclusion.

It is the assertion of <u>this</u> teaching that the following is supported by scripture:

1. Prior to the Rapture:
   a. Letters of acknowledgment and instruction are written to the seven Churches,
   b. There is a build-up of world conditions conducive to the emergence of a strong, world leader,
   c. A man steps on to the stage in the person of the Antichrist,
   d. A war in heaven takes place between Satan and Michael, God's representative, over the souls of the faithful,
   e. Satan is defeated and cast out of the heavens on to the earth, and
   f. The Rapture occurs.
2. Three and a half years of Persecution with Mercy.
   a. This is not the seven-year Tribulation Period.
      (1) From the Pre-Tribulation point of view, true Christians—the Saints/Overcomers/Gentiles—are removed before the Tribulation begins.
      (2) This is the Age of the Gentiles, during which the true believers are gathered to become the Bride of Christ.
   b. The Antichrist comes into full power and is heralded as a world savior.

---
* See timeline chart.

    c. The Woman (the Visible Church) goes into the desert with those left behind (the Tribulation Saints) to escape the persecution of the Antichrist.
    d. The Lamb takes the scroll and opens the first six seals:
        The 1st. Seal - The gospel is spread throughout the world,
        The 2nd. Seal - There are wars during which Babylon is destroyed,
        The 3rd. Seal - Great famines precipitate a requirement to take the sign of the Beast,
        The 4th. Seal - Death is released and the Tribulation Saints are martyred,
        The 5th. Seal - The Tribulation Saints are placed under the altar, and the unrighteous on the earth are condemned to God's outpouring of Wrath,
        The 6th. Seal - The Tribulation Saints are taken from under the altar into the Throne Room of God, 144,000 Jews are sealed against persecution on earth, a great earthquake takes place, and the moon turns to blood.
    e. Thus marks the end of the time of the Gentiles and the Age of Grace.
    f. There will be no more mercy.
3. Seven years of Tribulation—Daniel's Seventieth Week
    a. The seventh seal (God's Wrath) is opened, trumpets blown, and the seven angels pour out the bowls of plagues upon the earth.
        The <u>first trumpet</u> initiates the pouring from the <u>first bowl</u> that burns one third of the earth,
        The <u>second trumpet</u> causes the <u>second bowl</u> to pour out putrefied blood into one third of the oceans,
        The <u>third trumpet</u> sounds and the <u>third bowl</u> poisons one third of the rivers and springs to be polluted,
        The <u>fourth trumpet</u> and <u>fourth bowl</u> of plagues destroy one third of the sun and moon, and
        The <u>fifth trumpet</u> signals the release of locusts, resulting in a bowl of physical suffering from boils and sores.
    b. During this same period, the False Prophet comes on the scene, and a covenant is signed between the Antichrist and the Jews for three and a half years.
    c. At the end of this period, Satan takes over the body of the Antichrist and enters the temple to be worshipped as a god.
4. The second three and a half years of Daniel's Seventieth Week is called Jacob's Trouble.
    a. Satan, in the person of the Antichrist, turns his attention toward the annihilation of the Jews, as a race.

(1) In response, Two Witnesses appear and go about warning the Jews that they must return to God and accept Jesus, as the Messiah, or suffer the consequences of eternal death.

(2) They are put to death themselves at the end of three and a half years, but miraculously rise from the dead and ascend into heaven.

   b. During this period:

(1) The <u>sixth trumpet</u> sounds and one third of mankind is killed, and the <u>sixth bowl</u> of plagues is poured out on the Euphrates,

(2) The <u>seventh trumpet</u> and <u>seventh bowl</u> cause great earthquakes and hailstones to fall upon the earth.

5. Thus ends the Wrath of God and the Great Tribulation of the end times.
6. The Wedding Feast now takes place and Jesus takes the Saints as His Bride.
7. Together with His Bride, He returns to earth to fight the final battle with Satan and all his followers—natural and supernatural.
   a. They are defeated and Satan is bound for a thousand years.
   b. Death and the False Prophet are cast into the Lake of Fire, never to return.
8. The Judgments take place, and a thousand years of restoration begins.
   a. Satan is released, for a short period at the end of this time, and again attempts to create war, but is crushed and ultimately thrown into the Lake of Fire for all eternity.
   b. The battle between good and evil is over.
9. From this point forward, the Saints live with God, their Father, and Jesus, the Son in the New Jerusalem of the New Heaven.
10. Those Jews that accept Jesus as the Messiah shall live forever in their land on the New Earth, with David as their king.

World without End!

CHAPTER 19
God's Wrath

THE SEVEN BOWLS OF GOD'S WRATH (REV. 15:5 - 16:21)

THERE ARE CONSEQUENCES FOR THE choices we make in life—positive and negative. The Tribulation Saints, those who chose to accept Jesus as Lord regardless of cost, have been rewarded by being taken home to an eternity of joy and peace. Those choosing otherwise must now suffer the penalty for their resolve—God's wrath without mercy. Little do they know that their "god" will not offer them any solace or protection. They exist only for his purpose, and they are on their own from this point forward. This is heartbreaking, because they have no idea that what lies ahead is beyond their wildest imagination.

INTRODUCTION TO THE PLAGUES (REV. 8:2, 6; 15:5-8)

During the next seven years, not only will God pour out His wrath on the wicked of the world, but He will begin to deal with Israel as a nation—Daniel's Seventieth Week. The time of the Gentiles is finished, and God now focuses His attention on reclaiming His chosen people. They are a stiff-necked race, and it will take the persecution of the Antichrist, as well as the witnessing of two of their own, to open their eyes to their own blindness. God is patient, but He is also a God of justice. Consequently, there are hard times ahead.

John continues his description of what he sees—seven angels dressed in white linen robes coming out of the heavenly temple. Based on their appearance, these are most likely Saints on assignment. We were told in Rev. 8:2 that each is given a trumpet, and, as they sequentially sound their instrument, a specific action occurs on earth. From the perspective of earth, the down-turned bell of the trumpet appears like a bowl from which plagues of wrath are poured. God is still in control, and His power and glory—the "Shekinah" glory—are evidenced in the smoke drifting out of the temple. This cloud, which led the Israelites through the wilderness for forty years, assured them of God's presence. It will again until His Wrath is exhausted. No one is allowed to enter the temple to be saved until this has been accomplished.

1. The time has now come for the final "*Woe.*"
   a. Time has run out.
   b. God's Wrath, <u>without mercy</u>, is about to fall upon the world.
2. This is the period during which God begins to deal with Israel—Daniel's Seventieth Week.
   a. We are told in Rom. 11:26 that God will bring in Israel, when the time of the Gentiles is fulfilled.
   b. The time of Grace—the fullness of the Gentiles—is over.
3. John looks and sees the innermost, sacred sanctuary of the temple in heaven—the Holy of Holies.
   a. This is where the mercy seat is kept, and from whence comes all Judgment.
   b. Out of this place come seven angels dressed in white linen robes with golden sashes.
      (1) We have seen these messengers before and identified them as saints.
      (2) The saints are now going to play a part in the preaching, the warning, and the pouring out of judgment.
      (3) They have an important role, even after their resurrection.
   c. One of the four living creatures from around the throne gives each angel a golden bowl filled with God's Wrath.
   d. This compares to the golden censures of fire seen in the heavenly view in Chapter 8.
   e. A loud voice tells the seven "angels" to go out and pour the bowls of wrath onto the earth (Rev. 16:1).
   f. The familiar sounding of the trumpets and the pouring out of the bowls begins the last seven plagues that befall the earth and mankind.
   g. The temple fills with smoke, and *"no one can enter the temple until the seven plagues are completed"* (Rev. 15:8).
      (1) This can be interpreted to mean that no one else is saved until this time passes.
      (2) Thus, all who are left at this point have to suffer the great wrath of God.
      (3) There is no escape from this judgment.

GOD'S WRATH POURED OUT (REV. 16:2-17)

What John now shares are the concluding events leading to the Second Coming of Jesus Christ. Until thus far, the actions against mankind and the earth have been limited to convicting individuals of their sin in order to encourage them to exchange a commitment to the ungodly for an acceptance of Jesus Christ as Lord. From this point forward, however, the plagues that are released constitute an expression of God's fury and vengeance against man's sinful choices and conduct. Each occurrence reflects an increase in the intensity and frequency of His judgments. With the opening of the seventh seal, another comparison is revealed between that which is initiated in heaven by the seven angels and what is experienced on earth, as the plagues are poured out of each bowl of God's wrath. The details outlined in each description increases what we know about the end times.

1. The bowls of wrath described here are parallel with the sounding of the trumpets in Rev. 8.
   a. The announcement and action that is initiated in heaven, with the sounding of the trumpets, results in the outpouring of the plagues from the bowls, onto the earth.
   b. If one looks up from the earth into the down-turned bell of a trumpet, it would look like a bowl being emptied.
   c. The two actions are, therefore, comparable.
2. The first angel pours out the first bowl upon the land (Rev. 16:2; 8:7).
   a. As the trumpet causes the earth to burn, the plague causes malignant, loathsome, weepy sores all over the bodies of those who align themselves with the Antichrist and take his mark.
   b. This is reminiscent of the plague of boils that came upon the Egyptians (Ex. 9:9-11).
   c. The pain is unbearable.
   d. It is a result of fire and hail from heaven.
   e. In a nuclear age, this could be symbolic of radiation poisoning.
3. The second angel pours out the second bowl, and the seas are turned to blood like that of a dead man (Rev. 16:3; 8:8).
   a. This is not life-giving blood, but the putrid blood of death.
   b. It corresponds to the action of the second trumpet.
   c. As a result, every living thing in the sea dies.
4. The third angel pours out the third bowl, and the waters of the rivers and springs are turned to blood; all who drink die (Rev. 16:4; 8:10).
   a. God chose blood because it purifies, but also, those who shed the blood of the Saints deserve to die from drinking or again taking blood.
   b. The angel of the waters sees God's actions and praises Him for rightly judging the ungodly and purifying the earth.
      (1) Vengeance belongs to God, and He is just (Heb. 10:30).
      (2) His judgment is fitting to the crime, and those who have spilled the blood of the Saints get what they deserve.

(3) The martyred Saints agree, for they have been avenged.
5. With the <u>fourth bowl</u>, the <u>fourth angel</u> causes the sun to shine with such fierceness that all are scorched and tortured by the intense heat (Rev. 8:12; 16:8).
   a. Based upon the actions of the fourth trumpet, there are also times of extreme cold, and the people freeze when it becomes dark.
   b. The constant change from intense heat to extreme cold is torture.
   c. Despite their torment, the people still curse God and refuse to repent.
6. The <u>fifth angel</u>'s <u>bowl</u> of punishments even encompass the Beast and his kingdom (Rev. 16:16; 9:1).
   a. The entire world is under Satan's dominion by this time.
   b. This is evidenced by the fact that great darkness falls upon the land and increases the agony.
      (1) Satan is called the Prince of Darkness, so it is only reasonable that his kingdom should be so.
      (2) Joel 2:2 declares that the day of the Lord would be a time of darkness.
   c. With the sounding of the <u>fifth trumpet</u>, the locusts—evil creatures—come forth and torment with unbearable force.
   d. People are still, and increasingly, suffering from horrible sores all over their bodies, and they bite their tongues in anguish as they are further attacked.
   e. Death would be a relief at this point, but it is not an option, for death is removed for five months (Rev. 9:5-6).
   f. The earth becomes like hell, as the people blaspheme against God.
   g. They have rebelled for so long, they are beyond repentance.
7. The <u>sixth angel</u> pours out the <u>sixth bowl</u> at the sounding of the <u>sixth trumpet</u>, and the great river Euphrates is dried up (Rev. 16:12).
   a. This exceedingly wide and deep river separates the east from the west for 1,800 miles.
   b. Suddenly, just as God dried up the Nile so the Hebrews could come out of Egypt, the Euphrates is dried up to allow the armies of the east to join other nations in the Valley of Megiddo.
8. Suddenly, John sees three spirits, which look like frogs, come out of the mouths of Satan, the Antichrist, and the False Prophet, and they gather the armies of the world to the place called Armageddon..
   a. The Climax of the Ages is about to take place.
      (1) The day has come for the great battle between the Unholy Trinity and the power of God.

  (2) What appears to be at the command of Satan, however, is in fact according to the will of God (Ezek. 38:16, 23; 39:21-22) (Joel 3:9-12).
9. In the midst of describing this time of crisis, however, a third beatitude of Revelation is given.
 a. *"Blessed is he who stays awake...,"* so that he is ready for Christ's coming (Rev. 16:15).
 b. There is much to distract one during these years of extreme occurrences, and it would be easy to be caught unawares or unprepared, thus missing God's warnings.
 c. Knowledge of prophecy and preparedness alone will keep believers from being drawn into this time and being caught off guard (1 Thess. 5:2).
10. The <u>seventh angel</u> pours out the <u>seventh bowl</u> of wrath into the air.
 a. To this point, judgments have been poured onto the world of nature and mankind.
 b. God now deals with Satan's religious and political systems, the armies, and Satan himself.
 c. This demonic kingdom shall now come to an end.
 d. A loud, unidentified voice comes from out of the temple and says, with divine authority, *"It is done"* (Rev. 16:17).
  (1) The moment of climax has arrived.
  (2) As Jesus said from the cross, when He gave up His life, *"It is finished"* (John 19:30).
  (3) Again, the redemptive work is completed, and the final act of divine judgment takes place on the earth.
  (4) The earth is reclaimed and mankind redeemed.
  (5) The Day of Judgment has come.
 e. Lightning flashes, thunder peals, and a <u>great</u> earthquake, splits the city of Jerusalem into three parts (Rev. 16:18-19) (Ezek. 38:19-20).
  (1) As a result, it is raised up.
  (2) Springs of pure, living water flow forth to the seas in both the east and west (Zech.14:8).
 f. As these things take place, Jesus sets foot upon the Mt. of Olives, from which He ascended.
  (1) His very power and glory splits the mount, and He walks through the valley into Jerusalem (Zech. 14:4).
  (2) Having tested them, Israel now recognizes their Messiah, call Him by name, and know that He is their Lord (Zech. 13:9).
  (3) This is undeniably prophecy, as it is yet to be fulfilled.

    g. At the same time, all the cities of the world collapse and nations are destroyed (Is. 40:4) (Rev. 16:19; 19:15).
    h. The earthquake is felt worldwide, and the very islands and mountains of the world disappear (Rev. 16:20) (Ezek. 38:20) (Is. 24:19-20).
       (1) God now rights the world and puts it back on its axis, as it was at creation.
       (2) This is the way things were before the Flood—before the mountains and valleys were formed.
    i. One hundred-pound hailstones fall from the sky killing many of the remaining unsaved, as they continue to curse God (Rev. 16:21).
       (1) In Job, it tells of the hailstones that God has stored "*for that day*" (Job 38:22-23).
       (2) Job is the oldest book in the Bible, and God was prepared for the last days even when time began.
       (3) David too describes the events of the day of the Lord (Ps. 18).
    j. One city (Jerusalem) is only <u>partially</u> affected, and that for the better.
       (1) After the great earthquake, it stands higher than any other place and is more beautiful than ever before (Ps. 48:2).
       (2) It still has a purpose to fulfill.

THE PROPHESIED NATIONS (EZEK. 38:1-16)

Because scripture does not come out and specifically name the nations that will go into battle with Satan, against the Prince of Peace, it is necessary to put together references from across the Bible relative to who the "kings of the earth" or "kings of the east" are. In Rev. 6, following the opening of the sixth seal, John mentions that the kings, princes, and generals, as well as commoners, have to hide in the mountains and caves in order to escape the wrath that is being inflicted upon the earth. Because of the pain and suffering they experience, they are rebelliously anxious to do battle against the one they believe is responsible—Jesus, the one they curse.

    We are told by Daniel that there is a coalition of nations from the North and East out of which will come a mighty leader—Gog, along with Magog—who will gain control over them. Though the rulers of the nations willingly give their allegiance, he will use them for his own purposes. Ezekiel similarly refers to the nations prophetically. None of the prophets knew what would exist in the final days, but it is obvious that when that time comes, there will be political leaders from surrounding areas that will converge on the Holy Land and join forces with the Antichrist to do battle against a returning Christ and His heavenly army.

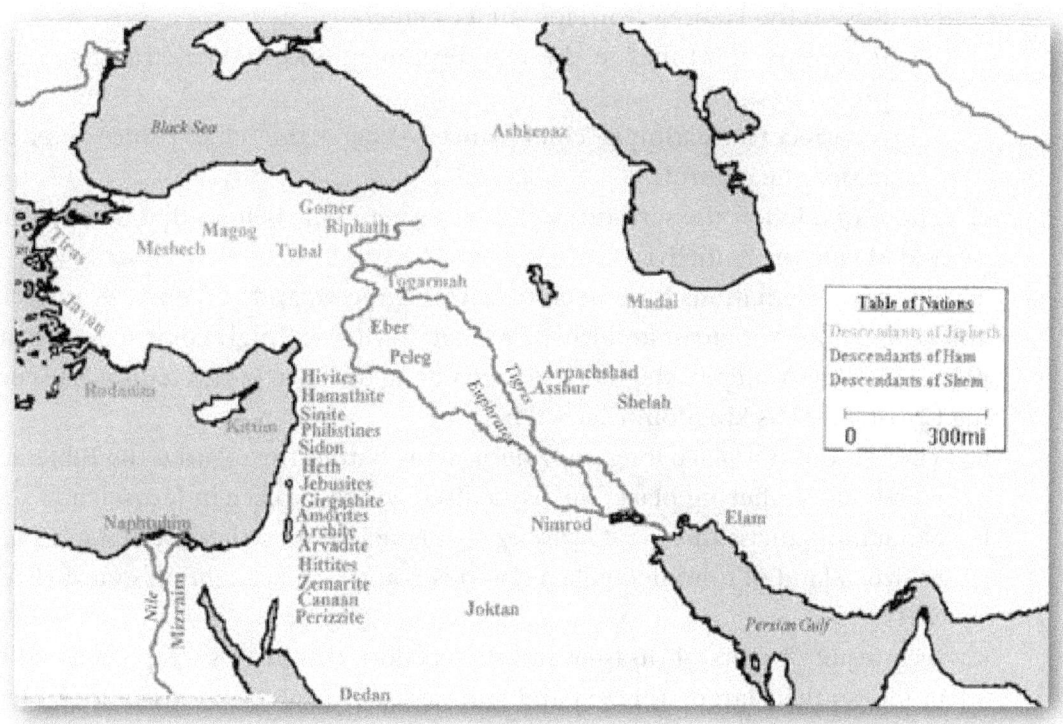

The armies who join forces will be great, and though Israel is small, they have God's protection, and Satan knows that. An attack on Jerusalem will have to be swift and overpowering. The hordes will come from the East, West, North, and South, with a full expectation of victory and great reward. Little do they know that they march to their death.

1. Who are the nations that assemble to do Satan's work?
    a. Old Testament prophecy says that Gog—the Prince of Rosh—Meshech, Tubal, and Magog gather the nations for the Battle of Armageddon.
    b. Once again, there are differing opinions as to who Gog and Magog are.
        (1) Because Gog is called Prince of Rosh, there is a very vehement, current-day interpretation that, since Rosh sounds like Russia, and has been such a powerful presence in modern-day political history, this is the nation that will be the destructive power described in prophecy.
        (2) Following this logic, Meshech could be Moscow and Tubal Tubalsky.
        (3) Such a conclusion, however, is purely arbitrary and not based upon the root meanings of the words.
        (4) You do not make prophecy fit your expectations and expect it to be accurate.

- (5) Rosh is the Hebrew word for "first or chief."
- (6) It appears 456 times in the Old Testament and never is translated as a proper noun.
- (7) A correct translation is "chief prince"—Gog is the "chief prince" over the nations he controls.
  c. Those who follow the scriptures, therefore, generally believe that Gog is Satan and Magog the Antichrist.
2. The kings of the nations have been deceived, enticed, and inflamed by miracles and signs by the Antichrist and False Prophet, so they willingly come together in a place called the Valley of Megiddo to wage war against the Jewish nation, the coming Christ, and His kingdom (Zech. 14:1).
   a. Though this is a place long known for many battles throughout the Bible, it is merely the gathering place; the battle itself will take place in Jerusalem.
   b. Satan must amass this great army against Israel, despite the fact that it is small in size, a land of unwalled-villages, and is going to be caught off guard (Ezek. 38:11).
   c. As a result of years of disaster and destruction, this army's weapons could be crude, so their large numbers and swiftness are needed to overcome the Jews (Joel 3:9, 10).
   d. God is with His people and they walk in His protection and power.
   e. Satan knows this, so he must command many nations in order to wipe out all the Jews, so prophecy is prevented from being fulfilled.
3. Ezekiel was looking into the future, where times would be so different he had no words to describe them.
   a. He could not know the names of the countries in the future that would constitute the lands of Gog and Magog.
   b. He divided them, therefore, into four groups:
      (1) Persia, Ethiopia, and Libya
      (2) Meshech and Tubal
      (3) Gomer and Togarmah
      (4) Sheba, Dedan, and Tarshish
   c. These represent the nations that come from all directions to join in the attack against Israel.
   d. The first three are in existence in Ezekiel's day and remain to the end.
      (1) The armies of Persia, Ethiopia, and Libya come from the south and east.
      (2) Part of them will come across the Euphrates that has been dried up for this purpose.

- e. For lack of a better way to identify them, the other nations are called by the names of their founders—the grandsons of Noah.
- f. From the north and northeast come the nations of Meshech and Tubal.
  - (1) This land is in the Caucasus Mountains between the Black and Caspian Seas.
  - (2) Though more recently a part of Russia, they will become independent again and voluntarily support the Antichrist.
  - (3) We have already seen this independence taking place.
- g. The land of Gomer includes Turkey and northern Europe.
- h. Gomer's son Togarmah settled the land of southern Europe—around the Mediterranean to Spain.
- i. Though the kings of Sheba, Dedan, and Tarshish come from the east, they are also from other parts of the world.
  - (1) Their location is unclear, though possibly they are from Africa, Arabia, and Gibraltar.
  - (2) These are not China and Japan, however, as some modern-day prophets contend.
  - (3) Though these countries may protest warring against Israel for a time, they do ultimately enter by another route to partake of the spoils (Ezek. 38:13).
4. As prophesied by Daniel and Ezekiel, these countries make up the four groups of nations gathered by the *"unclean spirits like frogs"* in Rev. 16:13-14.
5. Egypt and Babylon are not mentioned as a part of the army, because they are destroyed before the Battle of Armageddon takes place.
6. The reward to the nations, for responding to the command of the Antichrist, is to receive the spoils of war in Jerusalem (Ezek. 38:11-12).
   - a. Great deprivation prevails throughout the world at this point, but Jerusalem has been protected to some degree from that, because of the 144,000.
   - b. The rulers of the world now come to rape and sack the city out of need and jealousy.
   - c. They are even willing to join forces to surround the city in order to overcome it.
   - d. They do not know, however, that they march to their death.
   - e. They are merely Satan's pawns.
   - f. This is the final crisis of Israel.
     - (1) It looks as if the Antichrist is winning, because Jerusalem appears about to be conquered.
     - (2) The time of this event is just following the killing and resurrection of the Two Witnesses.

The Fulfillment of Prophecy

1. In order for the Bible to be reliable and true, prophecy must be fulfilled.
   a. If one part of it is changed, or does not take place, the Word is not infallible or trustworthy.
   b. Satan will go to any lengths, therefore, to change the course of events.
2. Knowing and believing the Word will prepare us to stand firm in the last day
3. Thus ends the Events of the Last Days from an Earthly Perspective.

PART V

The Tribulation as Seen from Satan's Realm

CHAPTER 20

Babylon

REVELATION 17: 1-18

JOHN'S VISIONS HAVE THUS FAR unveiled a glimpse of *"those things that must take place..."* before the Second Coming of Jesus Christ and the restoration of a lost and perverted world. Mankind, with the guidance and encouragement of the Evil One, has slowly damaged all that God created. Humanity has been the tool by which Satan has sought to eliminate all that God treasures. At the same time, however, God has taken advantage of Satan's schemes, in order to facilitate His own plan of redemption—His alternative strategy for reclaiming mankind from his own weaknesses and rebellious choices. God is a loving Father, and it is His desire that the lost should be saved. He knows full well, however, that not all will choose His plan of redemption. The battle for men's souls, and the restoration of a damaged world, is the content of "His[s]tory," as told in the Bible. The Book of Revelation is simply the last chapter—the victory of good over evil.

What John proceeds to describe reflects a third telling of what will occur during the end times. It is the interpretation of <u>this</u> study that John's vision now returns again to the days prior to the Rapture. This time it is from the perspective of Satan's domain. Upon careful reading of the scriptures, it is apparent that the sequence of events leading to the Great Battle line up with those viewed from heaven and then again from earth. As is evident throughout the Bible, the Word is consistent, and it is man's effort to make it say what he or she expects that causes the confusion. Nevertheless, we are told to *"lean not on our own understanding, but in all ways trust in the Lord."* Once more, we have the choice to elect what to believe—our own outlook or God's will.

BABYLON, THE SYSTEM (REV. 17:3-7)

It is important to remember that John's visions, in their entirety, are a wonder and mystery—just like Daniel's and Ezekiel's. The purpose of these visions is to foretell future events of which no one could have foreknowledge. For all these prophets know, the signs and wonders of the last days could occur momentarily, or not for hundreds of thousands of years. The Word tells us that not even Jesus Himself knows the day or time.

Besides the fact that prophetic literature is typically written in symbolic form, there is no way these men could know what the future times might be like, so it is reasonable that John's vision should continue to be described in symbolic terms.

There is much debate, therefore, over whether the Babylon of the Book of Revelation is real and true or merely symbolic of all that is evil. We know that it was real and powerful during Daniel's life, but as a city, it was destroyed in about 689 B.C. If we believe it will exist again in the end times, as the Word declares, we must then trust that at some point, it will have to be rebuilt and re-established as a world power, through and from which the Antichrist can rule. Based on the amount of time dedicated to this topic in the Book of Revelation (two chapters), it is not unreasonable to assume that Babylon is more than a symbol of Rome, or some other major city in modern times, as some believe. It represents a philosophy and religion, as well as a place and political ideology.

John picks up his account of what he sees by relating that the last of the seven angels that poured out God's Wrath from the bowls shows him a Woman with the title BABYLON THE GREAT written on her forehead. She represents the apostate world system and philosophy, and this angel explains the mysteries of this Woman and Beast upon which she rides.

1. Satan has waged war against Christianity and God, since almost the beginning of time.
    a. We will now see the end times, from Satan's perspective.
    b. In John's vision, the World Systems of Government, the New World Religion, and the City of Babylon are all ruled by Satan.
    c. His will be the last world empire before the return of Christ.
    d. In the last days, Babylon shall play a major role in Satan's plans.
        (1) This is partly evidenced by how much space is devoted to the topic.
        (2) Two chapters are spent on Babylon and its fall.
    e. In Chapter 17, we see Babylon throughout history.
    f. Chapter 18 reveals the form Babylon will take at the end of time, when she—the city—is destroyed for the last time.
2. As the scene opens, John is shown the heart of Satan's kingdom and the judgment that will come upon Babylon and the Beast upon which she sits.
    a. One of the seven "angels," previously seen pouring out God's wrath, tells John he will show him the woman, a harlot, who rides the Beast over many waters—masses of people (Rev. 17:1) (Jer. 51:8).

(1) This harlot is Babylon—the apostate world system—and she is drunk on the blood of the saints, is gaudy, and is holding a cup of evil and wickedness in her hand.
  (a) There is significant dispute over the belief that this city is not really Babylon at all, but <u>a type</u> of Babylon, and actually refers to Rome.
  (b) Some feel that it would not have been politically safe for John to say that the city was Rome, so he called it Babylon instead.
  (c) <u>This</u> study, however, again takes the scriptures as *"faithful and true,"* and chooses not to make prophecy fit a speculation.
(2) As in the past, the "waters" can refer to great masses of people.
  (a) This woman exercises control of, and influence over, many nations of people.
  (b) Some believe this reference to water stems from the fact that ancient Babylon was built upon a network of canals.
  (c) Also, because of the belief of some that Babylon really refers to Rome, it is often viewed in relation to the Tiber River.
(3) The rulers and kings of these people of all nations have joined forces with her and seek to share all that she has to give; her power is immense.
(4) They prostitute themselves with her in order to share in her power and wealth.
  (a) Harlotry is repeatedly used throughout the Bible in relation to idolatry and the whoring of the unfaithful after other religions.
  (b) Babylon is the Great Harlot and representative of the greatest rejection of God's will ever seen.
  (c) To the ungodly of the world, she appears to have much to offer.
  b. The Beast, upon which the woman rides, gives her that wealth and power to seduce the nations.
3. Once again, John is taken in the spirit—this time into a wilderness (Rev. 17:3).
  a. This is not a particular wilderness, so it is not a specific place.
  b. This is the realm of Satan.
  c. It is a place of temptation and interaction with demonic power.
    (1) It is a place of confrontation with satanic forces.
    (2) Even Christ sparred with Satan in this place (Matt. 4:1).
  d. As God has always had a plan for the warring of good against evil, Satan also has had a plan.
  e. Through the ages, there has been a system of God and a system of Satan, and they have functioned side by side.
  f. What John sees is this horrible spirit of Babylon.

4. Physically, Babylon was the area around the Garden of Eden.
   a. It is where Satan first came and made an attack against mankind.
      (1) It is where sin first occurred (Gen. 3:6).
      (2) It is where the first murder took place (Gen. 4:8).
      (3) It is where sin increased until God took vengeance in the Flood (Gen. 7:10).
   b. After the Flood, everyone on earth knew God.
      (1) Noah and his family were all that were left.
      (2) As the population of the world grew, Satan again began to pollute the life of man.
   c. In this same area, the city of Babylon was built.
      (1) King Nimrod, a wicked, vile man, commanded his people to build a mighty city and tower to prove their might.
         (a) He felt threatened by <u>someone</u> he believed was coming to interfere with his rule.
         (b) As a consequence, he had 70,000 baby boys killed, just as the Pharaoh of Egypt and King Herod did in their times.
         (c) In every case, <u>someone</u> great did follow—Abraham, Moses, and Jesus.
         (d) Satan has always known that his adversary is coming again.
      (2) Nimrod led his people to exalt themselves.
         (a) They developed supernatural powers and knowledge, and wished to stay together and expand on those powers to become even greater.
         (b) A sign of that greatness was a tower they began to build, supposedly to honor God, but they were using supernatural, occultic knowledge to do so.
         (c) It was Nimrod's desire to rule over this extraordinary achievement and establish a world government.
         (d) None of the world governments throughout history (Egypt, Persia, Rome, Greece), however, have ever been Godly. This one was not either.
      (3) It was God's plan that man should multiply and scatter throughout the world.
         (a) The strategy for Babylon was contradictory to God's wishes for man.
         (b) For extraordinary reasons, God took extraordinary steps to confound this plan.
         (c) Because the people were united in their goals and their language, God caused there to be confusion in their speech. Suddenly they could not understand one another nor work together (Gen. 11:7).

(d) The tower they had been united in building thus became known as the Tower of Babel (Gen.11:1-9).
(e) Because of the disruption that this caused, the people began to move away and establish themselves in communities in other parts of the world.
(f) <u>This</u> was according to <u>God's</u> plan.

5. Unfortunately, but obviously with God's knowledge, as the people moved away from Babylon, they took their perverted, false religion with them into the world.
   a. This Babylonian religion was the religion of Satan and included:
      (1) Idolatry
      (2) Human sacrifice
      (3) Occultism, sorcery, and
      (4) Satanism.
      (5) It is <u>self</u>-worship—evidenced in the New Age Movement of today.

6. In the last days, Satan, as the Antichrist, does not start out in this area, but when he comes into full power, he moves his capital back to Babylon.
   a. He ensures that the city is rebuilt and is more magnificent than it had ever been previously.
      (1) This has to occur during the times of prosperity and safety, as such a feat would not be possible during wars and chaos.
      (2) The Antichrist will have the riches of the world at his disposal, and he will see that this glorious city is reconstructed.
      (3) When we see this happen, we should look up, because the time of our Lord's coming—the Rapture—draws nigh.
      (4) If we check our times, even now the restoration of Babylon has begun in Iraq.
      (5) Based upon the devastation of the last days and the outpouring of the Wrath of God, this rebuilding could not occur just before the Second Coming.
   b. Repeatedly, John calls this city Babylon.
      (1) If it were Rome, or some modern-day city, he would have said so.
         (a) When we have been shown a sign of something other than what is previously described, we are told it is a "sign" or "like."
         (b) In this case, the city is identified as Babylon, not like Babylon.
         (c) The woman that represents Babylon has "BABYLON THE GREAT" written on her forehead. We are told who Babylon the Great is and how and why she falls (Rev. 17:5; 18:2, 8).
      (2) If we are not to change God's word, as He instructs, Babylon is Babylon.

      c. It will become the political and religious center of the world.
- (1) This area is a crossroads into Europe, the Middle East, Asia, and Africa.
- (2) Satan will be King of Babylon and from it have power over all nations.

7. At this point, Satan has taken control of the body of the Antichrist and becomes a man.
   a. This will be him who suffered the fatal wound and "*who was, but wasn't, but is*" (Rev. 17:8).
   b. He is "*...also an eighth, and is one of the seventh...*" (Rev. 17:11).

THE WOMAN (REV. 17:1-18)

As John describes the Woman he sees riding on a scarlet beast, the fact becomes imminently clear. She is the total opposite of the Woman we saw previously going into the desert. This Woman is Satan's counterfeit of God's creation—a harlot that seduces the rulers of the nations to follow the Beast upon which she sits.

Here again John is not seeing an actual woman, but an image or representation of the times and conditions of the last days of a perverted and damaged world. It is important, therefore, to analyze the attributes of these symbolic women in order to grasp the severity and true nature of the conditions. Only with such understanding is it possible to make an informed choice about who and what to believe and follow. These are not decisions to be taken lightly or with temporary consequences. They determine one's eternal life.

1. The Woman John sees in Chapter 17 is contrasted with the Woman in Chapter 12.
   a. They are both seen in the wilderness.
      (1) The first is fleeing persecution.
      (2) The second is doing the pursuing, in order to persecute the first.
   b. They are both clad in fine garments.
      (1) The first is clothed with the sun—heavenly light.
      (2) The second is arrayed in purple, scarlet, gold, precious stones, and pearls—all ornaments from the earth and below.
   c. One is pure, the other a harlot.
   d. One is hated by the earth, and the other is coveted by it.
   e. One is carried on celestial wings, the other by the power of the Dragon.
   f. One has a crown with 12 stars; the other has the name of the Destroyer on her forehead.
   g. One is finally seen in the heavenly city—the New Jerusalem—the other in a seemingly glorious, earthly city, which shall be destroyed for its wickedness.

h. One reigns forever, the other is judged forever.
   i. The one is the Mother of the Godly—the faithful. The other is the Mother of the ungodly, or Satan's organization—the faithless.
2. Everything that God has created, Satan has duplicated with a counterpart.
3. No other city throughout history was considered the Mother of harlots and abominations—only Babylon.
4. As mentioned before, there are those who believe the harlot is Rome.
   a. Rome's influence was not felt, however, by *"...all of the inhabitants of the earth," "...through all the ages."*
   b. The evil, pagan, satanic system of Babylon was begun in the earliest of times; it is still felt and influences the world today.
   c. This is not true of Rome.
5. *"In her*—the harlot— *was also the blood of prophets and saints, and all that had been slain (martyred) upon the earth"* (Rev. 16:6; 17:6).
   a. Many of those prophets and martyrs died long before Rome was ever established.
   b. Rome was merely <u>a type</u> of Babylon.
6. This Woman also sits upon *"many waters...," "people, and multitudes, and nations, and tongues"* (Rev. 17:15).
   a. This is far beyond Roman influence.
   b. There are many nations and peoples over which Rome never ruled.
7. The perversion of all governments and peoples stems from the Woman—Babylon.
   a. The Woman—Satan's system—rides on (rules) all of the empires, by their own choice.
      (1) They are her servants and lovers.
      (2) They support her, and she gives them riches and power in payment.
   b. In her hand is a cup full of abominations, and she is drunk from the consumption of them (Rev. 17:4).
      (1) She shares this corruption with the rulers of the world, and they are intoxicated into committing adultery with her and the ways of Satan.
      (2) As a result, they too will drink of the undiluted cup full of the wrath of God (Ps.75:8) (Is. 51:17).
      (3) They think they are getting the power and riches of Satan, but that is short lived. In the end, they will get God's wrath, undiluted by mercy.
      (4) This is the same cup that Christ had to partake of at the cross.
         (a) He did not agonize over the physical torture of whippings, the nails, and thorns—a torture that others have suffered.

  (b) He had to endure the full wrath of God, in order to take our place and punishment.
  (c) This is the cup He asked the Father to take from Him, but *"...not My will, but Thy will be done"*(Matt. 26:39, 42).
  (d) This is the fullness of "forsaken," and why He had to go down to hell (Matt. 27:47).
  (e) This is wrath reserved for the unrepentant, and, if we do not accept Christ's gift of sacrifice and atonement, we must experience that judgment and wrath ourselves—for eternity.
 c. We either sit at God's table and drink of His cup of mercy, or we sit at the table of the Antichrist, and drink of the wrath of God.

THE BEAST (REV. 17:3, 8-18)

The Woman is not the central figure in this scene, however. She may reign supreme over the religious and philosophical aspects of this vile kingdom, but she actually only exists to support the Great Red Dragon upon which she rides. He is the power and authority over all sin and corruption—past, present, and future. While she acts through the False Prophet, she exists only at the will of Satan, the Beast. As soon as he is finished with her, or she has served her purpose, she is gone.

 The Dragon with the seven heads and ten horns represents the political head of a despotic world system. He is both the king over the nations that bow down and worship him, as well as the kingdom through which he controls them. This Beast is Satan himself in the person of the Antichrist—the one who *"was and was not and yet is (or will be)."* Just as this describes the Antichrist, it also describes Babylon, the city and system of government. Grand in the days of Daniel, defeated and destroyed by the Persians, it will rise again in the last days. Only a biblically minded individual will put together all of the clues throughout the scriptures concerning the end times and recognize that the time of redemption draws near.

1. The Beast, upon which this Woman sits, is the Antichrist/Satan incarnate.
 a. It is the Beast with the seven heads and ten horns seen earlier by Daniel (Dan. 7:4-6).
 b. The seven heads—mountains—are world governments seen throughout history.

    Egypt   Medo-Persia
    Assyria   Greece
    Babylon   Rome
    And one yet to come

(1) Mountains have often been used to mean governments (Ps. 30:7) (Dan. 2:35).
(2) Each of these world governments has been ungodly.
  (a) Plagues came against Egypt and her gods.
  (b) The Assyrians were known for child sacrifice.
  (c) Babylon, Medes and Persians were occultic, perverse, and corrupted.
  (d) The Greeks had their gods.
  (e) The Romans adopted Greek gods and incorporated them into their own.
(3) There has not been a <u>world</u> government since Rome.
  (a) It is just one of the mountains, however.
  (b) It is not the entire Beast.
(4) Daniel said there would not be another world government or religion after Rome, until the Antichrist.
  (a) Constantine tried and failed.
  (b) Napoleon tried and failed.
  (c) Hitler tried and failed.
  (d) Communism tried and failed.
(5) Some ask about America, and although it is clearly turning from the fact, it was built on a godly foundation.
  (a) America never <u>said</u> it planned to take over the world.
  (b) There is really no reference to America in this book of prophecy.
  (c) That does not mean we will not feel the impact of the end times, however.
 c. Of the seven heads, or mountains—governments—five are fallen and no longer world empires, one—Rome—<u>is</u> when this was written, and one is yet to come—the kingdom of the Antichrist.
2. The Beast also has ten horns.
 a. These ten horns are ten kings, or contemporaneous rulers, who align themselves with the Beast to do his bidding in the last days.
 b. Where they once had sought after and prostituted themselves with the Woman, they later turn on her and destroy her.
  (1) This they do at the direction of the Antichrist.
  (2) The Woman, like the original Beast from the sea, becomes so honored and revered that it too infuriates the Beast, who, though he is the source of her grandeur, is almost disregarded.
    (a) This is the same situation that occurred with the Antichrist, when Satan took over his physical body in order to be able to experience being worshipped.

- (b) When the political power (Satan) no longer needs the philosophy and religious power (the Woman), she can be eliminated or destroyed.
- (c) His jealous need to be honored and exalted causes Satan to destroy even his own servants.
- (3) All of this plays into God's plan to have the Woman destroyed, for she is responsible for the persecution and killing of any and all who do not accept Satan's new world order.
- c. The ten horns are also delegated to wage war against the Lamb, at His return, and they willingly give their allegiance to the Beast.
  - (1) Though their end will be annihilation and destruction, in their blindness, they are deceived and comply with Satan's agenda.
  - (2) They cannot imagine that they are merely his pawns and will go to their death—both physical and spiritual.

CHAPTER 21
Babylon, the City

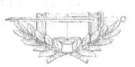

THE CITY OF BABYLON (REV. 18: 1-24)

THE CITY OF BABYLON THAT has lain in ruins for thousands of years will most likely be rebuilt sometime during the prosperous times leading up to the period of tribulation. This effort has even today been started by the Iraqis. As we approach the last days, a coalition of ten nations will also contribute to the creation of this city as a great political, economic, religious, and cultural center. At that point it will be under the command of the Antichrist, to construct a world capital from which the Beast can rule. Because demonic powers from the past have only lain dormant in this region, it will be a perfect site from which an evil and sinful Spirit, such as Satan, can reign.

1. The perverse system and world religion empowered by Satan will again settle in an actual city.
    a. The city of Babylon becomes the capital of the Antichrist in his full power.
    b. To do so in the last days, it must be restored (Is. 13:6).
    c. It was destroyed in the past, but will exist again when the time is right.
    d. Its fall in the past was not complete.
    e. Shepherds continue to tend their sheep in this region, and Arabs still set up tents in the place of Ancient Babylon.
    f. If you keep up with the news, it seems that Iraq has already begun to restore this area.
2. This city shall be magnificent again beyond belief.
    a. It will be a center of the new world religion.
    b. It will be a commercial and transportation center of the world (Ezek. 26:15-18).
    c. It will develop into a center of culture and the arts.
    d. It shall become an entertainment and tourist center of the world.

THE FALL OF BABYLON (REV. 18:2-24)

The Woman, who also represents the City, as well as the philosophy and new world religion of Satan's kingdom, the New Babylon's future is also doomed. Spread by the Second Horseman from heaven and proclaimed by the Second Angel on earth, war is an inevitable outcome of the violence and greed of the existing society. The fall of Babylon is predestined. Prophesied in John's visions, the destruction of this glorious, but evil city will occur. However, not only will the city itself fall into ruins again, but the citizens will suffer the outpouring of God's Wrath, primarily ending in death. Throughout the wicked world, there will be plagues, extreme temperatures, earthquakes, and giant hailstones. Nothing and no one will be safe, and like other cities around the world, Babylon will fall, both physically and culturally. It will again become a wasteland and ruins—and great will be its fall. Because of their blindness, all who align themselves with her grandeur and opulence will mourn her loss.

1. In his vision, John sees a glorious being with great authority come down out of heaven.
    a. While this being is described as "an angel," it could actually be Jesus Himself again, considering how He is described as full of glory.
    b. He has been seen as an "angel" before in this vision, so it is not inconceivable (Rev. 14:15).
    c. He illuminates the entire earth.
    d. Only He has the power of judgment that is about to be released on Babylon.
    e. However, this is more likely the Second Horseman released from heaven declaring mighty wars and the Second Angel seen from earth proclaiming the fall of Babylon.
2. In any case, the Being cries *"Fallen, fallen Babylon the great..."* (Rev. 14:8; 18:2) (Is. 21:9) (Jer. 51:8).
    a. Not only the false system of worship falls, but the great city itself.
    b. The Beast himself, in conjunction with the ten kings, actually plays a role in the downfall of the Woman—Babylon—to prove his power (Rev. 17:16-17).
3. Before the destruction of the city, the "angel" calls any of the children of Abraham who reside in this city, to come out before they too suffer the destruction—plagues—that are about to occur (Rev. 18:4).
    a. As a great commercial city, one could expect to find many Jews in this city, so this is not unrealistic.
    b. The time of the Gentiles has been fulfilled, so God again acknowledges His chosen people and attempts to protect them.

4. This was actually foretold in the Old Testament (Jer. 50: 4-9, 51: 6 & 45).
    a. The Euphrates dries up, the crops fail, the shipping is cut off, and there is great famine, death, and mourning.
    b. In the midst of this, a great earthquake takes place, the city burns, and all nations are rocked to their very foundations—both literally and symbolically.
    c. The prophecy of Isaiah 47:1-15 becomes a reality.
    d. Just as Babylon once laid waste to Jerusalem, so _it_ now is brought to destruction again (Jer. 51:24).
5. The great city that attracted the nations of the world to serve her, share in her wealth and power, and exalt her above all is now destroyed, because of her sin and perversion.
    a. Such shall also be the end for all who participate in her ways.
    b. *"The wages of sin is death..."* (Rom. 6:23).
6. The great rulers and merchants of the world, who align themselves with Babylon, mourn her destruction, because of the impact that it has upon them (Rev. 18:11).
    a. Babylon becomes a great consumer of all the riches and commodities of the world, and the loss of that outlet affects every producer, shipper, and accounting house in the world.
    b. Even the laborers of many nations and businesses feel the consequences, as they lose their jobs.
    c. The greediness of the world causes it to weep for Babylon.
    d. It happens so quickly, all who are left are in shock.

After Babylon

As those who are still left on the earth, including the kings of the nations, see that judgment has even befallen the great Babylon, they either tremble in fear or rage in anger. Many of the armies are already on their way to the Valley of Megiddo, and they have to believe that through some supernatural power their mighty Commander—Satan, the Antichrist—will lead them to victory over Jerusalem and the heavenly army. They have been promised great rewards for their allegiance, but based on what has just happened to Babylon, there is a crack of doubt in their armor. The Evil Duo—the Antichrist and False Prophet—must further deceive and manipulate them into believing they will be victorious in the long anticipated battle between good and evil.

1. Even though Babylon, the city and the system, which represented the ultimate in wickedness throughout the ages, is destroyed, there is still evil on the earth.

a. Through all the famine, disasters, and devastation that take place around the world, Israel has been protected from much of it, and still has food and goods not available in the rest of the world.
   b. The rulers of the nations want to move in and take possession of what is there.
2. Using this covetousness, Satan calls all nations to meet in Israel at the Valley of Megiddo, in order to go into battle against Jerusalem.
   a. To get what they want, the kings and rulers of the world allow themselves to be further used by Satan for his purpose.
   b. Satan's objective is to fight against Jesus, and stop Him from taking control of the earth.
   c. The armies of the world assemble to do battle, thinking that, along with Satan, they are actually going to win.
      (1) These armies are made up of kings, generals, and strong men drafted to fight.
      (2) These are not <u>all</u> the unbelievers remaining on the earth.
      (3) Those left, after the war and the final judgments, are those over whom the Saints will rule and reign.
   d. Satan has just destroyed Babylon, which became his rival, and now he believes he can use these armies to wage war on God's elite.

A Time of Praise (Rev. 19:1-6)

While those on the earth mourn and lament the destruction of Babylon, there is great rejoicing in heaven. A great voice shouts to all those before the throne that God is to be praised, because Babylon, the prostitute of the world, has been judged, condemned, and destroyed. The apostles and prophets have been avenged and the score settled for the persecution of the Saints. Never again will people live, love, and enjoy life in that City, as they once did.

This is not the first praise celebration we have seen in heaven. In Rev. 4:11, the Lord was praised for His creation. In Rev. 5:12-13, there was praise over His plan of redemption, and now there is rejoicing in the salvation of God's good over evil. As Judge, He has proven that *"Vengeance is mine; I will repay."* The very center of evil and corruption has been destroyed, and all of God's people rejoice. Along with the twenty-four elders and the four living creatures, the multitudes of heaven—great and small—say, *"Hallelujah, Amen."*

1. At the same time that all of the lamenting over the fall of Babylon takes place on earth, a great celebration takes place in heaven.

      a. The vile system, (philosophy, religion, and center of Satan's kingdom) is destroyed.
      b. At last the faith and testimonies of the saints and prophets of God are fulfilled.
      c. The sorrow of the unsaved world is contrasted with the joy of the faithful in heaven.
2. John hears, coming out of heaven, great multitudes saying, *"Alleluia,"* which means *"Praise Ye Jehweh."*
      a. These are the voices of the angels, the saints, and the martyred—all of God's own.
      b. There is praise and thanksgiving for what has just occurred and for what is yet to come.
      c. In all of the New Testament, this is the only place you see the word *"Alleluia."* In six verses, it appears four times.
      d. The first *"Alleluia"* is because God has provided salvation—victory over the evil forces of Satan.
          (1) Glory is about to be revealed in a new way.
          (2) *"True and righteous are His judgments"* (Rev. 19:1-3).
      e. The second *"Alleluia"* is because the harlot that corrupted the earth throughout the ages has been destroyed.
          (1) Babylon has been removed, and in memorial, smoke will rise forever, as a reminder of its destruction.
          (2) Man must never forget the repulsiveness of Babylon.
      f. The third and fourth *"Alleluias"* are because the reign of Jesus on earth is about to take place.
          (1) The governments of the world have always been corrupt in some ways.
          (2) The New Kingdom of Jesus Christ will be unlike all that have come before.
          (3) This reign was even prophesied and described in the Old Testament (Ps. 72:1-20).
      g. The Elders and Living Ones around the throne lead the rejoicing and bow down in worship.
          (1) As in Chapter 1, they are ever praising God.
          (2) They say *"Alleluia"* because the Lord God Almighty reigneth, and they rejoice in His glory.
          (3) They then add *"Amen,"* meaning *"So be it. It is true and certain"*—a statement of confidence in God's truth.
3. The word *"Alleluia"* is a universal word found in almost every language and is used when God's enemies have been put down or defeated.

  a. There is power in the word, and the use of it in praise causes Satan's power to be weakened.
    (1) God inhabits our praise, and the use of this word adds power to those prayers.
    (2) Satan hates it, for it renders him powerless in God's presence.
    (3) This is why we are told to *"...praise the Lord without ceasing...and...in all things give thanks."* (1 Thess. 5:17-18).
    (4) Even in the worst of circumstances, God has made provision and is sufficient.
  b. To curse and complain about problems is to employ Satan's tools and invoke his presence into our lives.
4. A voice now comes out of the throne telling <u>all</u> of God's servants to praise Him even more—great and small.
  a. It is not clear whose voice this is.
  b. It is most likely the voice of Jesus, however, acknowledging His Father.
5. With that command, there is an even mightier sound of the multitudes saying *"Alleluia,"* because the Lord God Almighty is ready to assume the kingdom and begin His reign.

CHAPTER 22
The Marriage

THE MARRIAGE (REV. 19:7-9)

THE MUCH-AWAITED HIGHLIGHT OF JOHN'S prophetic vision is about to take place—the marriage between Jesus, the Bridegroom, and the Church, the Bride. This is the ultimate reunification ceremony between God and man. *"That which God has united, let no man put asunder"*(Mark 10:9). Predictably, in His all-knowing wisdom, God knew from the beginning of time that man would sin and cease to be perfect. This sin—a disobedient and rebellious acceptance of Satan's temptation to eat of the forbidden fruit in the garden and throughout the ages—would precipitate a separation that man, by his own efforts, could never repair. This separation—man's sin nature—has and will continue to exist until the final battle of good over evil is accomplished. Only the sacrificial Lamb is capable of restoring the union that is broken. The Wedding that John now observes is a formal display of the Bridegroom, as the Lamb, healing that wound for eternity.

Not all who attend the marriage ceremony, however, are a part of the Bride or Groom. Some are honored guests who have been invited and blessed to be chosen worthy of attendance. Because this celebration is planned and given by the Father of the Groom—the Creator Himself—He alone knows who is a part of the Bride and who are friends and witnesses. Our opinion is purely speculation and irrelevant.

THE BRIDEGROOM AND BRIDE (REV. 7:7-9)

Jesus, the Lamb, has been ready for this day for eons. He understands what He has yet to do, and He is ready. The joyous day has arrived. The Bride—those believers who come to Christ between Pentecost and the Rapture, plus the Tribulation Saints—is also ready. Dressed in fine, white linen with no stain or wrinkle, she has been cleansed and made holy—sinless through the sacrifice of her intended, the Lamb. She awaits His arrival, as do the guests who are blessed to be invited to the wedding. As mentioned previously, all in attendance are not merely the Bride and the Groom. Although there is much debate over who is on the guest list, one can be assured that each is honored to be a witness to the marriage ceremony and invited to the feast that follows. It is proposed that the guests are the redeemed of other ages—the patriarchs, the prophets, the Old Testament Saints. They may also be persons who made last-minute decisions, at the fall of Babylon, to acknowledge God and Jesus as Father and Son, or who prepared themselves for the eventuality that all that they had heard was true. Additionally, there are God's chosen people, the Jews, who ultimately accept Jesus as the Messiah. In any case, we know that all who are in attendance are there by invitation and have accepted the request that they join in the celebration.

1. The time for the marriage between Jesus and His Bride has finally come, and she is ready.
2. This is the marriage of the Lamb, not the King.
    a. Because of His love, He sacrificed His life to purchase her—to pay a ransom for her life.
    b. He will reign with her as King, but wed, as the Lamb.
3. The Bridegroom
    a. There is no question but that this is Jesus Christ—Son of God, our Lord and Savior.
    b. It was for His Bride that He died.
    c. In the parable of the Ten Virgins, they wait for the coming of the Bridegroom, and go out with friends to meet Him and welcome Him, when He arrives (Matt. 25:1-13).
        (1) They are not the Bride, but her friends and attendants.
        (2) They seek to be blessed just to accompany Him to the wedding.
        (3) They are a part of the wedding party, but are not the Bride or Groom.
4. The Bride
    a. She already is in heaven awaiting her Bridegroom.
        (1) She is adorned in a fine, white, linen gown—reserved for the Saints.
        (2) She does not have to come in her own garments, but has been given her raiment by the Bridegroom.
        (3) She is clothed in His righteousness.
        (4) All the Bride has to do is say "Yes" to the Bridegroom's proposal.
        (5) He does everything else.
        (6) She is there because of <u>His</u> works, not her own.
            (a) The greatest deception of our time is that we get to heaven by our own works and by being good.

                (b) In actuality, our only responsibility is to accept the Bridegroom—Jesus Christ.
        b. As just mentioned, not all who attend the wedding are the Bride or Groom.
            (1) By this time, all who are true and faithful to the Lord are in heaven, but not all are of the same degree of honor or nearness to their Lord.
            (2) Not all have the exalted position of the Bride.
            (3) Those redeemed in the Old Testament, or who are found ready and watchful at His coming, are guests and witnesses at the marriage, along with any who accept Him as Lord and Savior following the resurrection of the Tribulation Saints.
            (4) They are equally blessed to be present at the wedding feast and to attend, but their rewards are different.
            (5) God decides who shall be crowned and glorified as priests and princes — the elect, the worthy.
            (6) They make up the Bride.
            (7) John says, *"Blessed are they who are called to the... marriage of the Lamb,"* not *"... they who are called to be the Bride"* (Rev.19:9).
                (a) This is the supreme beatitude, for there is no greater blessing.
                (b) Participation in the wedding at all is an honor and makes an individual a member of the wedding party.
                (c) All those present share in the glory of the occasion.
                (d) Not only is everyone there invited, but the King of the Universe honors and serves them.
                (e) This is the greatest blessing.

THE WEDDING AND THE FEAST (REV. 19:9)

It is Jewish tradition that marriages are arranged at birth, and this Wedding is no exception. Because God gave mankind a free will to make choices, He knew from day one that not all would elect to follow His will and plan for their lives. He, therefore, established a plan to save and reward those who do. The marriage ceremony is a part of that reward. Jesus said to His disciples in the Upper Room that He would not eat or drink with them again until the Kingdom of God came, and this is that next meal. The Feast, following the marriage ceremony, reflects the joyous celebration of this occasion. Jesus and His followers are reunited, and the banquet is sweet.

It marks the beginning of an eternity of fellowship, praise, and worship. It is a thanksgiving feast that the pain and suffering of life, in the natural, is over. All who belong to the

Bridegroom are His forever. The banquet is the symbolic culmination of God's restoration of mankind.

1. According to Jewish custom, marriages were arranged for couples—often at birth.
   a. At an appointed time, they become betrothed, and this is a binding agreement.
      (1) The marriage between Jesus and the Church was also arranged from the beginning of time.
      (2) God chose even then who would be the Bride.
      (3) Betrothals were often lengthy, to allow the couple to grow up and give the bride's parents time to accumulate a dowry.
      (4) When the time comes, the bride is taken to the groom, and *his* family throws a huge ceremony and feast to celebrate the marriage.
   b. In the case of the marriage between Christ and His Bride, He loves and wants her so much that He also willingly pays the price of the dowry Himself, which He did on the cross.
2. First, the Bridegroom comes; the marriage takes place, and the feast begins in celebration.
   a. It is catered by the Creator of all things.
   b. There is nothing missing from this marriage feast.
3. With it comes much rejoicing, which John hears.
4. The Bride and Groom are not alone at this feast.
   a. Their guests and attendants are many.
   b. All are there, basking in the redemption for which they hoped and suffered.
   c. At the Last Supper Jesus promised that He would eat with His own again, when the kingdom of God comes (Matt. 26:29) (Luke 22:18).
   d. This is that day.

FELLOW MESSENGER (REV. 19:1-10)

As John observes the glorious celebration and hears the rejoicing of the multitudes at the wedding, he is told by an "angel" that what he sees and hears is real and true. They are greatly blessed to be invited to the wedding supper of the Lamb, and they should respond with shouts of thanksgiving. Unsure about who the angel is, John bows down in worship. The messenger assures him, nevertheless, that he is merely a fellow servant and only God is to be worshipped for this prophecy which is the testimony of Jesus Christ.

1. John is overcome by what he sees and hears, and bows down in worship before the angel who has revealed this to him (Rev. 19:10).
    a. The angel, however, insists that he is but a messenger and fellow brethren.
    b. Only God should be worshipped, not him.
        (1) It is obvious from the scripture that the worship of "saints" is in direct conflict with the Word.
        (2) Any justification to the contrary is in error.
2. Revelation is the testimony of Jesus Christ and the fulfillment of prophecy.
    a. The purpose of that prophecy is to point to Jesus, not to world affairs or speculated future events.
    b. It is the reason for <u>this</u> study in particular.
    c. Any prophecy that does not concentrate on the person of Jesus Christ is in error and misses the point.

RIDER ON A WHITE HORSE (REV. 19:11-16)

The primary purpose of John's prophetic vision is to prepare mankind for the Second Coming of Jesus Christ. During His life on earth as a man, He came to reveal God in all His glory and majesty, to demonstrate God's love and mercy through His own teachings, and serve as the sacrificial payment for man's sin—past, present, and future. As a Lamb without spot or blemish, He became sin and gave His life that we might be saved and have eternal life. Having accomplished that assignment, He returned to heaven and His position as a part of the Godhead. His work is not finished, however. He promised that one day He would return again—this time as Warrior and Judge. Only then would God's plan of redemption and restoration be completed.

Before this can happen, however, we are told that the Church will become the Bride of Christ, and along with the rest of the wedding party, accompany Him when He returns for the second time. He will then wage war against the kings of the earth and their armies, as well as the principalities and powers of darkness, who follow Satan, their Master. This battle will put an end to the conflict between good and evil, once and for all. As His Bride, those who give their lives to and for Him will rule and reign <u>with</u> Him in the New Jerusalem for all eternity.

There is little defensible argument that the rider on the white horse is any other than Jesus Christ Himself. Based on His description, His demeanor, and His actions, what John sees is a conquering hero, who rides into battle and wages a victorious war against the Enemy and his followers. This was what the Jews expected at His first coming. It was not the time, however, and they did not recognize Him as their Messiah. This time He comes as the KING OF KINGS AND LORD OF LORDS. Nevertheless, He does not come merely as the King of the Jews, but the King of the world.

1. When the wedding and feast are over, John sees the heavens open, and a rider on a white horse come forth.
    a. As He returns, He is called by three names:
        (1) Faithful and True (Rev. 19:11)
        (2) Word of God (Rev. 19:13)
        (3) KING OF KINGS AND LORD OF LORDS (Rev. 19:16)
    b. In Rev. 4:1 heaven opens to let the church in; here, heaven opens and Christ rides forth in victory, to judge and make war (Jude 14-15).
        (1) This is why those left on earth will wail and mourn (Rev. 1:7).
        (2) With Him are "...*the armies which are in heaven, clothed in fine linen, white and clean...*" (Rev. 19:14).
        (3) Because the marriage between Christ and His Bride has taken place, and the wedding party ride out of heaven <u>with</u> Him, it is hard to justify a Post-Tribulation Rapture.
        (4) Those still on earth at this point are the unsaved, upon whom He comes to wage war.
    c. Based upon John's description, it is safe to assume that this is Jesus Christ Himself.
        (1) His eyes are full of fire, which represents perfect knowledge.
        (2) On His head are <u>many</u> crowns, signifying complete victory, power, and authority.
            (a) The Dragon had seven crowns, as the possessor of seven great world powers.
            (b) The Beast had ten crowns, as he combines ten sovereignties.
            (c) Jesus now has <u>all</u> of the crowns, and He is not only Judge and General, but also the King Himself.
        (3) He is *"Faithful and True"*—a minister of righteousness.
            (a) In Him is no deceit.
            (b) This is in contrast to the Dragon—the Deceiver/False Christ—and his companion, the False Prophet.
        (4) He comes in righteousness and has authority and sovereignty over everything in heaven and earth.

(5) He wears a robe stained with blood, because He has shed blood both physically and mentally in order to overcome evil.
    (a) This is His blood, as well as that of those He conquers.
    (b) <u>He</u> judges and wages war at this point, not the Saints (Is. 63:1-4).
    (c) <u>He</u> wears the bloody garment that they might have white, spotless robes.
    (d) All that He does is so we might be cleansed and have everlasting life with Him.
(6) Out of His mouth comes a sharp sword (His Word), which strikes down the nations.
    (a) This is the word of wrath and destruction.
    (b) With His mouth, He created the world, and with His mouth, He will destroy it.
    (c) *"His word is quick and powerful and sharper than a two-edged sword"* (Heb. 4:12).
    (d) Men, who will not bow to the Word and receive the Gospel, will be slain by that same Word.
(7) Upon Him is written a name that only He knows (Rev. 19:12).
    (a) We too shall be given a new name that was selected for us before time began.
    (b) Until 'that day' we are given His name (Christian) to identify us.
(8) The white horse portrays a military image and denotes royalty, justice, and righteousness.
(9) He returns to take possession of all that has been lost.
(10) The rider is coming to put down evil and fight both a physical and spiritual, holy war.
(11) He will rule with a rod of iron and tread on evil with the wrath of God Almighty.
(12) This is the culmination of every prophecy and promise of the Bible.

c. <u>His</u> name is the *"Word of God"* (Rev. 19:13).
  (1) All things are made—and destroyed—by Him.
  (2) *"In the beginning..."* and in the end.

d. On His robe and thigh is written, *"KING OF KINGS, AND LORD OF LORDS"* (Rev. 19:16).

e. This is His name, His title, and His authority.
  (1) To pray in His name is imperative, vital, and gives us power.
  (2) Such prayer has the power to change lives and circumstances.

2. Jesus is not alone; however. His Bride and His army follow him into battle.
   a. These are the Saints of all time—the faithful, the Overcomers.
   b. He is coming back <u>with</u> them, so they obviously have had to have gone <u>to</u> Him previously.
   c. It is with them that He shares His authority and rulership for all eternity.

CHAPTER 23

The Battle of Armageddon

THE FINAL CONFLICT (REV. 19: 17-21)

ONE OF THE MAJOR THEMES of the Bible is the conflict between God and Satan, ultimately played out in the conflict between Christ and the Antichrist. At this point, the time of retribution has arrived. Except for the nation of Israel, all that is left on earth is sin and corruption, and it must be eliminated by force. Jesus as King—Warrior and Judge—will carry out that action. The armies of Satan, the Beast, and the False Prophet have been gathered in the Valley of Megiddo for the Battle of Armageddon. As with every corrupt government throughout the ages, they have been deceived into believing that they can be victorious and walk away with the spoils of war. Little do they realize that they are only pawns in Satan's war against the Lord God Almighty—Father and Son. For that reason, they march unknowingly to their deaths.

Surprisingly, there will not be much actual fighting. It will all be over in an instant, through the deliverance of a Word. Jesus is the Word of God, and just as a Word brought the universe and all creation into existence, so shall it be destroyed and made new.

THE FEAST OF THE BIRDS (REV. 19:17-18)

Before the battle begins, however, John sees an angel standing in the sun, who calls together all of the birds of prey of the region to come to another feast. Unlike the one we just saw in heaven, this is not a feast of celebration; it is one of desecration. Those who are about to die will themselves be the supper. The birds will devour the remains of all that have committed and aligned themselves with evil. Such will be the only reward that Satan, the Antichrist, and the False Prophet can deliver. *"The wages of sin is death."*

1. The marriage supper has taken place in heaven, and now another great feast is about to begin on earth.
    a. The first is a time of blessing and joy.

b. The second a time of judgment and sorrow.
2. John sees an angel standing in the sun, who calls together all the birds of the air (Rev.19:17-18).
   a. Much of the earth and its inhabitants have perished during the past seven years.
   b. An exception has been the birds of prey.
   c. They have found much to feed upon and have multiplied and flourished.
   d. They are now about to have their greatest feast, and they come, circle, and wait.
3. The Great Battle is about to commence, and the birds are called to feast upon the fruits of the war.
4. They are poised ready to devour the destroyed bodies of the kings, generals, and mighty men—all the peoples, who do battle with God—great and small.
   a. Even their horses will be food for the flesh-eating birds of the world.
   b. The very bodies of all of those going to war for Satan shall be desecrated.

Christ Returns (Rev. 19:11-16)

The Valley of Megiddo is merely the gathering place for the great armies that come from the east, west, north, and south. Under the control and direction of the Antichrist and the False Prophet, they march into Jerusalem to fight for what they believe will be victory. It, in fact, will be, but not theirs.

At first, the armies seem to be in control—the city captured, homes ransacked, women raped, and half of the population sent into exile. According to God's plan, however, those overcome are not His children in spirit. They are a part of the sinful world. The ones who truly belong to Him are still under His protection. Then the unexpected happens. Jesus, in all of His power and authority, steps down onto the Mount of Olives, speaks a mighty Word, and the battle is over. Lightning flashes, thunder roars, the heavens shake, the earth quakes, and mountains are moved.

The armies are slain, but the Antichrist and the False Prophet, though men, are left standing in their defeat. Unlike the troops that followed them into destruction, the two Commanders will never die. They are seized by Christ and cast into the Lake of Fire.
They will exist in this place forever and never escape. Their judgment is swift and everlasting.

1. As He ascended, Christ now descends to the Mount of Olives, and the battle begins.
   a. When He sets foot upon the Mount, it splits apart under the weight of His glory.

b. He has come to destroy and restore.
   c. The details of this battle are described in Zech. 14:1-21—an Old Testament prophecy.
   d. It marks the beginning of the political regeneration of the earth.
   e. The fulfillment of *"Thy kingdom come...on earth..."* will finally become a reality.
2. With a word, a breath, the war is won (2 Thess. 2:8).
3. The Dragon, the Beast, and the False Prophet are all present, leading their armies into battle.
   a. Despite their seeming power and authority of the past, they and their armies are soon overcome.
   b. Ezek. 28:1-19 tells of the downfall of Satan—*"the King of Tyre"* (Is. 24:21-24).
   c. Is. 14:3-21 also describes Satan and his fall.
      (1) Even the world will see him as no more powerful than they.
      (2) He will be weak and defeated.
   d. The Beast and the False Prophet are thrown alive into the Lake of Fire.
      (1) Some say the Beast is a system—Communism or the New Age Movement.
         (a) Before a system is removed, overcome, or destroyed, however, the <u>persons</u> fostering it must be eliminated.
         (b) The Beast is that <u>person</u>.
      (2) He is a man resurrected from the dead by Satan's power, and cannot be slain.
      (3) The False Prophet deceived men with his miraculous signs and caused men to worship the Beast; his fate is, therefore, the same.
      (4) They alone go <u>alive</u> into the Lake of Fire and brimstone (Rev. 19:20).
   e. With their two leaders gone, the remnant is killed and devoured by the birds.
      (1) Rebellion against God is death.
      (2) Those who will not have Christ over them will perish.
   f. <u>The Battle is over</u>, and Christ and His Bride are victorious.

SATAN BOUND (REV. 20:1-3)

Before life on earth under the demonic influence of Satan can end, however, Jesus Christ must do one more thing. He must bind Satan in such a way that he cannot interfere with the intended restoration of the earth. For God's plan of regeneration to be accomplished, the source of all evil must be restrained from hindering the rebuilding of God's New World. Only Jesus has the power and authority, as well as the keys to the Abyss, to bind the Enemy of God and man in chains. This He does and locks him away for a thousand years. At the end of that period, he will be released *"for a short time."* God still has a mission for him. Just to show that the Evil One's nature does not change, and never will, we will see him attempt to use man for his own purposes, one last time. Again, he will attempt to gather the naive of the world to wage war against God and Jerusalem. Once again, he will be defeated, and this time he will be cast into the Lake of Fire, along with the Antichrist and False Prophet, for all of eternity.

1. After the Great Battle, John sees an "angel" come out of heaven with chains and the key to the Abyss (Rev. 20:1-3).
2. "Hell" has become a rather generic term for that place under the earth, which is the unseen world of evil beings—the dwelling place of Satan and his demons.
   a. The Hebrew of the Old Testament and Greek of the New Testament have somewhat contributed to this—Hades (Greek) = Sheol (Hebrew) = Hell (English)
      (1) Hades/Sheol is not really hell, or a final place of judgment.
         (a) It is a place where the departed (dead) spirits, good and bad, go until the resurrection of Christ.
         (b) Since that day, it is the place where only departed unbelievers go to await their judgment.
      (2) Paradise
         (a) Until Christ's resurrection, Hades was divided into two areas—Paradise and Hades.
         (b) Paradise was that section where the good/believers went.
            i. It is where Abraham and Lazarus, etc. went.
            ii. Jesus went into Paradise with the thief, when they died on the cross.
            iii. He then brought those pious dead out with Him, when He was resurrected.
            iv. At that point, Paradise moved from Hades to heaven.
      (3) The Abyss
         (a) The Abyss might be considered pre-hell.
         (b) It is the place where the demons, and particularly evil persons, are held prisoner until the final judgment.
         (c) It was from this place that the spirit-locusts came at the sounding of the <u>fifth trumpet</u> (Rev. 9:3).
         (d) This is where Satan will be bound for 1,000 years.

(4) "The Lake of Fire" = Hell = Gehena = the Grave
   (a) This place burns with fire and brimstone.
   (b) Into this place, the Beast and False Prophet are thrown alive following the Great Battle.
   (c) It is the place of eternal punishment—the final Hell.
   (d) Satan too will one day be placed there, followed by all of the wicked, after they have been judged.
   b. One of the lies of Satan and the world is that he will be "king" in this place, and all who follow him will be rewarded, both in this life and after.
   (1) In actuality, "hell" was created <u>by God,</u> as a place of eternal punishment <u>for Satan</u> and his followers.
   (2) God is Lord even in hell.
   (3) Satan's punishment will be the greatest of all.
   (4) He has nothing but eternal torment to offer those who do his work and follow him.
3. The angel John sees is most likely Christ Himself, as He alone holds the keys to Death and Hades (*Rev.* 1:18).
4. It also seems reasonable that Christ, against whom Satan wages war, would carry out the act of confining him.
5. The "angel" lays hold of the Dragon—the old serpent, the devil, Satan—binds him in chains, and locks him in the Abyss for a thousand years.
   a. The Dragon has had authority over the earthly sovereignties until this point, but with them gone, he is powerless.
   b. He cannot carry out his evil without the help of earthly followers.
   c. The reference to him as a serpent refers to the fact that he has existed, and been active, since the beginning of human history in the Garden of Eden.
   d. As the devil, he is the liar and slanderer of man—to God and others.
   e. His many names are all aspects of his evil nature.
   f. He has been the accuser and adversary of mankind throughout human history.
   g. He is not bound at this time as punishment, however, but so he cannot deceive the nations for the next thousand years of restoration.
6. God still has further use of him.

PART VI
The Final Events
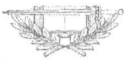

CHAPTER 24
The Millennium

THE PERIOD OF RESTORATION (REV. 20:1-15)

THE CONFLICT OF THE AGES—GOD against Satan, good against evil—is over. Christ is victorious and God's will has been done —"*on earth as it is in heaven.*" Jesus has come to reclaim that which was lost to evil in the Garden of Eden. *"It is finished."* And yet... Christ cannot return the earth to His Father as it was in the beginning. As a consequence of man's response to Satan's bidding and the outpouring of God's wrath upon a wicked world, the earth has been devastated. Cities have been destroyed, the land laid waste, the waters of the rivers and seas polluted, and there are human and animal remains everywhere. The world is anything but beautiful and pristine, as it was created in the beginning. This is not the gift Jesus wishes to present to His Father. Throughout the scriptures, we are told that all things will be made new, but how will that happen—only through time and the efforts of many.

Following the Battle of Armageddon, there will still be nations of people on the earth. Not all die during the period of tribulation and outpouring of God's wrath. We are told that a quarter of the wicked are killed with the opening of the fourth seal and another third at the sound of the sixth trumpet. God alone knows whom to destroy and who should remain—who will be obedient and faithful and who easily led astray. Those left are carefully chosen and have a mighty responsibility ahead. It is their assignment to rebuild a new world. That will take time, energy, and wisdom, as well as guidance and instruction. It is for this purpose that the Saints were saved. It is not man's ultimate destiny to sit on clouds and play harps forever, or even stand before the Throne of God praising Him every moment. Being saved and going to heaven is not about seeing loved ones, understanding all mysteries, and spending eternity in a state of rest and peace.

It is clear that there are many still alive on the earth at this time, and they have faith that a better day is possible—that there is Someone to guide and lead them to it. By God's will and mercy they manage to survive the time of wrath. They are "good" people who have not followed or condoned the wicked ways of the world, but, though they believe there is a God, they simply consider themselves non-religious. For that reason, they have not bothered to make a commitment to Jesus Christ. This is why they are still on the earth and not in heaven, or in the grave. They have somehow managed to avoid being required to decide whether to take the mark of the Beast or not. In any case, they now are open to growing in wisdom and knowledge of the One who has orchestrated all that they have seen and endured. Nevertheless, they do not know where to begin. They sincerely desire to be a part of rebuilding a New World—one that is pleasing to God who saved them for this purpose. The guiding of these people may well be part of what the Saints are destined for—to rule and reign with Christ and act in His behalf.

The process of restoration will take 1000 years. During this time, Jesus and the Saints will live among the people. The entire world will acknowledge God. Jesus will be Lord and He will govern with a rod of iron. Because He is righteous and acts from a position of authority, all will honor Him—this time by choice. Mankind will still have a human nature, however, and not all will make wise choices. Nevertheless, Christ and the Saints will sit on seats of judgment and deal with the issues that can disrupt life in the New World. The swift application of justice, and a requirement that each be held accountable for his or her actions, will reduce the temptation to do wrong. Sin will lessen, but not be totally gone. During this period of reconstruction, Satan, the Father of Evil, Lies, and Deception is put away, so that he is not free to influence mankind to carry out his evil plans. Only under these conditions can *"all things be made new."*

VIEWS OF THE MILLENNIUM

As we have seen, there are differing interpretations of how the Period of Tribulation and the outpouring of God's wrath upon the nations play out. There are also varying views relative to the 1,000-year millennial period—what is its purpose, when does it occur, and who are the participants? In most cases, these views are reflective of personal and/or corporate opinions and agendas. Although they are not salvation issues, it is unfortunate to realize that these differences are divisive, even within the Church. Throughout history, they have actually caused schisms within the Church that have a negative impact on the non-believing world. Why should one accept or believe a particular point of view as truth, if the church body itself does not agree on what the scriptures mean? It is important, therefore, that each individual become knowledgeable and familiar with what the Word actually says. <u>This</u> study is presented for the purpose of facilitating that understanding. The Holy Spirit must then guide one's choice of which interpretation to accept.

1. The period that follows the Second Coming of Jesus Christ is called the Millennium, which in Latin means *"a thousand years."*
   a. The millennial kingdom is the end of the "old" world, as we now know it and the beginning of the "new."
   b. It is a time of restoration and reconstruction.
2. The Pre-millennial View of this period is that there will be an actual 1,000-year reign of Christ on earth preceded and inaugurated by His return.
   a. With Him will be the resurrected Saints, who will reign with Him over the nations.
   b. At the end of the 1,000 years, there will be a second resurrection of those who did not belong to Christ.
   c. This will be followed by the Great White Throne Judgment.
   d. At that point, a new heaven and a new earth will become a reality for eternity.
3. The Dispensational Pre-millennial View also gives great significance to the prophecies of the Old Testament concerning the nation of Israel.
   a. It sees its reemergence today as having relevance for the future of the Church.
   b. This view is also a part of the belief in a Pre-Tribulation Rapture in which Christ comes for His Saints prior to the tribulation, or outpouring of the wrath of God.
4. A Post-millennial View acknowledges a 1,000-year reign of Christ, but it is to come after the millennium.
   a. According to this view, the millennium will be a golden age of a victorious Church.
      (1) In the early Church, the first 1,000 years of Christian history, beginning with the resurrection of Christ, is considered to be the millennium.
      (2) Some believe that it began with the edict of Constantine, when he put an end to the persecution of Christians.
      (3) Others believe that this golden age of the Church began with the expansion of the missionary movement in the 19th Century.
   b. This outlook claims that <u>man</u> will build a kingdom on earth, and when <u>he</u> gets things straightened out, Jesus will come again. (Heaven help us!)
   c. This is the 'Kingdom Now' theology.
   d. Many of the political activists of today are postmillennialists.
5. The Amillennial View contends that the Bible does not teach a literal millennium.
   a. There will be no true 1,000-year reign on earth.
   b. It is all just an allegory—an interesting story.

  c. Everything is interpreted as a symbolic fulfillment of the struggle between good and evil.
  d. It does propose, however, that there is a decisive binding of Satan's powers, for a time.
6. Some believe this all parallels the seven days of creation.
  a. 4,000 years before Christ.
  b. 2,000 years of Christian history.
  c. 1,000 years of Christ's reign.
7. All of these theological differences have caused a great deal of divisiveness between Christians with regard to doctrine.
  a. This is extremely unfortunate, though understandable.
  b. There must, therefore, be some latitude in interpretation, as this is not a salvation issue.

THE THOUSAND YEARS (REV. 20:1-15)

Despite one's view of whether there is a literal period of one thousand years, during which Satan is confined in the great abyss, or what occurs during that period, and who is present, there is consensus that, following the defeat of the Devil and his armies, there will be a time of restoration, peace, and order. During this period, Jesus will literally come down from heaven and rule the entire earth, along with the Saints, from the city of Jerusalem in Israel. A new government will be established and *"the government will be upon His shoulders."* He and the Saints will guide those remaining to rebuild a world that operates justly, honors God, obeys Christ, and lives according to God's will and commandments. There will be no other kings and no other religions. He and He alone will be the KING OF KINGS AND LORD OF LORDS. Everyone will know and serve Him, and He will have dominion over all. It will be a period of renewed peace and joy. There will be no more war or conflicts between men or beasts. After all that the people have gone through, they will rejoice in this new world, as it is restored to a renewed environment and society. Life will not yet be perfect—that day is still to come—but it will be approaching it. All that preceded is for the purpose of fulfilling God's perfect plan—a plan that only demonstrates His great love for us.

1. "A thousand years" is said six times in the Book of Revelation (Rev. 20:1-6)
  a. Though a day is *"...as a thousand years"* to the Lord, it is not likely that only one day is meant in this case (2 Pet. 3:8).
    (1) We do not believe Christ was in the grave for 3,000 years.

(2) Why should we believe 1,000 years is one day in this situation?
(3) What would be the purpose of imprisoning Satan for one day?
    b. There is work to be done, and Satan must be put out of the way in order to allow it to be accomplished.
2. Time is nothing to God, but it does not mean that, if He gives you a specific time, you should expect it to mean whatever *you* wish.
3. This period is a time of restoration.
    a. During the Tribulation, there is much destruction on the earth.
        (1) The plagues, the earthquakes, the hail and fire, and the great battles that take place destroy great numbers of people and the works of man.
        (2) There are still people, however, remaining in the world, who must readjust to the times.
        (3) It will take those who are left seven months to merely bury the dead (Ezek. 39:12).
    b. Because many men perish during the prior seven years, the population of the earth will be greatly diminished, and there will be seven women to every man (Is. 4:1).
        (1) They will help to rebuild and repopulate the earth.
        (2) People will live longer and be fruitful.
        (3) It is God's plan that there always be people on the earth.
        (4) Why would He go to such great pains to create and carry out His plans, if it was His intent to destroy it all again at some point?
        (5) The Word even says, "Unto Him be glory…throughout *all* ages, world *without end*" (Eph. 3:22).
    c. While there will still be death, as in the beginning, people will live much longer lives (Is. 65:17-25) (Zech. 8:1-23).
        (1) They will die of natural causes, not because of sin.
        (2) Death will merely be a natural consequence of a long life.
    d. This will be a time of perfect government.
        (1) Under the guidance and direction of Jesus Christ, the restoration of a new and perfected earth will begin.
        (2) There will be true justice under the rule of Jesus and the Saints.
            (a) It will not be temporary.
            (b) It will increase and last forever (Is. 9:7).
        (3) Peace will be restored—peace between men and with nature.
        (4) Because man is not perfect, however, problems and disputes will arise, but they will be dealt with swiftly and justly.

Thrones of Judgment (Rev. 20:4)

As mentioned earlier, whenever we are told *"and then John saw...,"* it indicates that he is shown a new vision or new scene. Like Jesus, the Saints come alive to return to earth to live amongst those who survived the Tribulation. In their glorified bodies, they assist Christ, as promised, in the ruling and judging of the nations. This explains why John sees multiple thrones and those who sit upon them. We are told that they are given the authority to judge. He also sees those who were beheaded, or martyred, for not taking the mark of the Beast in order to save their lives. Theological analyses of this group vary significantly, and in some cases are extremely complex. The bottom line, however, is that repeatedly, the Saints—whether those Raptured or Tribulation Saints—are promised that they, along with Christ, will rule and reign over the nations. It is their reward for faithfulness, to join in the judgment, guidance, and direction of the nations, as the world is restored. What John sees is further evidence that the scriptures are honest and true.

Very likely, not all Saints will have the same level of responsibility during the millennium. The reason being that some of them will be spirit-filled, long-term Christians, who gave their entire lives in the service of Christ, while others may be brand-new Christians that know little about the Word or the teachings of Christ. They too will require some guidance and instruction in order to grow into their promised positions. Additionally, there may even be individuals who lived wicked lives, but repented and turned to Christ just before their demise. In any case, many, including Saints, will need significant shepherding and tutelage. This must fall to someone, so, in addition to ruling and reigning over the nations, the Saints may also be assigned to educate and nurture new citizens of the kingdom. For that reason, ruling and reigning will entail judging, governing, teaching, guiding, counseling, demonstrating, disciplining, etc. Obviously, we must not spiritualize that life in the hereafter will be merely a restful vacation.

1. John sees these thrones upon which are seated those who have been given the authority to judge.
    a. He also sees ones martyred for holding fast to their faith during the tribulation.
        (1) It is not clear if there are two groups being described here, or whether the individuals are simply doing different things.
        (2) If there are two groups, the Raptured Saints seem to be sitting on the thrones of judgment, while the Tribulation Saints (those saved after the Rapture) are ruling and reigning.
        (3) There were many prophecies in the scriptures that the Overcomers would receive these rewards (Dan. 7:18, 22) (1 Cor. 6:1-3).

b. John does not see just one throne for the conquering King, but <u>thrones,</u> for all those who share in His authority (Rev. 20:4).
c. The time has come for Jesus to rule and reign on earth along with those who were repeatedly promised this position—the redeemed.
   (1) This is why the thrones are not empty.
   (2) "They (the Overcomers) sit upon them," in His company (Rev. 20:4).
      (a) Though all the evidence points to the fact that these are the true and faithful followers of Christ—those who have overcome through the ages—there again is not total agreement.
      (b) Other interpretations theorize that these merely represent:
      Souls of martyrs
      Principles of the martyrs
      Christianity as an institution
      The Gospel over the nations, etc.
d. During the great Battle of Armageddon, not all on the earth are slain.
   (1) It is the kings and generals, with their armies, that go into battle that are destroyed in the war.
   (2) Unless the nations of people over whom they ruled died in the outpouring of God's wrath, they still exist.
   (3) God determines who each will be.
e. The Conqueror now must guide those remaining into a new and better world order.
   (1) It is said of the Rider on the White Horse that *"He will rule and shepardize with an iron rod"* (Ps. 2:9) (Rev. 12:5; 19:15).
   (2) This does not mean slaying them, but helping, guiding, and directing them into a better life according to God's plan.
   (3) What we see is a Good Shepherd, as He uses His staff to guide, direct, protect, and pull back wayward lambs.
   (4) This is a time of preservation and reconstruction rather than destruction.
   (5) First was the striking down of the enemy with the two-edged sword, then comes the shepherding with a strong arm and iron rod.
   (6) It is obvious that it will take much work and great effort to restore order where there has been chaos.
f. Despite the fact that the Unholy Trinity has been removed, there will still be sin and death in the world, because, as mentioned before, man is flawed.
   (1) He is not perfect, and his flesh alone will cause him to sin.
   (2) God created man with a free will, and he often chooses un-Godly ways.
   (3) Both sin and death will diminish greatly, however.

g. There will also be a new government established during the millennium.
   (1) Sin will be dealt with swiftly, and sentencing will be immediate.
   (2) Man will be obliged to obey the law or pay the consequences, which will be harsh.
   (3) The innocent will be avenged in the present, not the future.
   (4) The Saints will share in this judgment process.
h. In Rev. 2:26-27, Overcomers are told that they shall be given *"authority over the nations to shepard them..."*
i. Not only are the Saints, as a body, given this dominion, but particular mention is made of those who were martyred for not worshipping the Beast.
   (1) Better than anyone else, they understand that wrongs can be righted.
   (2) They experienced forgiveness first hand and will be credible encouragers to any other sinners.
j. We now have the beginning of a perfect government on earth for the first time, since the downfall of Adam and Eve.
   (1) Everything will be lawful, quick, and just.
   (2) There will be no death for these thousand years except for transgression, disobedience, or natural causes.
   (3) This will be a step toward the perfect days still to come.
   (4) It is the period of regeneration.

CHAPTER 25

The Judgments

THE JUDGMENTS

THE DAY OF JUDGMENT IS at hand. In fact, there are three judgments—the Judgment of the Saints, the Judgment of the Nations, and the Great White Throne Judgment. In John's visions, the Judgment of the Saints has already occurred. We are told of this in Rev. 12:7-12, when Satan engages in a spiritual war with Gabriel and the forces of heaven. He accuses mankind of every sin he or she ever committed since Adam and Eve, and argues that they are not worthy of God's acceptance as His children. Nevertheless, he is defeated by the fact that man is not judged by his own righteousness, but by the righteousness of Jesus Christ.

The second judgment—the Judgment of the Nations—comes at the beginning of the millennium and judges those <u>still living</u> who refuse the gift of salvation offered by Jesus Christ. The third judgment—the Great White Throne Judgment—takes place at the end of the thousand years and judges the <u>unsaved dead</u>. These are the wicked, or people who never responded to God's offer of salvation, thus remaining in the grave throughout the Rapture, the tribulation, and the thousand years. God alone, who makes judgments based on His love, mercy, and demand for justice, decrees their reward or punishment.

JUDGMENT OF THE SAINTS (REV. 12:10)

As we have seen previously in Rev. 12:10, the Judgment of the Saints has already taken place. Just before the Rapture, in an attempt to prevent it from happening, Satan goes into heaven to accuse the brethren of every sin man has ever committed. It is his intent to show that even the most devout followers of Christ are not worthy of the position and rewards promised to them. He is convinced that nothing can out-trump his arguments that man is a sinner and does not deserve God's mercy. Nevertheless, he is defeated because he forgets that Jesus has already paid the price for our redemption, and we are not judged based on our own deeds, but by the righteousness of our Savior. Therefore, Satan loses the debate—the War in Heaven—and is further cast down onto the earth. So ends the Judgment of the Saints.

1. We see that in Revelation, we are told of <u>three judgments</u> and two resurrections.
2. In Rev. 12:10, Satan accuses the saints, before God, of being sinful and unworthy of the promises made concerning them. This is the <u>First Judgment</u>—the Judgment of the Saints.
    a. Throughout history Satan keeps track of all our sins and misdeeds and uses them as a defense against any arguments made on our behalf.
    b. God's plan is perfect, however, and, as believers, we are not judged for our unrighteousness, but for the righteousness of Jesus Christ.
    c. Deeds are not an issue at this judgment.
    d. We are given the opportunity throughout our life to choose to be judged either by our own works or by the shed blood of Jesus Christ.
    e. This judgment takes place just before the Rapture and again at the collecting of the souls of the martyred saints under the altar (John 5:24-25).
        (1) The Judgment of the Saints precipitates the First Resurrection, at which point they are physically raised and granted eternal life (Dan. 12:2) (John 5:28-29).
        (2) Both the *"living and dead in Christ"* are judged by God and found worthy, because of their testimony and the price paid by the blood of the Lamb.
        (3) They are determined to be deserving to be the Bride and to rule and reign with Christ throughout eternity.
        (4) As a result of the First Judgment—the War in Heaven—Satan is proven a liar and is hurled from the air to the earth, where his days of power and authority are numbered and further diminished.

JUDGMENT OF THE NATIONS (MATT. 25:31-33)

The second of the judgments—that Judgment of the Nations—is actually foretold in Matt. 25:31–33. It is a judgment of those remaining on the earth following the Battle of Armageddon. Those still living are described as the "sheep" and the "goats." Because most of the "goats" are no doubt Gentiles who reject God and give their allegiance to the Beast, this is sometimes called the Judgment of the Gentiles. They are willing to take the mark of the Beast and join in the torment of those being martyred.

The "sheep" on the other hand are people who help and even comfort those persecuted by the Antichrist and his forces. They do not take the mark of the Beast, but, by either neglect or lack of opportunity, they do not make a profession of faith either. For this reason, they are not allowed to go to heaven, but <u>will</u> *"inherit the kingdom prepared from the foundation of the world"* (Matt. 25:46). They also will ultimately be assured eternal life.

1. As described in 1 Cor. 6:2, the <u>Second Judgment</u>, which takes place at the <u>beginning</u> of the millennium following the Great Battle of Armageddon, judges those still alive on the earth, for their deeds (Joel 3:12).
    a. This will be the Judgment of the Nations, or Gentiles, who refused to accept salvation, thus were followers of the Beast, but somehow survived the plagues of the tribulation.
        (1) Some—the goats—actively persecuted the believers and denied them any help.
        (2) Others—the sheep—were more compassionate and offered aid to the persecuted.
    b. This judgment, described in Matt. 25:31-33, is referred to as the *"sheep and the goats judgment."*
    c. It is based upon *"How did you treat my brethren,"* and nothing more (Matt 25:31-46) (Mark 9:41).
2. Those who did not accept Jesus as their Savior, but lived "good" lives and ministered to their fellowmen are now granted life in the New Earth and ultimately, eternal life, under the rulership of Jesus and the Saints.
    a. These are not the saved, or a part of the Bride, but those who are rewarded, as a result of God's infinite mercy.
    b. Salvation is only granted, before the Rapture or the collecting of those under the altar, to those who confess Christ as their Lord and Savior.
    c. Eternal life, however, is given to everyone—either on earth or in hell—for not living an evil life or for supporting the ways of the Devil.
3. Those who expressly reject Christ, and act as an agent of the Beast, are now condemned to spend eternity in hell—aware of, but separated from, God and Christ.
    a. A full knowledge of what they have done is a part of their punishment.
    b. They will go through everlasting condemnation for their own choices.

CHAPTER 26

After the Thousand Years

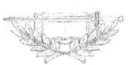

SATAN'S DOOM (REV. 20: 1-3, 7-10)

BY THE END OF THE thousand years, the earth will again be like new. The environment will be renewed. There will be peace with little or no crime or wars. Prosperity will abound and all will feel safe and secure. Most importantly, however, everyone will know Jesus Christ. Although external temptation to sin has been removed, man will, nevertheless, still struggle with his own human nature. God never removes free will. For that reason, there will continue to be some on the earth who are rebellious by nature and reject the favors of life, including Christ. This is either based on ignorance of what occurred prior to the millennium, or due to an innate defiance of guidance and direction. They are the ones who will be open to rebelling against God should the opportunity arise. That opportunity is provided.

Satan is again set free, but does not escape from the abyss on his own. He is purposely released to do what he does best—to deceive. The thousand years in captivity does not change either his nature or his purpose. Upon being let loose *"for a short time,"* he again entices the discontent, the rebellious, and the disobedient, from around the world, to follow him into battle against the earthly city of Jerusalem. This will be a test of the loyalty and devotion of the nations. Through the manipulation of his pawns, Gog and Magog, Satan again attempts to wage a war against God's people. Once more God grants mankind the freedom to choose whom to follow—Jesus Christ or Satan. The rebellion does not last long, however. God's mercy reaches its limit. Fire comes down from heaven, wipes out the armies, and Satan is thrown into the Lake of Fire, along with the Beast and the False Prophet. There they will be tormented *"for ever and ever."* He, who deceived the angels and mankind alike, in actuality, only deceived himself.

1. At the end of the thousand years, Satan is released from imprisonment in the Abyss *"for a little while."*

    a. John says in Rev. 20:3 that, *"he must be released for a short time."*
        (1) During the thousand years, the world is restored to its original condition, without the interference of Satan.
        (2) Upon his release, however, he expends his last moments of freedom to again deceive the nations and seduce many into rebellion against Christ.
        (3) This is to demonstrate his unchanging nature and man's continued vulnerability to his lies and sin.
    b. This time, Satan does not go to "kings," because there are no mortal kings left.
        (1) He goes directly to the people and attempts to persuade them to overthrow the government of the King of Kings.
            (a) These peoples are called Gog and Magog, but it is not truly clear who they are.
            (b) They may or may not be the Gog and Magog mentioned in Ezek. 37:1-14.
            (c) They are, however, more easily seduced, because they had less involvement in the first rebellion.
            (d) They did not have the same awareness of, or suffer the same level of impact, of the Great Battle of Armageddon.
        (2) It is, therefore, easier for Satan to convince them that they can be successful, just as he did as the Antichrist.
    c. These armies of the deceived again enter the holy land and surround the citadel of the city God loves—Jerusalem.
        (1) Nevertheless, it is a useless act.
        (2) Fire comes down from heaven, and they are totally annihilated.
        (3) All those left on the earth now acknowledge Jesus as their one and only Lord and Master.
    d. Satan, the Deceiver, is *"cast into the lake of fire and brimstone,"* along with the Beast and the False Prophet (Rev. 20:10).
        (1) This is the *"everlasting fire, prepared for the Devil and his angels"* (Matt. 25:41).
        (2) It is their eternal reward.
2. Thus ends the last rebellion to be seen upon this planet.
    a. It marks the last sin and the last deaths.
    b. The earth has been restored to near perfection.
    c. Its ultimate state of utopia will now be achieved in the New Heavens and New Earth.

THE GREAT WHITE THRONE (REV. 20: 11-15)

What John now sees is fearsome to behold—a Great White Throne upon which Jesus, under the authority of the Three-in-One, sits in judgment of the wicked dead. Unlike the judgment, which took place earlier, when the "dead in Christ" were judged, there is no evidence of a rainbow of hope around this throne. That was in heaven. This is in some unknown place and is dazzling white in its glory. The condemned that stand before it have nowhere to hide. The sea, the graves, and Hades give up their dead—the unsaved and wicked who rejected God and His Word throughout history. This is the <u>second resurrection</u>—the "resurrection of damnation," as well as the final judgment (John 5:29).

In order to make His judgments, He who sits on the great throne opens two books. *The Book of Life,* which holds the names and deeds of every soul who has ever lived, and *The Lamb's Book of Life* that contains only the names of those who accept the gift of salvation. They committed to obedience and faithfulness to God and His Son, thus making up the multitudes from every nation and tongue that will spend eternity in the New Heaven and New Earth.

Those found guilty at this judgment are cast directly into the Lake of Fire. At this time, the body and soul are brought together in bodies that cannot be destroyed. They will last an eternity, in order to endure the everlasting punishment of fire and brimstone, as well as separation from what could have been. This is the <u>second death</u>. Mankind is promised a destiny of either heaven or hell, based upon his or her own freewill choices in this life.

1. The Great White Throne is the <u>Third Judgment</u>.
    a. At the end of the millennium, Jesus is able to tell God that all has been restored.
        (1) As prophesied, He returns a near perfect world to God, His Father (1 Cor. 15:24-29).
        (2) All that is left is the destruction of death.
    b. Now comes <u>the judgment of the unsaved dead</u>, who slept through the Rapture, the tribulation, and the 1,000 years.
        (1) The sea, the grave, and Hades give up their dead to be judged for their deeds.
        (2) Those who did not hear <u>His</u> voice remained until this day, and they now stand before the throne to have their place in eternity decided.
    c. Even the good, the fair, the honest, but the unredeemed, stand on their own merit to have their place in eternity decided.
    d. Satan opposed the Judgment of the Saints and condemned them for their works, because he did not want them to be found worthy of the rewards God had in store for them.

(1) He does <u>not</u> speak out in condemnation, or on anyone's behalf, at this judgment.
(2) He does not care about the lost. They have never been a threat to him.
(3) He knows those being judged at this time are already condemned by their own works.
2. This judgment is carried out by Jesus, on behalf of God.
   a. John sees Him who sits upon the great throne—the eternal Godhead.
   b. It is He whom we first saw in the throne room in heaven (Rev. 4:2-6).
   c. He, as the Father, the Son, and the Holy Spirit, does the judging at this point.
   d. His presence is so awesome that the very earth shrinks back from it.
3. The <u>second resurrection</u> now occurs (Dan. 12:2) (John 5:28-29).
   a. All, throughout history, who have remained dead, are now resurrected to come forth to stand before the throne of judgment.
   b. They are the ones who chose not to accept the redeeming grace of salvation during life, and are now about to be judged according to their own works.
      (1) These sinners, great and small, now await their punishment.
      (2) It is such choices and sin that will separate the sinner from God for eternity.
   c. Those who have sinned grievously, who knew what was right but did not do it, who knew of Christ and yet denied Him, are judged more harshly than those who simply did not know Him (Luke 12:47-48) (John 12:46-49).
4. Two books are opened in order to make these judgments (Rev. 20:12).
   a. *The Book of Life* includes the names of everyone throughout the history of mankind, who has ever lived.
      (1) The only way one's name can be blotted from it is to <u>choose</u> to sin against God and man (Ex. 32:33).
      (2) God is merciful and He gave us a free will, so our eternal destiny is in our own hands.
   b. *The Lamb's Book of Life* holds only the names of those who accept Christ as their Lord and Savior.
      (1) These were chosen by God—from the foundation of the earth—to inherit the kingdom.
      (2) They chose the redeeming grace of God and became the saved, not because it was pre-ordained or inevitable, but because God <u>knew</u> they would.
      (3) They wear the mark of Christ, are the Bride, and are sealed by Him.
      (4) Those, whose names are in this book, are judged according to Christ's deeds and His righteousness, not their own.

(5) No matter how virtuous one's life may have been, his/her name is not in the *Lamb's Book of Life*, if he or she chose not to accept Jesus as Lord.
5. God is a merciful God, however, and those who tried to "be good," but were unsaved, can never be a part of the Bride, but they may be spared eternity in the Lake of Fire.
   a. If God so decides, they could become a part of the Nations that will live on this earth and over whom the Saints will rule.
   b. Again, man's own actions and choices determine his destiny.
6. As are those who die without Christ, Death and Hades are thrown into the Lake of Fire in the company of the Unholy Trinity.
   a. This is the <u>Second Death</u> (Rev. 20:14).
      (1) The Lake of Fire and the Second Death are synonymous.
      (2) The Second Death is a spiritual death, as opposed to the first, which is physical.
         (a) Those who are born once shall die twice.
         (b) Those who are born twice shall die but once.
      (3) This is not annihilation, but an eternal, unending existence separated from God.
   b. The last enemy has now been eliminated—Death (Is. 25:8).

Punishment or Rewards

As God, Jesus came from heaven. As man, He lived on earth. As sin, He descended into hell. There is nothing He does not know. So who better should determine our final punishment or rewards. Before His death, He told His disciples that He would go to make a place for them. Having experienced both heaven and hell, He knows which outcomes will be most appropriate for every soul that ever lives. He will make His judgment from a position of love and righteousness. There will be no justifiable arguments about His decisions and no one to make them. His Word is the "*first and the last.*"

1. The entire theme of the Book of Revelation is that ultimately, all are responsible to their Creator.
   a. All will stand before Him, at some point, to answer for their decisions and works.
   b. Mercifully, judgment will be swift and just, because God sees and knows all.
2. Because God is merciful, there is a gradation in punishment as well as in rewards.

      a. While one's good works alone are not enough to save one from going to the same place as the worst sinner, the level of punishment does differ.
      b. The mildest hell is still hell.
3. Even those who are God's own, who spend eternity with Him, are rewarded differently relative to their works.
      a. Crowns, positions, and authority are given accordingly.
      b. Christ's righteousness, however, provides everlasting life, and that is what counts.
4. We must consider whether our own goodness and good deeds merit us reward or punishment.
      a. All will receive exactly what their works deserve, unless they accept the salvation offered by Jesus Christ.
      b. It is not enough to just "be a good person."
5. If we stand upon the righteousness of Jesus Christ and receive judgment according to virtue, how will we each fair?
      a. Eternity is at stake.
      b. Is it worth taking a chance?
6. The execution of the White Throne Judgment is immediate.
      a. The condemned are hurled into the Lake of Fire.
      b. What this place is, is not known, but it is a place of everlasting woe, pain, suffering, chaos, and confusion.
      c. It is eternity without God, or any of His blessings.
7. Our choices are ours to make.

CHAPTER 27
All Things Made New

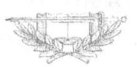

THE NEW HEAVENS AND NEW EARTH (REV. 21: 1-27)

IF WE LOOK BACK OVER history since God's creation of the universe and mankind, it is enlightening to note just how grossly we have failed to wisely manage the opportunities and experiences of this life that were so lovingly given to us. The state of the world and its condition today is definitely evidence that we have made some exceedingly serious mistakes and often used very poor judgment. Consequently, it is not unreasonable to reach a possible, hypothetical conclusion. What if this has been merely a stage and dress rehearsal for another life—a new life—a life that is not corrupted by sin or human frailties? What if the trials and tribulations we face are God's way of teaching us how to overcome our own human natures and the temptations of the world and Satan? He created us with free will, and because He knew we would often make bad choices, stumble and fall, He provided an opportunity for us to grow and mature in wisdom and knowledge, in order to do it better another time. (This is not referring to reincarnation.) In God's infinite love, He wants us to learn to seek Him when times are difficult, or we make bad choices and act out. It is His desire that we understand that. If we will but repent for our rebellious and sinful ways, He is faithful to forgive, and we can still receive the gift of salvation and eternal life. That "new life" is exactly what we have been promised—a life in the New Heavens and New Earth. There we can live in the presence of God the Father and God the Son, for all time.

It may be purely speculative thinking, but it seems that perhaps what John has recounted is that this time of preparation or probation—the period of generation, destruction, and regeneration—passes and "is finished." All who choose to be saved are judged worthy of spending eternity with the Three-in-One. A repentant Jewish nation accepts Jesus as their Messiah and is given their promised land "forever." Sin is removed from the earth, the wicked judged and sent to their eternal punishment. God's plan is fulfilled, and He then reveals the New Heavens and New Earth—all for a perfected mankind. That which God intends, shall be so.

1. John finally sees this "new heavens and a new earth" (Rev. 21:1) (Is. 65:17).
   a. Many in today's society argue that after the millennium the earth ultimately comes to an end.
   b. God consumes the heavens and the earth in fire. <u>Everything</u> is burned up (2 Pet. 3:10-12).
      (1) There is no recorded cataclysmic event that occurs between the 20th and 21st chapters of Revelation, however, that says anything about the <u>earth</u> being destroyed by fire or any other means.
      (2) This is another attempt to interpret the Bible to fit man's belief.
   c. Nevertheless, if one reads on, this is not how the story ends.
   d. There will be <u>new</u> heavens and a <u>new</u> earth <u>afterwards</u> (2 Pet. 3:13).
   e. The old shall merely pass away.
      (1) It is not destroyed in the sense of being annihilated, but it is made new.
         (a) The Greek word *luo* actually means, "dissolved, changed, or loosed."
         (b) All is not gone; it is just made different.
         (c) It is loosed from the bondage of sin and changed from its degenerated state.
      (2) The earth and mankind are returned to their original state of perfection.
      (3) When loved ones pass away, they merely pass into a new realm, as does the old world.
      (4) What is generated, at the beginning of time, degenerated, but is now regenerated.
      (5) This is the result of God's plan of redemption for all things defiled by Satan and sin.
      (6) The earth is cleansed, and the last are judged in the Great White Throne Judgment.
      (7) For a thousand years, Christ and the Saints, along with those remaining on the earth, work at this restoration.
      (8) The heavens and earth are restored, and there now may be <u>a new beginning</u>.
   f. Not only does the Word say this, but it is unbelievable that God would go to such lengths to restore His original, perfect creation and then destroy it completely afterwards.
      (1) The earth is the site of God's greatest creation.
      (2) It is where Jesus lived and died for man's redemption.
      (3) It is the site of the greatest war of all time between the powers of good and evil.

(4) Would God care so little about a people and place He put so much into, just to destroy them yet again?
g. The teaching of Revelation is that *"one generation passeth away, and another generation cometh, but the earth abideth <u>forever</u>"* (Eccl. 1:4) (Eph. 3:21).
   (1) We are told that *"the meek shall inherit the earth,"* and *"the righteous will inherit the land and dwell in it <u>forever</u>"* (Ps. 37:9, 29).
      (a) For this to happen, the earth must continue to exist in some form.
      (b) Christ and His Bride are to reign <u>forever</u>, and that is not possible if the land and peoples over whom they are to reign are gone.
h. The nations, who dwell on the New Earth, will be made up of several types of people, as mentioned previously.
   (1) The blessed, but not the first-born—those who were friends of the Bride—shall live on the earth.
      (a) They too have been redeemed and made new.
      (b) They live in joy and peace, as in the Garden of Eden.
      (c) The nations on earth shall *"build houses and inhabit them,"* as well as increase without end.
   (2) This is also true for the nation of Israel—the kingdom of David, which is an everlasting kingdom.

"They shall dwell in the land that I have given unto Jacob my servant, wherein your fathers have dwelt; and they shall dwell therein, even they and their children, and their children's children <u>forever</u>; and my servant David shall be their prince <u>forever</u>" (Ezek. 37:5).

"But Israel shall be saved in the Lord with an everlasting salvation; ye shall not be ashamed nor confounded <u>world without end</u>" (Is. 45:17).

"And He shall reign over the house of Jacob <u>forever</u>, and <u>of His kingdom</u> <u>there shall be no end</u>." (Luke 1:33).

   (3) If God's word is Truth, then it is not just truth when it is convenient.
2. Satan's intent since the Garden of Eden was to destroy mankind as a race and take dominion over the earth.
   a. If, in fact, man ceases to exist and no earth remains, then, to an extent, Satan is victorious.
   b. He causes a situation that requires God to destroy His own creation.
   c. Satan is not that powerful.
3. Since before the foundation of the earth, for everything that Satan attempts to do to man and the earth, God has a better plan,
   a. Jesus, as God, was called Wonderful Counselor.

            (1) This is the extraordinary, marvelous "planner"—the Creator (Is. 9:6).
            (2) All things are created by Him, and <u>nothing</u> shall defeat His plan.
            (3) Before creation began, He wrote our names in the palm of His hand (Is. 49:16).
            (4) We are *"the apple of His eye,"* and He wants us to desire His best.
        b. God even created Lucifer, who was beautiful—the bearer of light, and the closest of all created beings to the throne—before man.
        c. He intended from the beginning that His Son should not be alone, however, and should have a Bride.
            (1) Since mankind was also a created being, he or she was lower than the Son, and automatically unworthy to be His Bride.
            (2) Lucifer did not realize that, however, and when he learned that man would take a place higher than his, he became angry and began to formulate his own plan.
            (3) Because of his pride and rebellion against God's will, he, along with a third of the angels who joined him, were cast out of heaven.
        d. God, however, already had <u>His</u> plan.
            (1) He gave man a free will and the capacity to choose to acknowledge his lowliness, and thus be changed into the likeness of God—to accept the redemptive power of Jesus Christ.
            (2) Man was created with a strength and character to overcome the efforts of Satan to defile him.
            (3) Every time we overcome the temptations and persecution of Satan, remain faithful and true to God and His Son, we become more worthy to be the Bride that God intended us to be.
        e. God's plan is perfect and will not be defeated.
    4. John says that as he looked at the new earth and the new heavens, he saw no seas (Rev. 21:1).
        a. The sea is mentioned separately in the creation (Gen. 1:6-10); it is also mentioned separately here.
        b. With the shaking of the earth by the last mighty earthquake, the mountains and the valleys were flattened, the earth righted on its axis, and the all-consuming fire that spread across the earth caused the waters of the oceans to evaporate (Rev. 16:18-20).
        c. The result is that the polluted seas are gone, just as the polluted atmosphere is gone.

d. As in the beginning before the Flood, however, there are pure waters in the heavens above the earth and in the subterranean depths of the earth (Gen. 7:11) (Job 38:8).
   e. The lakes, rivers, and springs, which do remain, provide the world with all the water it will ever need to survive and prosper.
   f. There are just no longer any great bodies of useless space occupied by water.
5. The thousand years is now over.
   a. Jesus and His Bride have completed their task of overseeing the restoration of the world.
      (1) All <u>new</u> things have not been created; "*all things have been made new*" (Rev. 21:5).
      (2) God Himself says this is trustworthy and true, and "*It is finished*" (Rev. 21:5-6).
         (a) This is the third time we hear "*It is finished.*"
         (b) Jesus said it as He gave up His life on the cross (John 19:30).
         (c) As the last bowl of wrath is poured out upon the earth, it is shouted from the throne in heaven (Rev. 16:17).
         (d) And as the restoration of the earth and mankind is completed, God says it yet again (Rev. 21:5).
         (e) As we have seen before, the Jewish method of expression is to repeat something two or three times for emphasis—"*Verily, verily...,*" "*Woe! Woe! Woe!*"
         (f) He leaves nothing undone.
         (g) Once more, He says, "*He is the Alpha and Omega—the beginning and the end*" —again three times (Rev. 1:8; 21:6; 22:13).
         (h) In each case, His plan is victorious over Satan's plan of destruction.
   b. Jesus turns God's restored gift back over to Him.
   c. And the Saints are about to receive their final promise (Rev. 2:7; 21:7).
      (1) As Overcomers, they are to inherit all that God has promised—rest, peace, joy, and life everlasting, with God the Father.
      (2) He shall live with them forever and be their God, and they His sons.

THE NEW JERUSALEM (REV. 21:2-27)

John is now shown the most spectacular vision of all. The heavens have been made new, and he sees a glorious city come down out of heaven and settle above the earth. He is told by a loud voice that this is the New Jerusalem—that place which Jesus told His disciples

He would go to prepare for them. This magnificent city is the new dwelling place of God, where He and His Son will live forever with the Saints. What John sees is the *"city of the living God,"* where He will again walk and talk daily with His own—just as He did in the Garden of Eden. Christ has created this perfect dwelling place for a perfected mankind.

This New Jerusalem is magnificent in size and description. There is no more death, or pain, or sorrow, and God Himself wipes away all tears. Here is the new life that we are promised to inherit, if we will but love the Lord and persevere in His name. This is a holy place and all that dwell within it are holy. There is no need for a temple, because God and Christ are everywhere among the people. They are the temple, and there is no need to seek Him in a particular place.

The city appears to John to be like a radiant bride prepared for her bridegroom. Just as the Woman riding on the Great Red Dragon was manifested in the city of Babylon, so the Bride of Christ—the Saints preserved for this day—are seen in and as the New Jerusalem. The Woman on the Dragon was destroyed, but all in the New Jerusalem shall live forever and remain fresh. The Saints are given glorified bodies like that of Jesus following His resurrection, and no matter the age or physical condition at death, those destined for this eternal home will live forever at the height of their physical, mental, and spiritual maturity.

The voice, which John hears, is obviously Christ, as He identifies Himself as *"the Alpha and Omega, the beginning, and the end."* Once more, He says, *"It is finished."* The Overcomers now inherit their promised position as *"joint heirs with Jesus."* All things that belong to Him, *"whether things present, or things to come...,"* are theirs—ours, if we choose to believe.

Nothing sinful or unclean exists in this place—particularly those things that are particularly abhorrent to God:

- The cowardly are not faithful enough to stand firm in the face of tribulation, loss, or ridicule.
- The unbelievers know God, but reject Him.
- The corrupt, murderers, and immoral are naturally sinners.
- Those involved in the occult look to demonic powers.
- And because God is Truth, He hates liars.

These *"all fall short of the glory of God,"* and can never enter this place.

1. John sees this Holy City—the New Jerusalem—come down out of the clouds with his own eyes and is awestruck (Rev. 21:2).
   a. It is a heavenly, celestial city of divine creation—beautiful, pure, righteous, and moral.

b. It is not the Jerusalem of the earth, but a New Jerusalem, which will be the new and final dwelling place of God and the Saints.
c. This city, which hangs above the earth, is to be the eternal home of God, the Bride—the Saints,—and the Bridegroom—Jesus (Heb. 13:14).
   (1) It shall be the new seat of government, and from this place, they all will reign over the nations forever.
   (2) This is the Saints' eternal reward for remaining faithful and overcoming the temptations of Satan and the world.
   (3) They have received crowns, but in this place, they will lay them at the feet of their Lord. He is Almighty and sufficient.
2. A voice from heaven says that God now dwells with His people (Rev. 21:3) (Heb. 11:10; 12:22).
   a. Where they once saw Him only through faith, now they can see Him in person and be in His physical presence.
   b. In the earliest days, His dwelling place was a tent—later a tabernacle.
   c. After Jesus came, it was within the life of Jesus Christ.
   d. Following His resurrection, God dwelt in the Church—the community of faith.
   e. In the Old Testament God was found in a place.
   f. In the New Testament, it was wherever His people were.
      (1) *"Where two or more are gathered, there am I"* (Matt. 18:20).
      (2) God is in His people.
3. In this new place, there will be no more death, or pain, or sorrow (1 Cor. 15:26).
   a. That is gone forever, and God shall wipe away all tears (Rev. 21:4) (Is. 25:8).
      (1) The trials and tribulations of life were for the purpose of teaching us to depend upon Him.
      (2) When He is all we have, He is all we need.
      (3) If we come to know Him through the sorrows of life, we will know Him in His entirety forever.
      (4) What a glory and small price to pay to spend eternity in His presence.
   b. This is perfect joy.
4. The whole purpose of God's redemption is to bring man back into fellowship with Him.
5. We are told that it is those who overcome that will inherit this new life.
   a. Within the new city will be both Old Testament saints and the faithful of the New Testament.
   b. All who have remained true to their Creator will dwell in this holy city.

THE CITY OF GOD (REV. 21:9-27)

It is interesting that one of the seven angels that poured out the last plagues upon the earth a thousand years previously said, *"Come hither"* to John, in order to show him the *"whore of Babylon."* Now, another of them tells him to *"Come hither,"* to show him *"the Bride, the Lamb's wife."* Both times, he sees a great city—Babylon and the New Jerusalem. In prophetic form, if one is literal, they both must be. Each is magnificent in its own right, but the first is destroyed for its wickedness, and the other will last forever, because of its holiness. One is the seat of the source of all evil and the other the eternal kingdom of the God of all creation.

John is taken to a high place outside of the great city and is shown every detail of this new capital of the earth. He is overwhelmed by its size, the spectacular materials out of which it is constructed, its design and physical layout, as well as the impact of God's glory within the city and upon the earth below. He also sees those who dwell in this mighty city and the life they live.

1. One of the seven angels who poured out the bowls of plagues, comes and leads John to a mountain or high place, for a panoramic view of the Holy City.
2. The New Jerusalem is the counterpoint—the antithesis—of Babylon.
   a. They are both a moral/immoral system and a city.
   b. One exemplifies all that is good—the other all that is bad.
   c. They have dimensions, walls, gates, and streets.
3. This is a city that God has promised and created for His people (John 12:22-23).
   a. Just as He created every inhabitant of the city, He also creates his or her final dwelling place.
   b. He is always faithful to His word.
4. This grand city, laid out in a cube, is 1,500 miles in diameter and 1,500 miles high (Rev. 21:16).
   a. It would stretch from New Hampshire to Florida and the Atlantic to Colorado.
   b. Because it will be equally high, and the inhabitants will be unfettered by gravity, there will be more than adequate room for this static number of people—their number will never increase.
   c. The size of this city would hold 58,000,000,000 people and still allow ¼ of a mile between each of them.
5. A great wall encircles the city and is 200 ft. thick (Rev. 21:17).
   a. The wall is made of jasper and shimmers with God's glory.
   b. It has twelve foundations, and the names of the twelve Apostles are written upon them (Rev. 21:14) (Eph. 2:20).

(1) Some were apostles to the Jews.
(2) Some were apostles to the Gentiles.
(3) The foundations represent New Testament Saints of the Lamb.
c. Each foundation is made of a different, precious stone or jewel.
1st. = jasper (red)   7th. = chrysolite (pale green)
2nd. = sapphire (deep blue)   8th. = beryl (grey)
3rd. = chalcedony (emerald)   9th. = topaz (blue)
4th. = emerald (green)   10th. = chrysoprase (green)
5th. = sardonyx (red)   11th. = jacinth (purple)
6th. = carnelian (copper)   12th. = amethyst (purple)
d. These shimmering colors again bring the rainbow into this new place.
e. The twelve gates are made of a single pearl and have the name of one of the twelve tribes written on them (Ezek. 48:31-34).
   (1) This indicates the inclusion of Old Testament Saints.
   (2) God is inclusive, not exclusive like man.
   (3) Pearls were not precious to the Israelites, but God uses them for a purpose.
      (a) Pearls are the result of an injury.
      (b) This could be representative of God's response to their injury of Christ.
      (c) It is a constant reminder that we do not deserve to be in this place.
      (d) We are there because Jesus paid the price for our redemption.
6. The streets of the city are made of pure gold.
   a. They are a translucent, glimmering gold, however, through which the other colors shine.
   b. The light from this city shines <u>down through</u> the streets and lights the entire earth and the nations who dwell upon it.
7. All of this size and the precious, costly elements used to build the New Jerusalem give evidence of the magnificence and splendor of this final home.
   a. The cities of the world seem like villages by comparison.
   b. This great city holds <u>all</u> of the people of the ages who have been faithful to God.
   c. Only God knows what that number will be.
8. John notices that there is no temple, because the temple is God Almighty and Jesus, the Lamb; they are present in this place (Rev. 21:22).
   a. Their glory provides the light for every corner of the city and the nations.
      (1) It is the same Shekinah glory that caused the prophets and the Apostle Paul to faint in its presence.
      (2) God is the light, and Christ is the lamp (Rev. 21:23).

        (3) The glory that man has never been able to look upon will be the light of this city.
        (4) It was even prophesied in the Old Testament (Is. 60:1).
    b. The nations of the earth shall walk in this light.
    c. The sun and moon may shine, but their light will not be needed.
    d. There will never be any night in this city, thus the gates shall never close (Rev. 21:25) (Is. 60:11).
        (1) Because this is now a perfect society, there will be no danger or need to ever close the gates against danger.
        (2) Only those whose name is written in the *Lamb's Book of Life* shall come in or out of this city.
            (a) This substantiates that it is the Saints that live in this city with God and the Bridegroom.
            (b) The Saints can come and go any place at will, in their transformed bodies.
            (c) The nations—those who now love the Lord and <u>are alive</u>, as well as the Jews—live on the earth <u>forever</u>.
9. <u>All</u> of the people in the heavenly city are righteous, pure, and honorable. They walk in the light and understanding of the Lord.
    a. Every level of person there, great and small, will bring their splendor—praise and worship—to God and the Lamb.
    b. Everyone and everything will then be holy.
    c. Nothing unclean, or no one unholy, will be allowed to enter this city (Rev. 21:27).
10. It is in this Holy City, the Church of the first-born—the Bride and Wife of Christ—shall live and reign with Him for <u>all</u> eternity.
11. What we see is a true paradise.
    a. Man began his existence in a paradise.
    b. It was a time of innocence.
    c. He then traveled through a long period during which that innocence was lost.
    d. He now comes full circle and again finds himself in God's place of perfection.
    e. <u>This</u> is God's plan for mankind.

THE RIVER OF LIFE (REV. 22:1) (EZEK. 47:1-6)

Thus far, John has only described the external magnificence of the Holy City, but now he shares the splendor of what he sees inside. The most obvious is a powerful, spectacular river flowing from out of the center of the city, to provide abundant, life-giving water to all who live in this place. It is conceivable that this river flows to the East, West, North, and South from its source, through the city, and then cascades down onto the earth below, providing additional water to maintain its lush environment.

John tells us that these are living waters, which have their source in the throne of God and His Son. The Creator Himself keeps the waters pouring forth, to assure that there is life without end, in both the city and on the earth—there is no more death. Just as blood mixed with water flowed from the side of Jesus Christ, so does this cleansing water flow from His throne. In both cases, it is intended to sustain eternal life for all of God's people.

1. To this point, John has seen the outside of the city from afar, but he is now shown its interior.
2. What he sees is a mighty river, as clear as crystal, coming out of the throne of God and His Son, the Christ (Rev. 22:1) (Zech. 14:8) (Ezek. 47:1-6).
    a. The Father reigns through Jesus and from that source comes living water — pure and precious.
    b. God tells us that He will give all Overcomers this water of life as a gift (Rev. 21:6-7).
    c. We will inherit these things as the sons and daughters of the Most High God.
    d. Water is essential to the life of man and the land, so it is not unexpected that a wonderful river should flow through this wondrous city.
    e. There are many interpretations of what this water is—joy and peace, abounding grace.
    f. Another interpretation is that it is the Holy Spirit.
        (1) It emanates from the Father and Son and flows through the very center of the city.
        (2) It brings joy, refreshes, and blesses all who drink from it.
        (3) It brings life to a people for whom death no longer exists.
        (4) This perspective is certainly not inconceivable.

THE TREE OF LIFE (REV. 22:2) (EZEK. 47:7-12)

John's eye is then drawn from the River of Life to the Tree of Life, which is seen in replicas lining both sides of the river. The very tree God planted in the Garden of Eden to preserve life is multiplied and is growing in this new Paradise. They produce twelve different kinds of fruit—one for each month of the year. Considering that time is mentioned, it would confirm that it actually moves on—forever. Not only do the trees add beauty to the city, they have life sustaining qualities. Even the leaves provide healing powers for those dwelling on the earth. God forgets no one.

1. On both sides of The River are specimens of the Tree of Life.
   a. Just as it was in the first paradise, the Tree of Life is again present (Gen. 3:22).
      (1) If we search through scriptures, we see that the Tree of Life represents wisdom, knowledge, happiness, and hope.
      (2) It is a mainstay of life.
   b. These are fruit-bearing trees and produce a different type of fruit each month.
   c. This life-giving fruit was promised to the Overcomers (Rev. 2:7).
      (1) We are not told whether the Saints eat, or not, but considering that they have glorified bodies, such as Jesus had following His resurrection, we do know that He ate at times.
      (2) Presumably, they can eat if desired; though it is not necessary to sustain life.
   d. The leaves of the trees also provide healing, or health, for the nations (Rev. 22:2).
      (1) While the fruit are a blessing to the Bride, the healing properties of the leaves are a blessing to those on the new earth—to the nations.
      (2) They preserve the health and comfort, which now shall abide everywhere, forever.
   e. Ezekiel saw a similar vision in Ezek. 47:7-12.
2. While sin entered into the first paradise, we are told that there never shall be sin in this new place (Rev. 22:3).
   a. Never again will the curse of sin, or darkness, or death overshadow peace, joy, and blessedness (Gen. 3:17).
   b. The final victory has been won.
   c. God's own will never fall again.
   d. This is a manifestation of "...*on earth as it is in heaven*" (Matt. 6:10).
3. The Tree of Knowledge of Good and Evil, which existed in the Garden of Eden, is not present here.
   a. We now have all knowledge.
   b. Evil no longer exists, as all things have been returned to a state of perfection in the New Jerusalem.

THE THRONES (REV. 22:3)

John reminds us that, in both the New Jerusalem and the New Earth, all sin is gone. There is no more death, the inhabitants remain ageless, all work is productive, knowledge is limitless, everything stays in perfect order, and time goes on forever. In the midst of this time and place is a mighty throne upon which the Eternal Father and Son sit. It is from this place that Christ will reign as King over all worlds, with the Saints in attendance. They are blessed to serve Him, and He writes His name on their foreheads so all will know to whom they belong—to bless is to be blessed. Regardless of where in all of creation they may go, they will be recognized as servants of the One True God.

1. Previously, we have seen various thrones upon which God/Christ/the Lamb have been seated.
   a. In the throne room in heaven, God Almighty sat, as a great light, in all His glory, while Christ walked among the "lampstands" (Rev. 4:2).
   b. On "the day of the Lord" the entire Godhead—the Father, the Son, and the Holy Spirit—sit upon the Great White Throne of judgment (Rev. 20:4).
      (1) It is the place of final judgment from which no man escapes.
      (2) The unholy-dead are sent directly into the "Lake of Fire."
   c. Now we are told of the final throne, in the New Jerusalem, upon which God and the Lamb, as King, sit with authority and power (Rev. 22:3).
      (1) From this place, they, along with the glorified Saints, will rule and reign together forever and ever (Job 36:7).
      (2) There will be no more false religions, no more faulty politics, no more tyranny, or rebellion.
      (3) All will serve with joyous obedience, for righteousness abounds.
         (a) To serve the Lord will be our joy.
         (b) At the same time, we are told that to serve is to be served, and that is our promise (Luke 12:37).
      (4) It is a blessing to be a servant.

FURTHER DESCRIPTION

John continues to describe this eternal home, by again stating that though the light of God's glory provides light to both the Holy City and the new earth, the Saints will no longer see any darkness. The nations of the earth, however, will continue to have day and night. They will have natural lives and bodies requiring sleep, and the Word promises that *"while the earth remainith, day and night shall not cease."* (Gen. 8:22).

The angel that has been revealing all these things to John, reassures him that they are *"honest and true."* From the beginning of his visions, John was told to *"Write, because these words are faithful and true."* He is here reminded of why he has been given this blessing, and he needs have no doubt. The very God of the prophets—the God who created and controls all that takes place throughout history—is faithful to keep every promise that *"must come to pass."* Nothing that He intends will be left unfinished. As a result of John's obedience, those who read and keep these words will also be blessed.

1. Because we are told that there will be no end to the increase of His government, we may need to examine our narrow belief that we are all there is, and this is the end of the story (Is. 9:7).
    a. There was history before the creation of man, and there must be history after Revelation.
    b. One theory might be:
        (1) While we once believed that the earth was the center of the universe and all things revolved around it, we now know that we are only a part of one galaxy among millions of galaxies.
        (2) According to a Harvard scholar in his book *Climactic Change,* at ½ million mph, it would take us 200,000,000 years to get around <u>our own</u> galaxy.
        (3) Therefore, based upon the law of probabilities, there <u>could</u> be 100,000,000 earths.
        (4) God created them all and perhaps this is the increase of His government, which has no end.
        (5) If we are not confined to the City, the gates are never closed, and we have bodies that are not restricted by time or space, perhaps we go to these other governments.
        (6) The battle of good and evil has been fought here; we are the Bride that has overcome, and live in the Holy City where we can see the face of God (Rev.22:40).
            (a) This makes us a unique and peculiar people.
            (b) We have His name on our foreheads, but because we are all a part of the Bride, we do not need that to identify ourselves to one another (Rev. 22:4).
            (c) Perhaps it is there so that when we go around the universe, those who see us will recognize us by this mark, as those who have survived the great conflict, and now live in the presence of God.
            (d) The story of this victory will last forever, and we will be known.
            (e) It would be an opportunity to serve the Lord by continuing to spread the gospel.
            (f) Obviously, this scenario is purely speculation and would generate much discussion and differences of opinion.
            (g) Nothing is impossible with God, however.

2. The angel that tells John all these things confirms that God's words are "*faithful and true.*"
    a. Three times throughout the book, we are told "*these things are faithful—trustworthy—and true*" (Rev. 19:9; 21:5; 22:6).
        (1) This is once for each member of the Godhead.
        (2) Either this book is divinely inspired, or it is a blasphemous forgery.
        (3) It is not our responsibility to change anyone, but we have been commanded to share God's Word (Mark 16:15).
        (4) The gospel and the Holy Spirit will accomplish that understanding and change, if it is to be.
        (5) In the end times, those who choose not to turn from their evil ways will continue to do so, and those who do will become better and more holy (Rev. 22:11) (Ezek. 3:37).
        (6) Everyone has been given the freedom of choice and will be judged accordingly.

CHAPTER 28
The Epilogue

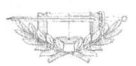

THE FINAL SCENE (REV. 22: 7-21)

REALIZING IT, OR NOT, JOHN observes the final revelation of Jesus Christ. Through the attending Angel, acting as a messenger, he hears Jesus say, *"I am coming soon." "Blessed is he who keeps the words of prophecy in this book."* Just as in the beginning of John's vision, we are told that all who read, hear, and keep the truths of this revelation will be blessed. Even as creation began—perfect and pristine—so does it exist in the end. Similarly, the Book of Revelation begins and ends with a blessing.

Throughout the ages, many will ridicule and reject what has herein been revealed, and we are instructed by Jesus Himself to guard against the attempts of the Enemy to keep the meanings of this prophecy in darkness. Only in this way can the Great Deceiver forestall the inevitable.

John again identifies himself to his audience—the Church—as *"I, John."* He knows full well that what he has seen, and been commanded to write, is almost beyond human comprehension. For that reason, he wants those who read and hear these words to know that they come from him, whom they know and love. It is vital to him that the churches trust that these are not the ravings of a madman. He too is overcome by what he has seen; and once again he falls down before the messenger, who repeats that he is only a fellow servant. God alone deserves our praise and worship.

The assignment John has been given—to share his visions with the Churches, as well as all who are yet to come—is an overwhelming responsibility. Because all of God's children are given the freedom of choice, some who read the contents of this book will elect to believe and receive it as truth, thus changing their destiny for the good. Others will not make such wise choices. In either case, eternity is at stake and we dare not tarry in making a decision. The time is short and Jesus Himself says, *"I am coming soon,"* and with Him, He brings judgment. We know this declaration is from Christ, because He identifies Himself as the *"Alpha and Omega."* He told us this at the beginning of the book, and He tells us again at the end. As Creator of all, He is the Alpha in Genesis and the Omega in Revelation. Of this, we can be assured, for as God, He can be none other than *"honest and true."*

At this point, we are given the seventh and last of the beatitudes of the Book of Revelation. John writes that, though we are blessed if we keep the commandments, only by having our robes—our very lives—washed in the blood of Jesus Christ, can we have eternal life and be granted the right to spend eternity in the Holy City. Once more, we have a choice. What will we do with that choice?

1. A review of what has been revealed through John includes:
    a. The universal Church from the days of John, the apostle, to Christ's coming for His people,
    b. His taking unto Himself those who are ready and have overcome the tribulations of life,
    c. The coming of the Antichrist, his captivation of the world, the manifestation of his evil plan, and his ruination,
    d. The leaving of others to suffer the judgments of the great Tribulation:
        (1) The breaking of the Seals,
        (2) The sounding of the Trumpets,
        (3) The pouring out of the bowls of God's Wrath,
    e. The final actions of Satan himself, his imprisonment for a thousand years, his loosing for *"a short time,"* and his foretold fate in the "Lake of Fire,"
    f. The shepardizing of the nations and the breakdown of their rebellion,
    g. The coming forth of the righteous new heaven and new earth, and finally,
    h. Redemption completed and paradise regained.
2. The Lord God of the prophets Himself sent the angel to reveal those things, which in Rev. 4:1 He said *"soon must take place."*
3. Now Jesus says, *"I am coming soon,"* and gives a benediction to *"he who keeps the words of the prophecy of this book"* (Rev. 2:16; 3:11).
    a. This is the only book we are <u>commanded</u> to read, and we are blessed for keeping it in our hearts.
    b. It is critical to our life—today and forever.
    c. We have a responsibility and a choice to make.
    d. We can heed this book and live our life in preparation for what <u>God</u> has told us "*...in Truth....,*" or, we can ignore it and take the consequences.
    e. The Revelation of Jesus Christ is a threat to Satan's plan, so if we ignore it, our choice is obvious.
    f. God has intended for His people to know and understand what is ahead, in order that we might make an informed decision about how to live our lives.

g. The greatest blessings are to be had by those who believe and keep what is revealed in this book.
   (1) To wait until Christ returns will be too late.
   (2) The time to understand is now.
4. John hears the Lord Jesus say, *"Behold I come quickly"* (Rev. 22:7).
   a. When He does come, it will be quickly, and it will be too late to repent and make a decision to follow Him or not.
   b. There will be no time to think about where we wish to spend eternity.
   c. We must make that decision today and live our lives in readiness, for we know neither the day nor the time of His return.
5. John is so overwhelmed by what he has been shown by the messenger that he falls down before him in worship.
   a. Though he meant no idolatry, he could not help but recognize that these were revelations from God.
   b. To correct any error, however, the angel tells him again that he is only a fellow servant, and God alone should ever be worshipped (Rev. 22:9).
6. John is then commanded to *"Seal up not the words of the prophecy of this book."*
   a. From the very beginning of John's vision, he is told to write down all that he sees and hears (Rev. 1:11).
      (1) He is to publish it to the Churches.
      (2) This is unlike Daniel who was told to seal his visions in his breast and not to write them or make them known (Dan. 8:26).
      (3) They were for the future, and the time was not right.
   b. John's desire to be recognized was not what caused him to reveal his visions, but a direct command from God.
   c. Again, we see that it is God's wish that we be informed about "the last days," so that we might be prepared to persevere.
   d. This book is God's blessing, and not meant to be an instrument of confusion.
7. The next statement concerning wrong doers remaining wrong doers, the vile remaining vile, the righteous continuing to be righteous, and the holy remaining holy, causes some confusion (Rev. 22:11).
   a. It refers to man's human nature and the fact that many will not heed these words.
   b. It also impresses upon John that this fact should not cause him to hesitate to make these revelations known.
   c. These words will either make men better, or worse, or have no effect at all.
   d. Their response is not John's responsibility.

8. To establish further that the time of coming is soon, Christ once again proclaims it (Rev. 22:12).
   a. With Him He brings not only judgment, but all of the rewards He has promised His own.
   b. Those rewards He will give out according to what each has earned.
      (1) This is not the gift of eternal grace.
      (2) Only Jesus Christ earned that for us.
      (3) These are rewards based upon our own deeds.
   c. To confirm His right to give these gifts, He states one last time that He is (Rev. 1:8; 22:13):
      (1) The Alpha and Omega,
      (2) The First and the Last,
      (3) The Beginning and the End.
      (4) There is no one before or after.
      (5) He is the Lord God Almighty.
9. In the final beatitude of the Book of Revelation, *"Blessed are those who wash their robes, that they may have the right to the tree of life...,"* we see that it is the only thing that will grant us entrance into everlasting life in the Holy City (Rev. 22:14).
   a. Only by that means are our garments made white and we be saved and made holy.
   b. To enable this to happen, we must wait and watch for His coming and believe upon Him.
   c. The alternative is that all who are sinners shall be left behind and condemned to an eternity of pain, suffering, and hopelessness.

THE CONCLUSION (REV. 22:16-21)

We finally come to the last words of John's account of the Revelation of Jesus Christ. They are also the last words of the last book of God's inspired scriptures. No further words are ever written, as a part of what we have come to know as the Bible—God's divine path of life—<u>from</u> Him and <u>back to</u> Him. His[s]tory of creation, de-generation, and re-creation here comes to an end, and all that God intended is accomplished. *"His will be done on earth as it is in heaven."* As *"in the beginning, there is the Word. The Word is with God, and the Word is God."* That Word is Jesus Christ, and just as at the beginning of His greatest revelation to mankind, He restates that, *"I am the Alpha and the Omega, the First and the Last..."* Only God Almighty can make such a claim. If this is not *"honest and true,"* then there is no Truth—Jesus Christ. Satan would reign victorious and God be the Great Deceiver. This is the decision we must make, and only the Holy Spirit can guide us to the Truth. If we choose Christ, we can then believe His last words, *"I am coming soon."* John, the Spirit, and all who are gathered in the presence of God the Father and Jesus the Lamb encourage us to *"Come"* and be partakers of the greatest gift ever given—eternal life. With that, John says, *"Amen, so be it."*

1. The conclusion of the Book of Revelation is similar in many ways to the beginning.
    a. The identity of the source is stated—Jesus.
        (1) He was given this name before He was born in human form (Matt.1:21).
        (2) It was stated that He would *"save His people from their sins."*
        (3) He still uses that name for Himself to the very end—*"I, Jesus..."* (Rev. 22:16).
        (4) He is our Savior, and He has the authority to direct the angels.
    b. The use of a messenger—angel—to communicate much of the testimony is pointed out.
    c. In some cases, the "angel" is Jesus Himself.
    d. A reference is made to John's seeing, hearing, and writing to the Churches.
        (1) If we are to be prepared for Christ's coming, we must know all that John is shown.
        (2) To be the Bride, we must be aware and informed in order to take action now.
        (3) The choices we make today, and the way in which we live our lives, determine our place in eternity.
        (4) Without the revelations of this book, we may not recognize the times or be prepared to overcome.
        (5) There is mercy in the gift of this book.
    e. Blessings are granted to those who give attention to the words that are imparted (Rev.22:14).
    f. A point is made of the nearness of the time of fulfillment of these prophecies.
        (1) We must be ready, for His return could come soon.
        (2) To postpone our preparedness could mean great loss.
    g. Christ again authenticates who He actually is and the names, or titles, by which He goes.
        (1) Lord God Almighty
        (2) The Christ
        (3) Son of Man
        (4) The Alpha and Omega—The First and Last—The Beginning and End
        (5) The Lamb/Savior
        (6) The Root and Offspring of David
        (7) The Morning Star

2. Man must desire the coming of Christ in order to be prepared.
   a. An invitation is also given by the Spirit and the Bride, to "*Come*" (Rev. 22:17).
      (1) All who hear these words say, "*Come*," to seek to drink from the living waters, and to come into communion with one another and the Spirit.
      (2) This gift is free, but we must, by faith, accept the giver as well as the gift.
   b. The promises of all of God's word are fulfilled in this book.
3. Because Revelation is an announcement of the "*true and trustworthy*" testament of the fulfillment of God's plan and purpose, a solemn warning is given (Rev. 22:18).
   a. Anyone who adds anything to it will have the plagues of this book added to him/her.
   b. Anyone who takes anything away will lose his/her share of everlasting life.
      (1) Salvation itself is at stake for changing any meaning of God's word.
      (2) This makes its wide variation in interpretations of such concern.
      (3) Our salvation is not dependent upon interpretations, but the words themselves must not be changed to support a point of view.
      (4) Herein is a curse that should not be taken lightly.
   c. To state as truth what is not truth, to denounce, condemn, reject, or minimize what God Himself has put forth is one of the highest crimes one can commit against God, and it will not go unpunished.
   d. The interpretations of this teaching are based upon the words, as stated, with no desire to add or subtract meaning, speculate upon interpretation, or claim anything other than what God has revealed to John.
4. Christ Himself adds a final summation to the content of this prophecy.
   a. Its entire purpose is to reveal Jesus Christ.
   b. The visions John has seen fit together to portray the final acts involved in the ending of this present world and the establishment of a new, eternal order.
   c. Jesus testifies to these things and says, *"Yea, I am coming soon"* (Rev. 22:20).
      (1) This is the hope of the Church and the promise of the Word of God.
      (2) We are free to accept it, or reject it; either way it is still the Word of God.
5. With that, John speaks for himself and all Christians, as he says, "*Amen. Come, Lord Jesus.*"
   a. There is nothing of greater desire than that God's Word should be fulfilled.
   b. This has been THE PLAN since before time began.
   c. That PLAN shall be fulfilled.
6. And to that, John adds his benediction:
   "*The grace of the Lord Jesus be with God's people. Amen.*"

BIBLIOGRAPHY

Bloomfield, Arthur E. *Before the Last Battle of Armageddon.* Minneapolis, Bethany House Publishers, 1971.

Gregg, Steve. *Revelation: Four Views. A Parallel Commentary.* Nashville, Thomas Nelson Publishers, 1997.

Interpreter's Bible; The Holy Scriptures. vol. XII. New York, Abingdon Press, 1957

Ladd, Gordon E. *A Commentary on the Revelation of John.* Grand Rapids, Wm. B. Eerdmans Publishing Co., 1972.

Morris, C. Leon. *The Book of Revelation: An Introduction and Commentary.* Grand Rapids, Wm. B. Eerdmans Publishing Co., 1987.

New American Standard: The New Open Bible Study Addition. Nashville, Thomas Nelson Publishers, 1990.

Phillips, John. *Exploring Revelation.* Neptune, N.J., Loizeaux Brothers, 1991.

Seiss, Joseph A. *The Apocalypse.* Grand Rapids, Kregel Publications, 1900 (1987).

Walvoord, John F. *Prophecy Knowledge Handbook.* Wheaton, Victor Books, 1990.

Sowa, Cynthia. *The Revelation of Jesus Christ.* Thousand Oaks, CA. Taped lectures, 1994/95.

Sproul, R.C. *Revelation.* Orlando, FL., Ligonier Ministries. Taped lectures, 1977.

Indexes

Subject Index

1,000 Years   242, 248-251
144,000   55, 94-97, 182-185, 195, 197, 200, 211
Abaddon   107
Abomination of Desolation   127, 182
Abyss   10, 105, 106, 129, 241-243, 259
After these things   10, 32, 62, 65-66, 67-68, 138
Alleluia   228-230
Alpha and Omega   29, 45, 269, 270, 281-282, 284, 285
Amillenialist View   19, 249-250
Anabaino   144
Angels   4, 26, 31, 65, 71, 72, 79, 82, 84, 93, 94, 96, 100-102, 106, 107, 110-114, 123, 125, 146, 148-149, 182, 188, 191, 195, 203-204, 216, 229, 234-235, 239, 242-243, 260, 268, 277, 279, 281-283, 285
    First Angel   83-85, 188-189, 205
    Second Angel   85-86, 190, 205
    Third Angel   86-87, 190, 205
    Fourth Angel   87, 88, 192, 206
    Fifth Angel   88-89, 192-193, 206
    Sixth Angel   89-90, 107-111, 206-207
    Seventh Angel   131-133, 207-208
Antichrist   9, 48, 56, 75, 78, 84, 86, 94, 97, 99, 103, 105, 106, 114, 117-118, 120-122, 123, 127, 132, 144, 151, 152, 156-157, 159, 161-168, 172, 175-182, 183, 188, 195, 199-200, 206, 208, 210, 211, 216, 219, 220, 222-223, 225, 227, 239-240, 256, 282
Apocalypse   14-15
Apollyon   107
Ark of the Covenant   50, 131, 166, 167

Babylon   154, 158, 164, 176, 211, 215-228, 272
Battle of Armageddon   88, 209, 211, 239, 240-241, 247, 253, 256
Beast   128, 154, 157, 175-181, 188, 216, 220, 222-224, 226, 236, 239, 241, 243, 256-257, 259, 260
Beatitudes   27, 76, 188, 190, 207, 233, 243, 281, 282, 284
Bible   5-7
Black Horse   86
Book of Life   33, 53, 55, 74, 147, 179, 261, 262-263, 274
Book of Revelation   14-16
Bowls   78, 200-201, 203-208
    First Bowl   200-201, 205
    Second Bowl   200-201, 205
    Third Bowl   200-201, 205
    Fourth Bowl   200-201, 206
    Fifth Bowl   200-201, 206
    Sixth Bowl   200-201, 206-207
    Seventh Bowl   200-201, 207-208

Bride 11, 88, 147, 184, 201, 231-234, 241, 263, 267, 269, 271, 278
Bridegroom 231-234

Cherubim 73, 74
Child 139-146, 149-152, 162, 169
Church Age 12-13, 19, 32, 38, 61-62, 82
Churches 30, 35-39
Conditions of the Times 127-129, 159-168
Covenant 70, 72, 112, 114, 118, 120, 127, 132-133, 167, 168, 200
Crowns 7, 40, 47, 71, 72, 73, 84, 141-142, 145-146, 220, 236, 271

Daniel 13, 24, 70, 153-158, 176, 177, 222, 223, 283
Daniel's 70th Week 91, 118-120, 184, 200, 204
David 8, 56, 77, 95, 119, 124, 133
Day of the Lord 10, 57, 82, 100, 126, 131, 206, 277
Days of Noah 161, 172-174
Dead in Christ 11, 65, 144, 170, 192, 256, 261
Devil 4, 10, 108, 145, 169, 243, 250, 260
Dragon 78, 140, 145-147, 152, 154, 169, 176, 177, 180, 182, 222, 236, 241, 243,

Earthquakes 9, 89, 93-94, 101, 102, 128, 131-132, 159, 160, 201, 226, 227, 251, 268
Egypt 102, 104, 132, 146, 152, 154, 157, 163, 164, 166-168, 178, 196, 206, 211, 222, 223
Elders 69, 71-73, 76, 78-79, 81, 98, 131, 185, 228-229
End Times 10-14, 19, 23, 26, 66, 114, 119, 125, 137, 153, 159, 161, 165, 201, 215, 216, 279
Ephesus, Church of 26, 39-42, 62
Ethiopia 167, 210
Euphrates 110, 132, 155, 201, 206, 210, 227

False Prophet 103, 159-160, 175, 180-182, 200, 201, 222, 227, 239-243, 259-260
Feast of the Birds 239-240
First and the Last 29, 32, 45, 284
First Judgment 256
First Resurrection 27, 170-172, 195, 256
Free Will 4, 137, 187, 188
Futurist View 19

Gentiles 13. 16, 36, 37, 90, 91, 97, 119-121, 127, 142, 154, 157, 184, 192, 197, 199-200, 204, 256-257
God's Plan 3, 4, 6-7, 31, 32, 55, 68, 75, 93, 96, 114, 129, 137, 147, 150, 154, 159, 160, 168, 169, 175, 176, 184, 217-219, 224, 233, 240, 241, 250, 251, 256, 267-269, 286
God's Wrath 13, 58, 65-66, 75, 81, 83, 90, 96, 101-102, 117-118, 132, 170, 171, 191-193, 200, 201, 203-208, 219, 237, 247, 269
Gog 208-211, 259-260

Hades 87, 192, 242, 243, 261, 263
Hail 102, 131, 132, 201, 205, 208, 226, 251
Harlot 141, 216-217, 220-221, 229
Harpazo 144, 170
Harvest 187, 191-192, 196
Heaven 67-74
Hell 45, 48, 106, 109, 110, 137, 146, 148, 190, 222, 242-243, 257, 261, 263
Historical View 18
Holy City 58, 119, 121-122, 269-274, 277-278, 282, 284
Holy Spirit 17, 28-29, 35, 53-54, 59, 61, 72, 77, 95, 123, 138, 139, 161, 169, 173, 175, 181, 248, 275, 277, 279. 284
Horsemen 82-88, 188-192
  First Horseman 83-85, 188-189

Second Horseman   85-86, 190
Third Horseman   86-87, 190
Fourth Horseman   87-88, 192

Idealist View   18, 183
Interpretations   4, 11, 13, 15, 16-19, 25, 27, 66-67, 71, 74-75, 84, 85, 96, 107, 108, 111, 125-126, 139-141, 143, 144, 160-161, 170, 172, 185, 196, 199, 209, 248-250, 275, 286
Isle of Patmos   23, 25-26, 43
Israel   18, 19, 90, 94-96, 118-122, 127, 132, 140, 142, 143, 145, 149, 154, 165-168, 183-185, 204, 207, 210-211, 228, 234-240, 250, 267

Jacob's Trouble   91, 120, 123-127, 200
Jerusalem   25, 58, 96, 120, 122, 128, 154, 164, 183, 207-211, 220, 227, 228, 235, 240, 242, 250, 260
Jews   8, 12, 29, 36-37, 90, 91, 94-97, 114, 118, 121-129, 132, 133, 165-168, 182-185, 200-201, 210, 232, 236
Jezebel   50-52, 141
John   8, 15-16, 17, 23-26, 29, 30, 32, 35-36, 40, 68-69, 114, 121, 173, 234, 281, 286
Judgments   31, 42, 113, 131, 192, 252, 256-257
First Judgment (Judgment of the Saints) 147-150, 255-256
Second Judgment (Judgment of the Nations/Sheep & Goats Judgment)   255-257
Third Judgment (White Throne Judgment) 249, 255-263, 277

Lake of Fire   87, 109, 182, 201, 240-243, 259, 261, 263-264, 277
Lamb, The   27, 74-79, 83, 93, 98, 131, 179, 182-184, 200, 231-234, 277, 285

Lamb's Book of Life   33, 53, 55, 147, 179, 261, 263, 274
Lampstands   30-31, 40, 70, 72, 125, 177
Laodicea, Church of   38, 39, 58-62
Last Days   4, 7, 9-13, 15, 28, 38, 58, 110, 114, 118, 121, 124, 141, 148, 153, 159, 163, 165, 171, 175, 181, 196, 208, 216, 219, 222, 225
Lightning   72, 101-102, 131-132, 207, 240
Little Horn   156-157, 163
Living Creatures   72-74, 79, 83, 85, 87-88, 98, 109, 204, 228
Locusts   105, 107, 200, 206, 242
Lucifer   4, 74, 145, 146, 268

Magog   208-211, 259-260
Medo-Persia   146, 155, 157, 158, 176, 222
Messiah   12, 13, 91, 95-96, 117, 118, 120, 123-124, 127, 129, 132, 140, 142-143, 168, 183, 201, 207, 232, 236, 265
Michael   148-149, 169, 199
Millennium   19, 247-254, 255, 257, 261, 266
Moses   61, 79, 94, 103, 123-124, 126, 127, 167
Mt. of Olives   207, 240
Mt. Zion   96-97, 167, 183, 195

Nations   8, 39, 79, 81, 85, 115, 118, 121, 122, 142, 146, 154, 157, 163, 170, 176, 188, 206, 208-211, 217, 220-222, 225, 227-228, 247-249, 252-254, 260, 263, 267, 271, 273-274, 277
New Earth   9, 12, 141, 201, 249, 257, 260, 265-269, 276, 277
New Heavens 9, 12, 119, 201, 249, 260, 265-269
New Jerusalem   58, 201, 220, 235, 269-278
New Songs   78, 183, 185
Nicolaitans   41, 47, 48, 52

Overcomers 11, 36, 39, 41, 42, 47, 49, 52, 58, 60, 62, 68, 72, 118, 147, 180, 199, 252-254, 269, 270, 275, 276

Paradise 242, 274-276, 282
Pergamum, Church of 37, 47-50, 62
Philadelphia, Church of 38, 39, 55-58, 61, 141, 163, 173
Post-Millennial View 249
Post-Tribulation 11, 66, 172
Praise 39, 55, 65, 73-74, 78-79, 93-94, 97-98, 131, 183, 185, 195-197, 228-230, 233, 274, 281
Prayers 29, 30, 71, 73, 78, 100-102, 120, 131, 152, 165, 230, 237
Pre-Millennial View 19, 249
Preterist View 18
Pre-Tribulation 10, 16, 65, 67, 78, 111, 165, 170, 199, 249
Prince of Darkness 149, 206
Prince of the Air 105, 147, 148
Prophecy 8-9, 12, 13, 15, 24, 27, 32, 35, 53, 68, 69, 75, 118-119, 154, 156, 160-161, 163-164, 167, 169, 175, 207, 209-210, 212, 217, 223, 235, 282-283
Prophets 7, 8-9, 12, 14, 23, 24, 51, 69, 103, 123-127, 132, 159, 175, 180-182, 200-201, 206, 210, 215, 221, 222-224, 229, 232, 273, 277, 282

Rainbow 70, 112, 261, 273
Rapture 12-13, 58, 61, 65-67, 78, 82, 85, 88, 97, 99, 111, 121-122, 142, 143, 144-145, 148, 149, 160-161, 162, 165, 169-174, 195, 196, 199, 231, 249, 255-257, 261
Red Dragon 145-147, 169, 174, 222, 270
River of Life 274-275

Saints 11, 29, 35, 69, 71-73, 78-79, 82, 85, 88, 97, 99-100, 102, 105, 119, 132-133, 141, 143-145, 148, 170, 175, 184, 188, 195-196, 199-201, 204, 206, 228-229, 232, 237, 238, 247-249, 250-256, 263, 266, 269-271, 273-274, 277
Sardis, Church of 37, 52-55, 61, 62
Satan 4, 9, 11, 24, 39, 46, 75-76, 103, 106, 108, 110, 120, 126, 137, 140, 145-150, 160, 162, 163, 164, 166, 169, 175, 177-182, 188, 200-201, 209-210, 215-222, 226-228, 235, 239, 242-250, 284
Satan Bound 241-243, 250-251, 259-260, 267
Scroll 74-76, 78, 81, 99, 100, 111-112, 200
Seals 18, 74-76, 78, 81-90, 99-110, 131, 282
    First Seal 83-85, 188-189
    Second Seal 85-86, 190
    Third Seal 86-87, 190
    Fourth Seal 87-88, 192
    Fifth Seal 88-89, 192-193
    Sixth Seal 89-90
    Seventh Seal 99-102
Second Coming 10, 14, 19, 27, 29, 36, 48, 119-120, 141, 154, 160, 195, 204, 219, 235, 249
Second Death 42, 47, 261, 263
Second Resurrection 249, 261, 262
Seraphim 73
Seven Spirits 28, 35, 53, 72, 77, 113
Seventieth Week 118, 120, 184, 200, 203, 204
Sheep and Goats Judgment 255-257
Shekinah Glory 31, 69, 112, 203, 273
Sheol 242
Signs of the Times 9, 10, 17, 56, 127-129, 159-168
Smyrna, Church of 37, 39, 42-58, 59, 62
Son of Man 30, 51, 157, 161, 191, 192, 285

Song of Moses   79, 196
Symbols   10, 17, 18, 30-32, 103, 139, 154, 176

Ten Virgins   173, 232
Things which are   35, 66
Things which shall be   35, 65
Thousand Years   242, 248-251
Throne Room   69-74, 94, 99, 137, 145, 296, 200, 262, 277
Thrones   71-72, 81, 132, 252-254, 276-277
Thunder   72, 83, 101, 102, 111, 113, 131, 132, 170-171, 183, 207, 240
Thyatira, Church of   37, 50-52, 62
Timeline   199-201
Title Deed   74-76, 99, 100, 112
Tower of Babel   218-119
Tree of Life   27, 41-42, 275-276, 284
Tribulation, The Period of   10, 12, 13, 93, 247, 248
Tribulation Saints   11, 13, 35, 38, 58, 66, 88, 94, 97-98, 142, 144, 150-152, 157, 180, 183, 185, 190, 191, 195-196, 200, 204, 231, 233, 252
Trumpets   18, 30, 65, 68, 97, 100-111, 141, 144, 170, 177, 200-201, 204-206, 282
    First Trumpet   102-103, 200, 205
    Second Trumpet   103, 200, 205
    Third Trumpet   103-104, 200, 205
    Fourth Trumpet   104, 200, 206
    Fifth Trumpet   105-108, 200, 206, 242
    Sixth Trumpet   109-111, 201, 206
    Seventh Trumpet   117, 131-133, 201, 248
Two Witnesses   114, 118, 123-127, 166, 168, 201, 211

Unholy Trinity   11, 103, 180, 181, 206, 253, 263

Valley of Megiddo   206, 210, 227, 228, 239, 240

War in Heaven   147-150, 174, 199, 255-256
Wedding Feast   201, 233-234
White Garments   54, 71, 88, 193
White Horse   35, 84, 235-237, 253
White Throne Judgment   249, 255-263, 277
Woe   104-105, 108, 111, 129, 132, 204, 269
Woman   139-144, 146, 150-152, 169, 200, 216-217, 220-224, 226, 270
Word of God   6, 16, 25, 31, 84, 85, 114, 181, 188, 236, 237, 239, 286
World Crisis   161-168, 172, 207, 211
Wormwood   104
Worship   25, 40, 47-49, 60, 69, 72-74, 78-79, 94, 98, 121-122, 131, 152, 167, 178-182, 189, 195, 197, 222, 228-229, 234-235, 241, 274, 281, 283
Wrath of God   13, 55, 57, 65, 66, 75, 81, 89, 90, 94, 101, 102, 110, 118, 132, 136, 170-171, 183, 187, 192-193, 201, 203-208, 216, 219, 222, 237, 247-249, 269

Scripture Index

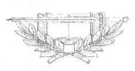

GENESIS
1:6-10....268
3:6....218
3:17....276
3:22....276
4:8....218
5:24....127
7:10....218
7:11....269
8:22....277
9:8-13....72
9:11....70
11:1-9....218-219
15:18....132, 167
17:8....132
22:7....77
49:9-11....77

EXODUS
7:1....
7:17....125
7:19-21....103
9:9-11....205
9:18-26....102
10:1....107
11:7....94
12:13....94
14:16....152
15:1-18....196
16:11-15....152
19:4....152
19:6....29
20:5....49
20:11....189
24:10....72
30:14....49
32:32-33....55
32:33....262

LEVITICUS
19:31....109
25: 23-55....75

NUMBERS
10:5-10....101
22:25....48

DEUTERONOMY
4:1....166
4:2....16
4:27....166
4:30....13

11:24....112
28:36....167
28:68....166
29:18-21....96, 104
32:11-12....152
34:6....126

JOSHUA
1:5....197

1 KINGS
17:1....125

2 KINGS
1:10....51, 125
1:12....125
2:11....126

2 CHRONICLES
4:1-2....72

NEHEMIAH
2:1-8....118, 120

JOB
5:17....37
36:7....277
38:8....269
38:22-23....208
41:1-34....177

PSALMS
2:9....253
13:1-6....89
18:13....72
29:3....31

29:4....112
30:7....223
37:9....267
37:29....267
48:2....208
69:28....55
75:8....221
89:37....28
97:1-4....72
103:19....69
110:1....31
115:16....52
146:6....189

PROVERBS
3:12....37
16: 4....100, 110
30:5....16

ECCLESIASTES
1:4....267

ISAIAH
2:19....90
4:1....251
6:1....69
6:2....73
6:6....73
7:14....7
9:6-7....7, 251, 268, 278
11:1....77
11:2-3....28-29
11:10....77
11:11-15....167
13:6 225

13:9-11....100
13:10-11....89, 90, 104
14:3-21....241
14:12....106
14:13-15....146
18:1-7....167
20:20....125
21:9....226
22:22....56
24:19-20....208
24: 21-24....241
25:8....263, 271
26:19....144
27:12-13....96
34:4....90
40:4....208
41:4....29
41:40....32
42:9-10....78
42:13....112
45:1-3....156
45:17....129, 267
47:1-15....227
48:12....32
49:16....268
50:3....90
51:17....221
53:2....31
53:3-9....7
55:11....31
60:1....274
60:11....274
61:6....29
63:1-4....237
63:3....193

65:17-25....251, 266
66:7....140

JEREMIAH

9:15....104
15:16....114
23:15....104
30:24....13
46:7-10....163
48:47....13
50:4-9....227
51:6....227
51:8....216, 226
51:24....227
51:45....227

EZEKIEL

1:1....68
1:5-10....73
1:5-24....73
1:7....31
1:10-11....72-73
1:26-28....69-70
2:1-10....74-75, 112
3:3....114
3:37....279
10:1....70
10:14....72
16:23....105
20:34-38....168
26:15-18....225
28:1-19....164, 241
29:12....168
34:11-13....168
34:23-34....211

36:3-5....166
36:25-28....8
37: 1-14....260
37:5....267
37:21-22....168
38:11....210-211
38:13....211
38:16, 23....207
38:19-20....207-208
39:12....251
39:21-22....207
43:2....31
47:1-12....275-276
48:31-34....273

DANIEL
2:19-28....154
2:31-44....154
2:35....223
2:42-44....146
7:2-7....68, 176
7:4-6....72, 222
7:9-10....31, 68, 70
7:13....8, 31, 192
7:18....252
7:22....252
8:17....32
8:26....283
9:24-25....118-120
9:27....127, 168
10:2....68
10:5-6....31
10:10-12....32
10:14....13
11:3-4....158
11:20....177

11:31....127
12:1....149
12:2....256, 262
12:4-7....68, 113
12:11....127

HOSEA
3:4-5....114, 132
3:5....124

JOEL
1:2-2:11....107
2:2....206
2:3-10....90, 110
2:31....90, 104
3:9-12....193, 207, 210, 257

AMOS
3:7....7
9:9....96

MICAH
5:2....7

ZEPHANIAH
1:8....54

ZECHARIAH
1:8....83
3:3-5....54, 125, 149
4: 3....125
6:1-8....83
8:1-23....251
12:10....124
13:9....207
14:1-21....207, 210, 241, 275

MALACHI
4:5....126

2 EZDRAS
2:42....98

MATTHEW
1:21....285
4:1....217
4:4....114
5:4-5....76, 114
5:9....143
6:9-13....79, 102, 131, 276
6:24....48
7:23-25....145
13:24-30....57
16:18-19....39, 70
18:20....271
19:26....108
19:28....72
21:2....70
22:1-14....55
24:4-39....8, 26, 41, 56, 57, 82, 84, 90, 104, 118, 127, 160, 161, 163, 165, 171, 172, 181-182, 192
24:44....171
25:1-13....56, 173, 232
25:31-46....256-257, 260
26:29....234
26:39....222
26:42....222
27:47....222
28:20....30

MARK
3:30....15
9:41....257
10:9....231
13:22....163
13:25....90
14:62....29
16:15....23, 279

LUKE
1:17....126
1:33....263
2:13-14....79
10:18-19....106
11:28....27
12:8....54
12:35-40....60, 277
12:39-40....161
12:47-48....262
13:25....56
21:8....7
21:24-26....89, 121
21:28....161
21:36....57, 171
22:18....234
24:44-49....126

JOHN
1:29....77
4:24....53
5:24-25....256
5:28-29....256, 261-262
8:44....146
8:51....87
12:22-23....272
12:46-49....262
14:2-3....29, 191
14:7....14
14:12....57

14:18....30
19:30....269

ACTS
1:11....29
2:19-21....90
17:11....37
20: 28-32....41
28:27-31....16

ROMANS
2:29....42
5:8-9....171
5:20....46
6:23....14, 76, 227
8:21....70
11:17-21....90
11:25-26....91, 204
12:19....89
15:12....77
16:25....14

1 CORINTHIANS
6:1-3....52, 252-253, 257
15:24-29....261, 271
15:51-52....65, 68, 144, 169-170

2 CORINTHIANS
6:4-10....46
15:20....28

GALATIANS
3:23-26....143
4:22....140

EPHESIANS
1:17....7
2:20....272
3:21....267
3:22....251
6:17....31

PHILIPPIANS
2:6-11....31
2:8-9....31
3:9....54

COLOSSIANS
1:16....71
1:18....28

1 THESSALONIANS
1:10....171
2:7....177
5:3....172
5:9....65, 171
5:17-18....70, 102, 230

2 THESSALONIANS
2:1-4....161, 164, 177, 182
2:8-9....164, 182, 241

2 TIMOTHY
1:7....7, 46
1:9....179
3:1-9....59
4:7-9....7, 59

TITUS
1:16....60

HEBREWS
4:12....31, 237
10:25....165
10:30....89, 205
10:36-38....165

11:5....127
11:10....271
11:30....100
12:6....37
12:22....183, 271
13:8....28
13:14....271

JAMES
1:2-3....46, 197
1:12....46
5:9....56
5:17....125-126

1 PETER
3:1-18....70

2 PETER
1:19-21....52, 81, 119
3:3-4....173
3:8....250
3:10-13....70, 266

1 JOHN
2:16....173
5:3-4....46

JUDE
14-15....29, 236

REVELATION
1:1....15, 26, 77, 101, 121
1:2-3....26-27
1:4-6....27-29
1:7....7, 8, 29, 39, 236
1:8....29, 269, 284
1:9....25, 27
1:10-12....29, 68, 72, 138, 283

1:13-20....31, 32, 35, 36, 39, 62, 67, 243
2:1....40
2:5....41
2:7-9....7, 29, 39, 42, 45, 54, 269, 276
2:11-12....7, 39, 47, 54
2:14....48
2:16....49, 282
2:17-18....7, 39, 51, 54
2:25-27....8, 142, 145, 254
2:29....7, 39, 54
3:3-6....7, 8, 39, 54, 55, 57
3:9....163
3:10....55, 57
3:11....8, 282
3:13-14....7, 39, 54, 59
3:16....59
3:20-22....7, 37, 39, 54, 60, 61
4:1....56, 66-68, 138
4:2-6....71-73, 262, 277
4:8-11....73, 78, 131, 196, 228
5:1....74
5:3-4....76
5:6-14....73, 77, 79, 131, 228
6:2-5....82, 188, 190
6:6-12....54, 82, 86, 88, 89, 131
6:15-16....85, 90
7:1....68
7:4....182-184
7:9....54, 66, 68
7:11-13....54, 71, 73, 98
8:1....82
8:2....100, 203
8:3-8....26, 101, 102, 103, 112
8:10....103, 205
8:12....104, 206
8:13....105
9:1-3....105, 107, 206, 242
9:5-6....87, 107, 108, 206

9:12-13....66, 110
10:1-3....26, 101, 111
10:5-8...113, 114
10:11...115
11:1-2....121
11:3-14....125, 168
11:7....128
11:12-14....128, 129
11:15....131
11:17....131, 196
12:1-2....142, 143
12:3-5....144, 146, 166, 253
12:7-8....149, 150, 255
12:10-12....149, 150, 151, 255, 256
12:15-17....138, 152
13:1-4....144, 176, 177, 178, 179
13:5-12....55, 179, 180, 181, 182
13:14-15....182
14:1-4....96, 184, 185, 188
14:6-9....188, 189, 190, 226
14:13-15....27, 101, 190, 192, 226
15:1-5....66, 68, 196
15:8....204
16:1-4....204, 205
16:6-8....186, 206, 221
16:12-14....206, 211
16:15-21....27, 87, 206, 207, 208, 268
17:1....216
17:3-6....217, 219, 221
17:8....178, 179, 220
17:11....178, 179, 220
17:15-17....221, 226
18:1-2....66, 68, 219, 226
18:4....226
18:8....219
18:11....227

19:1-4....66, 68, 73, 229
19:6-7....67, 196
19:9-10....27, 233, 235, 279
19:11-16....54, 85, 193, 208, 236, 237, 240, 253
19:17-18....239, 240
19:20....182, 241
20:1-6....27, 66, 241, 242, 250, 251, 252, 253, 277
20:7-10....259, 260
20: 11-15....55, 260, 262, 263
21:1....266, 268
21:2-4....270, 271
21:5-8....29, 47, 269, 275, 279
21:14....272
21:16-17....272
21:22-23....196, 273
21:25....274
21:27....55, 274
22:1-5....276, 277, 278
22:6-7....8, 15, 27, 102, 279, 283
22:8-9....25, 27, 283
22:11-13....8, 29, 102, 279, 283, 284
22:14....27, 284, 285
22:16-18....286, 287

www.ingramcontent.com/pod-product-compliance
Lightning Source LLC
Chambersburg PA
CBHW081217170426
43198CB00017B/2635